WORLD
ECO-CRISIS

International Organizations

in Response

Edited by

DAVID A. KAY and
EUGENE B. SKOLNIKOFF

with an introduction by
Maurice F. Strong

THE UNIVERSITY OF WISCONSIN PRESS

Published 1972

The University of Wisconsin Press
Box 1379, Madison, Wisconsin 53701
The University of Wisconsin Press Ltd.
70 Great Russell Street, London

First printing

Printed in the United States of America on .
Supple offset, a recycled paper

World Eco-Crisis reproduces the contents of the Spring 1972 issue of *International Organization*, published by the World Peace Foundation and the University of Wisconsin Press. This publication has been assisted through a grant from The Johnson Foundation (Racine, Wisconsin) as an expression of the Foundation's interest in the United Nations Year on the Human Environment.

ISBN 0-299-06151-5 cloth, 0-299-06154-X paper; LC 79-178153

John W. McDonald
Stockholm
Sweden

WORLD ECO-CRISIS

Bought — June 1972

Contents

Preface

It is becoming increasingly apparent that new technologies are global in nature and that even the intensive application of existing technology leads to transnational repercussions. The essays in this volume address themselves to the role, both existing and potential, of international institutions in coping with the environmental impact of the widespread application of an increasingly potent science and technology. This environmental impact is global in nature and is challenging us to develop the institutions and patterns of behavior necessary to manage a complex system of transnational effects that cut across the traditional boundaries of politics, economics, and the academic disciplines.

With a speed that reflects both the seriousness of the environmental problem and the extent to which near instant global communications have increased the level of international interdependence the subject of environmental pollution has raced to the top of domestic and international agendas. In fact, one of the early aims of the United Nations decision in 1968 to convene in 1972 a United Nations Conference on the Human Environment, to focus the attention of governments and public opinion on the importance and urgency of recognizing the impact of science and technology on man's environment, was largely achieved before the conference planning got seriously underway. The more fundamental aim of seeking the mechanism for diagnosing and managing this impact remains a continuing challenge for the Stockholm conference and beyond.

The authors of these essays draw upon a rich and diverse background of personal involvement and scholarship in the fields of science, social science, diplomacy, and international organization. We have urged them to consider the implications of environmental change for the international system from both a practical and a theoretical perspective. We hope that the results will prove useful both to policymakers and to students of international organizations. It is our belief that the Stockholm conference is only the start of a process in which international institutions, regional and global, are challenged by the technological imperative of global problem solving. We believe this challenge to be critical to the future survival and shape of the international system.

We wish to express our sincere appreciation to those who under the most severe of time constraints contributed to this volume, to the members of the Board of Editors of *International Organization* for their encouragement, and to Carolyn Leigh and Claire Gilmore for their editorial assistance. We also wish to thank the Johnson Foundation for its generous financial support of this endeavor. Each author's contribution is, of course, his own responsibility and does not purport to represent the views of any institution with which he may be associated.

DAVID A. KAY
EUGENE B. SKOLNIKOFF

PART I

INTRODUCTION

THE UNITED NATIONS AND THE ENVIRONMENT

Maurice F. Strong

MAURICE F. STRONG is secretary-general of the United Nations Conference on the Human Environment.

In these closing decades of the twentieth century modern man is a paradox of extremes. He possesses untold knowledge and wealth, but these have brought no universal end to the indignity of poverty and ignorance. He has conquered space, but on earth he is unable to overcome conflicts and inequities. His mastery of science and technology gives him unprecedented power, but his living world is threatened as at no time since his planetary home first gave him warmth and shelter.

Man's capacity to destroy is of course most dramatically manifest in his possession of the technologies of mass destruction—in particular those of nuclear and biological warfare—but the relatively recent emergence of the environmental issue has revealed the more subtle but no less dangerous risks he faces from the uncontrolled use or misuse of natural resources and the technologies of production. It is an issue that transcends political boundaries and stages of economic development.

Damaging conditions such as increasing salinity of fertile land, depletion of forest reserves, pollution of land and water supplies, maldistribution of populations, and the unanticipated and undesirable side effects of pesticides and fertilizers occur in a wide variety of countries, no matter what the state of their economy. Every nation is affected by pollution of the planet's atmosphere and of the oceans whether or not it contributes to that pollution. Some problems—such as air and thermal pollution—are most severe in industrialized nations; in others water-borne parasites and desert making are often born out of poverty itself and occur most frequently in those least able to afford the necessary measures to cope with them. Thus the subject of the human environment is global in character and of universal concern.

The human experience, of course, does not lack examples of attempts to generate popular enthusiasm and action by deliberate exag-

3

gerations of problems, and opportunities. Life is short, and every man's requirements are real and immediate. Questions of poverty and indignity, of economic underdevelopment and lack of opportunity, and of peace and war understandably weigh more heavily and urgently than a vaguer threat of ecological disaster. But it cannot be emphasized too strongly that these issues are in fact closely interrelated, and it is the combination of the achievement of the legitimate needs and ambitions of the present generation with the preservation of the interests of future ones that makes the environment problem so difficult, yet so crucial, to resolve.

The fundamental priority is to enhance the quality of life now and to ensure that actions to achieve this do not compromise the interests of future generations. The task may be simply posed. Its solution is infinitely more complex. The basic issue posed by the environmental crisis is how man is to manage the world's first technological civilization in which he has the power to shape his own future—the power to create and the power to destroy.

It is important to emphasize that, in using the phrase "the human environment," it is necessary to include all elements, both natural and man-made. It embraces urban and rural poverty as well as the dangers of atmospheric pollution from automobiles and factories. It includes the discovery and development of natural resources as well as the inefficient and wasteful use of presently exploited resources. It covers air, water, and soil. It includes the methods by which food production can be increased as well as study of harmful agriculture and practice.

Inherent in the concept of the human environment is that it involves concern for man's present circumstances as well as for his future hazards. This concern must be seen against the background of a much wider and deeper concern about a world in which a small minority lives in unprecedented comfort and in which the vast majority lives in conditions which have hardly improved over the past century. Glaring disparities between wealth and poverty have always existed, but they have never been so sharply and massively demonstrated as they are now; the problems of the human environment cannot be separated from the problems manifest in this imbalance, and it is essential that they be viewed—and resolved—in wide and comprehensive terms that look to interrelated solutions.

Man's life and well-being depend on a healthy equilibrium between his activities and the natural environment. Population growth and the intensification of man's activities through the processes of urbanization, industrialization, and agricultural development have vastly accelerated the pressures he is exerting on such vital resources as soil, water, air, minerals, and plant and animal life. Serious depletion of nonrenewable resources is already evident in many areas, and in some cases the deterioration beyond which damage is irreversible may be reached in the near future if nothing is done to correct present trends.

These pressures can be mitigated by reductions in population growth and in those activities which give rise to environmental degradation and resource depletion as well as by changes in the practices and technologies man employs. It is likely that all of these courses ultimately will be necessary, but the degree to which any of them need be accepted by each nation at a particular time will vary widely.

The more industrialized countries which enjoy the principal advantages and wield most of the power made available to man by science and technology have special responsibilities in this respect. Many of the activities that are largely responsible for the global environmental problems are among those which have produced today's unprecedented levels of wealth and power for the industrialized countries. Thus, if there are to be certain limitations on economic growth, they should logically apply first to such countries. But it would clearly not be realistic to look at this as being feasible or necessarily desirable in the short run. Much more promising are the possibilities of designing ways of reorienting and redirecting economic growth in the more industrialized countries toward environmentally compatible activities and toward greater satisfaction of nonmaterial needs, of their seeking a more balanced distribution of population and industrial activity, and of adopting practices and technologies that are less damaging to the environment. Such measures will in themselves require a major redeployment of man's energies and resources, but it is undoubtedly within the capacity of his creative genius if he has the political will to do it.

Many environmental problems are local and capable of local solution. Others can be resolved by national action. If the problems are wider, regional organizations are available. It may be fairly asked, therefore, what need is there for the active involvement of the United Nations? To answer this question it is necessary to point out that the unity of the natural environment creates a chain of cause and effect relationships which link many local and global concerns and actions. Also, the very scale and complexity of the subject in itself call out for the pooling of international knowledge and experience. Our lack of knowledge of many crucial areas requires the initiation of international research and inquiry. The potential global consequences of wrong decisions are such as to make global consultation and cooperation essential. Finally, the United Nations system provides the only available machinery for the degree of global consultation and central coordination that the problems urgently require. The question that is posed is simply whether mankind is to continue heedlessly as it has done in the past or whether it is to evolve a new understanding of the perils of this course. Such awareness, and the action to implement it, must be *global* if the future is to be effectively safeguarded. These factors do not merely justify United Nations action; they require it.

It is evident that the achievement of a new course presents a multitude of problems. The 1972 United Nations Conference on the Human Environment, although of high importance, will represent only one step on a long and arduous road. But it must be taken, and the very process of preparation for the conference has already resulted in a degree of global participation and active involvement which provides hope and encouragement. Our concern must be for advance. The concept of respecting and protecting the human environment has as its objective the fulfillment of the legitimate immediate ambitions of individuals and nations as well as the interests of future generations. The rectification of past errors, wherever possible, has as its object the provision of better opportunities for development and progress.

In this sense, therefore, the Stockholm Conference on the Human Environment will be neither a beginning nor an end but an unprecedented opportunity to break new ground in the management of a world in which all of us live.

In this world a reversion to the narrow concepts of national interests that have proven so destructive in the past would be tragic. The only realistic and durable concept of our international community must be one based on cooperation and sharing between equal partners which see their relationship as mutually beneficial and necessary to their common survival and well-being.

But the concept alone will not be enough. We have to realize this fundamental truth of our day in the 26 years since the larger ideal of world community inspired the architects of the UN. We know now it will only be achieved by a new sense of realism in dealing with a world that is vastly different from the world in which the United Nations was born. It is a world in which man has the tools with which to shape his own future. It is a world of unprecedented peril and of unparalleled promise—the realizable promise of a better life in larger freedom for all mankind.

Perhaps it is not too much to hope that the environment issue will be the key to the realization of this ideal. The ultimate test of Stockholm—and of the UN—will be the extent to which it does. At stake are the progress and welfare of mankind.

PART II

PRESENT AND FUTURE DIMENSIONS
OF THE PROBLEMS OF ENVIRONMENT

POPULATION, RESOURCES, AND TECHNOLOGY: POLITICAL IMPLICATIONS OF THE ENVIRONMENTAL CRISIS

Nazli Choucri, with the research assistance of James P. Bennett

NAZLI CHOUCRI is assistant professor of political science at the Massachusetts Institute of Technology, Cambridge, Mass. JAMES P. BENNETT is a graduate student in the same department. The investigations reported in this article are based on current work with Robert C. North, Stanford University, Stanford, Calif. Earlier studies and related materials are noted appropriately.

Virtually everyone recognizes the existence on an environmental crisis in the world today, but many uncertainties remain concerning the precise nature of this crisis and its domestic and international implications. This much is clear: The world's population is continuing to grow at an alarming pace; finite resources are being utilized at exponential rates; and technological advances are contributing to negative ecological outcomes. These trends have been documented extensively. Their political significance, however, has received little attention if only because the visibility of the problem is such a recent phenomenon. This article is addressed to some of the political consequences and international implications of the environmental crisis.

I. INTRODUCTION: PROBLEMS AND PERSPECTIVES

The magnitude of man's impact on his environment necessitates a readjustment of current perspectives on ecological issues and a redefinition of our conventional views concerning social and political order, both domestic and international.[1] We are now confronted with the need to examine the effects of variables that have been generally viewed as nonpolitical in nature. The problem is to specify those ways in which international politics and the environmental crisis are interrelated and to chart the linkages between ecological and political perspectives. Networks of interdependence are intricate and complex;

---

[1] See *Man's Impact on the Global Environment: Assessment and Recommendations for Action,* Report of the Study of Critical Environmental Problems (Cambridge, Mass: Massachusetts Institute of Technology, 1970); *Environmental Quality: The Second Annual Report of the Council on Environmental Quality, together with the President's Message to the Congress* (Washington: Government Printing Office, August 1971); and Walt Anderson, ed., *Politics and Environment: A Reader in Ecological Crisis* (Pacific Palisades, Calif: Goodyear Publishing Co., 1970).

an issue that might appear to be only of national concern may have global implications. But it is naive, premature, and empirically invalid to suggest that the environmental crisis will necessarily result in greater international cooperation. The opposite is equally plausible. A realistic assessment of the present situation must weigh the evidence between these two hypotheses. This article takes one step in this direction by summarizing the relevant evidence pertaining to various aspects of the environmental crisis and by highlighting the actual as well as the potential political implications. We do not anticipate arriving at any clear answers, but we must begin to put the pieces together by identifying those parameters that are critical for both research and policy planning.

The interrelationships between man's impact on his environment and his attempts to manipulate and control that environment provide the key for defining the problem. Of the numerous relevant dimensions the most basic and the most critical are those related to population dynamics, resource constraints, and technological developments. These may be thought of as distinct vectors of the environmental crisis, but their interdependence makes the resulting dynamics highly interactive. Sources of environmental problems attributable to population growth can rarely be distinguished from the effects of technological advancement or the underlying resource base. It is also difficult, if not impossible, to isolate the political consequences of population growth from those pertaining to technology or to resources. The population equation is generally defined in terms of the accompanying resource and technology calculus. For purposes of analysis, therefore, it is difficult to examine independent, intervening, and dependent effects without becoming entangled in dynamics of feedback and reciprocal causation.

We break down the problem to discuss: 1) the international implications of population dynamics, resource constraints and distribution, and technological developments; 2) the interdependencies and reverberating effects associated with efforts to cope with any one dimension singly; and 3) the ways by which the conduct of research in the academic community may address itself more clearly to environmental problems. A social science perspective is adopted here, but a certain amount of technical and scientific detail is also necessary for any analysis of this kind. Our concern is with the political—and potentially conflictual—implications of the present global predicament. A prime objective will be to highlight the implications for more technologically developed as well as less developed societies. In this regard our empirical analysis will center specifically around Japan, the People's Republic of China (Communist China), the Union of Soviet Socialist Republics, and the United States.

II. POPULATION DYNAMICS: MEASUREMENT PROBLEMS AND POLITICAL ISSUES

There are many uncertainties regarding the precise nature of the population problem and extensive disagreement as to the optimal mode of analysis to employ. The issue is inevitably defined in terms of referent variables (i.e., space, food, and resources) and as a problem of variable dimensions (i.e., levels, rates of growth, distributions, compositions, densities, or movements), all of which depend largely upon the choice of referent variables. To complicate matters further there are considerable statistical uncertainties pertaining to population projections and estimates of the earth's carrying capacity, and there are economic, political, and cultural uncertainties concerning potential sources of constraints on population growth.

Turning first to statistical uncertainties, we observe that existing data on levels and rates of growth, and on projections and expectations, are fraught with ambiguity and error occasioned as much by the difficulties of compiling accurate statistics (or gauging the range of measurement error) as by the choices of intervening sociological or economic indicators. United Nations projections, for example, are generally based upon the assumption of continuing progress in economic and social development and upon the continued availability of needed resources.[2] Variability in these assumptions inevitably colors the nature of the projections and, by extension, our assessments of the problem.

The United Nations Statistical Office publishes three variants of world, regional, and national population projections. These are designed to represent different assessments of error around the most plausible estimates. They are useful for research and policy planning, but considerable caution must be exercised concerning their potential sources of error. UN statistics are generally based upon the official data of member countries. Possible errors or deliberate modifications of official statistics make it difficult to assess their accuracy. In addition, since population projections are intimately tied to economic and social projections, errors in estimates of growth and development are invariably felt in demographic assessments. In view of these ambiguities some experts have concluded that we are "playing with predictions that are wrong and have always been wrong."[3] More im-

[2] United Nations, Department of Economic and Social Affairs, *World Population Prospects as Assessed in 1963* (Population Studies, No. 41) (United Nations Publication Sales No: 66. XIII. 2 [UN Document ST/SOA/Ser. A/41]) (New York, 1966), p. 6.

[3] M. C. Shelesnyak, ed., *Growth of Population: Consequences and Controls: Proceedings of the First Conference of Population Held at Princeton, New Jersey, September 27-30, 1968* (New York: Gordon & Breach, Science Publishers, 1969), p. 57.

portant, however, is the direction of error: To date, population projections have consistently *underestimated* potential rates of growth.

Alterations made in the UN projections between 1963 and 1968 are illustrative of possible errors (although there is no assurance that the projections corrected in 1968 will prove more accurate than their predecessors). "By 1985 . . . the revised projections add 187 million (4.0 per cent) to the world total as assessed in 1963, of whom only 19 million are in the more developed regions (1.5 per cent of their total) and 168 million in the less developed regions (4.8 per cent of their total)."[4] Such adjustments result mainly from modification of mortality and fertility assumptions in less developed countries.

There are related statistical uncertainties involving the earth's capacity to sustain the burgeoning population. According to some calculations the food supply might be increased ninefold with the cultivation of all possible land and the utilization of considerable technological advances; given adequate distributions, such levels of output could sustain a global population of 30 billion.[5] At present rates of growth this level would be reached within 100 years. Estimates of the earth's carrying capacity, however, have also been conservative. Partially biased or more optimistic assessments of carrying capacity center around 40 billion. The difficulty with all of these estimates is that they often disregard synergistic effects and chain reactions involving technological innovations and utilization of untapped resources. Such effects might enable the earth to support an even larger population than has been estimated to date. Conversely, synergistic effects could also exacerbate an already critical situation.

In view of these statistical uncertainties, coupled with basic definitional and empirical disagreements concerning optimum population levels, it is difficult to assess the validity of either optimistic or pessimistic views. Also, the concept of "optimum" is fraught with built-in conceptual problems many of which are related to the referent variable. The basic question is: "Optimum with respect to what?" The economic optimum is not necessarily congruent with the political optimum. At the level beyond mere subsistence the optimum may be culturally and sociologically defined; it is thus impossible to employ this concept as a useful measuring instrument for a precise definition of the population problem.

If we assume that growth cannot continue forever, we must examine the mechanisms by which added population places undue

[4] United Nations, Population Division, *World Population Prospects, 1965-1985 as Assessed in 1968* (Working Paper, No. 30) (New York, 1969), p. 7.

[5] In this regard see United States House of Representatives, Subcommittee of the Committee on Government Operations, *The Effects of Population Growth on Natural Resources and the Environment, Hearings,* 91st Cong., 1st sess., September 15-16, 1969, p. 5.

pressures on material and psychological needs and constraints upon further growth. But where are the sources of constraints to be found? Basic to the constraint question are the dual vectors of absolute global *shortages* of life-sustaining materials versus imbalances in regional *distributions*. In each case experts tend to identify the sources of potential dislocation with 1) food, 2) availability of resources, and 3) general environmental quality. But there is strong disagreement concerning the relative importance of each factor in constraining population growth.

Let us turn first to the political implications of the food situation. Studies undertaken by the Food and Agriculture Organization (FAO) have found the relationship between population growth and food needs to be one of almost perfect positive correlation. Future trends in food demand are almost totally dependent upon future populations. At the 1965 United Nations World Population Conference it was estimated that in order to meet food needs with a modest improvement in the quality of diet "the total food supplies will have to be increased by 43 per cent by 1970, 103 per cent by 1980 and 261 per cent by 2000."[6] Because of cultural problems and the long time lags involved birth control or fertility reduction cannot be considered an immediate solution to expected food shortages. Viewed in these terms, two perspectives on the food issue converge: the technological feasibility of increasing supplies versus the sociological feasibility of constraining demand and adjusting tastes to novel diets and substitute crops. It is not uncommon for technological solutions to be neutralized by cultural opposition.

Much of the prevailing optimism concerning the food situation emanates from technological considerations. Marxist spokesmen are perhaps the most positive when appraising the future capabilities of food production. From their perspective the critical issues pertain to distribution and management and not to the earth's productive capacity.[7] Yet, the proposition that the world is becoming increasingly unable to feed itself is also rejected by authorities in the West. The key issues are less those of distribution than of damage to the earth occasioned by the extensive use of fertilizers and accompanying strains on yield and productive capability. In these terms technological advances allow for increased yield; but yield increase often produces added burdens on the earth's capabilities.

---

[6] United Nations, Department of Economic and Social Affairs, *Proceedings of the World Population Conference, Belgrade, August 30-September 10, 1965* (United Nations Publication Sales Nos: 66.XIII.2-5 [UN Documents E/CONF. 41/2-5]) (New York, 1966), Vol. III: *Selected Papers and Summaries of the Papers for Meetings,* p. 421.

[7] K. M. Malin, "Food Resources of the Earth," in ibid., p. 390.

When viewed in a regional context, however, the food problem assumes new dimensions revealing a serious gap between developed and developing countries in their ability to meet their food requirements. The interactive effects of the food and technology gaps make each even more salient than would otherwise be the case. The inevitable interjection of political discourse when confronting these differentials adds further uncertainty to an already complex system of relations.

Of the many factors in the food problem the transfer of food is especially fraught with critical international implications. The salience of the food issue in developing societies is such that in today's world the development of international guidelines for food distribution ranks in importance with the need for guidelines in international transfers of knowledge and skills. In this context the domestic situation of donor countries is an important factor influencing the possibilities for the development of international food transfer guidelines. For example, the ability of the United States to supply a substantial part of the future world deficit is undoubtedly curtailed by the expansion of urban areas at the expense of cropland. Despite technological advances it is expected that future demands for recreation will further restrict agricultural output. In this respect it is estimated that, by the year 2000, "satisfaction of all projected demands would mean the use of every acre in the 48 contiguous states, including deserts, mountain peaks, and marshes. Even at that, there would result a net shortage of 50 million acres. . . . Excluding recreational needs there would still be a shortage."[8] We need not generalize from the United States case to Canada or to other donor countries for this much is clear: Levels and rates of population growth, in combination with levels and rates of technological development, give rise to demands that increasingly call upon the utilization of land for purposes other than agriculture.

Another key factor in the food transfer equation pertains to the usages of fertilizers. Aside from the problems of fertilizer shortages, of shortages in component minerals, or of the unanticipated negative consequences of fertilizer usages the increased fertilizer usage in recipient countries occasions corresponding increases in fertilizer imports. The case of Communist China may be the rule rather than the exception as the implications of growth trends reveal. Although it was in a position of agricultural self-sufficiency in the 1950s, Communist China is now dependent upon imports of grain and fertilizers. In view of present population projections it is expected that Com-

[8] Hans H. Landsberg, *Natural Resources for U.S. Growth: A Look Ahead to the Year 2000* (Baltimore, Md: Johns Hopkins Press [for Resources for the Future, Inc.], 1964), pp. 173-174.

munist China will need to increase its grain output by 50 to 60 million tons in the 1970s, requiring in the process 20 to 30 million tons of chemical fertilizers per year.[9]

The world's oceans have been proposed as a substitute for land in food production, but their contribution has been overestimated. At least within the next ten to twenty years they cannot be considered as economically realistic sources of food for mankind. Furthermore, basic international differentials in the distribution of knowledge and skills contribute to further inequalities in the eventual uses of oceans. Land-based production is still the only viable alternative.[10] Also, while migration of population within national boundaries might alleviate some regional shortages, migrations alone cannot be viewed as a globally applicable solution to national problems. Invariably international linkages will become more rather than less salient.

In view of these considerations we are forced to note the obvious: In many countries the meeting of food needs increasingly involves imports. International implications of national needs must be carefully examined. In the absence of international guidelines for the transfer of food and fertilizers such needs inevitably involve dependency relationships. We know that dependency relations are not new, but it is important to realize their potential implications. Recent investigations have indicated that the dynamics of conflict are invariably embedded within situations of dependency and that these are reinforced when dependencies extend across several issue areas thus possibly institutionalizing hostilities rather than diluting them.[11]

III. POLITICAL IMPLICATIONS OF POPULATION DYNAMICS: NATIONAL AND INTERNATIONAL PERSPECTIVES

Statistical uncertainties are matched by equally great uncertainties regarding the socioeconomic and political implications of continued population growth. The basic malthusian thesis that indefinite population growth will bring widespread poverty is applicable only under conditions of isolation from international trade, minimal standards

[9] Victor-Bostrom Fund and Population Crisis Committee, *Population and Family Planning in the People's Republic of China* (Washington, Spring 1971), pp. 12-13. This is an estimate of total annual fertilizer needs.

[10] The effects of the Green Revolution are not to be denied. But implications in the context of related factors, such as population growth and technological growth (or lag), are more ambiguous. See Graham Jones, *The Role of Science and Technology in Developing Countries* (New York: Oxford University Press, 1971).

[11] For a summary of recent findings see Robert C. North and Nazli Choucri, "Population and the International System: Some Implications for United States Policy and Planning" (Paper prepared for the National Commission on Population Growth and the American Future, August 1971).

of living, marginal flexibility in technology, and low energy output. In such cases fluctuations in food availability have direct effects on the number of people depending upon a given set of resources. Today such conditions are most closely approximated by the close to subsistence levels of many Asian and African countries. However, if one of these factors is absent, the malthusian rationale is undercut by the possibility of modifying the underlying resource base.[12]

In negating the malthusian premise the marxist perspective defines the problem in terms of distribution: If resources and technology were properly utilized and distributed, the entire population of the world could subsist on existing resources. The concept of absolute overpopulation is, in principle, denied. Missing from both the malthusian and the marxist perspectives is a sufficient appreciation of the implications of differential levels of technology and their repercussions on the viable resource base and on the external environment.

The nonmalthusian view, propounded by Jean Mayer, considers the relationship of changes in levels of wealth to changes in levels of population. The case is made for population control on exactly the inverse of the basic malthusian premise: Controlling the number of the rich is deemed far more crucial than controlling the number of the poor. This view highlights a basic reality of our times for the rich consume more, pollute more, and discharge greater amounts of waste in the atmosphere. In terms of the environmental crisis population control is a more critical problem in developed societies than in less developed societies in which technological deficiencies and low energy outputs do not cause large-scale, negative environmental outcomes. However, with increasing industrialization pollution and waste may not be readily avoided.

Yet, population control alone is not an adequate solution. Without resorting to the extremes of Paul Ehrlich's position it might be emphasized that population growth occasions a nonlinear, negative impact on the environment.[13] Thus, it is imperative that population, resources, technology, and environmental effects be considered jointly. No less important is a reassessment of the social, economic, and political rules and regulations that were developed at a time when the environmental crisis was less pronounced. We are presently witnessing the cumulative effects of dynamics that were set in motion much earlier than has been recognized. Indeed, the effects of population growth are characterized by long time lags. Inadequate assessments

[12] Edward A. Ackerman, "Population and Natural Resources," in *The Study of Population: An Inventory and Appraisal,* ed. Philip M. Hauser and Otis Dudley Duncan (Chicago, Ill: University of Chicago Press, 1959), pp. 637-638.
[13] Paul R. Ehrlich and John P. Holdsen, "Impact of Population Growth," *Science,* March 26, 1971 (Vol. 171, No. 3977), p. 1212.

of the problem might activate causal chains of reactions whose implications might not be fully understood and of whose consequences we
are not fully cognizant.[14] Equally important is an emerging appreciation of 1) what it is that we need to be asking, 2) what it is that
we need to know, and 3) what it is that we do know about the
political implications of the present environmental crisis.

At a general level of abstraction recent trends seem to indicate
that increased population means more government and that more
government means greater regulation of individual behavior. The
trend toward centralization emerges as much from the increasing complexity of social organization as from the recognition that resource
constraints imposed by growing population need to be subject to discipline regarding their uses.[15] But there is no indication that this trend
toward increased centralization continues on the supranational level.
Scarcities might well obstruct the development of international organizations.

Among the most critical implications of increasing populations
for political systems and social institutions are the following: Population growth places unavoidable and increasing demands for goods
and services upon national government.[16] In underdeveloped countries
it is generally the lowest economic or politically powerless groups
which remain unattended in the allocation of resources and wealth.
Severe problems of governmental management that result from population pressures are especially evident in countries that are both large
and less developed. Aside from pressures on the allocation of resources
numbers alone are not crucial to the political process in developing
societies. But they are increasingly important in developed societies
in which political participation is high and in which demands can be
expressed proportionately to numbers. Related to this is the consideration that governments find themselves in a position to manipulate the population issue in desired ways. In countries where there
are insufficient job opportunities there is a tendency to channel excess manpower into the educational system, thus overburdening educational facilities and artificially underemploying labor.

However straightforward these implications might be, their ramifications in terms of political instability or violent behavior are highly
ambiguous. Indeed, there is no evidence that population densities

[14] Statement of E. F. Watt, *The Effects of Population Growth, Hearings,* September 15, 1969, p. 33.
[15] Emilio Q. Daddario, "Technology and the Democratic Process," *Technology
Review,* July-August 1971 (Vol. 73, No. 9), p. 20.
[16] Myron Weiner, "Political Demography: An Inquiry into the Political Consequences of Population Change," in *Rapid Population Growth: Consequences
and Policy Implications* (Baltimore, Md: Johns Hopkins Press, 1971), pp. 567-
617.

per se lead to instabilities. Those correlations that do exist are spurious and do not hold cross-culturally. Many densely populated areas of the world have been highly stable, and many of the most unstable areas in Latin America and Africa have low population densities.[17] More rigorous, multivariate, statistical analysis of the relationship between density and internal violence or instability has reinforced this singular absence of relationship, causal or otherwise.[18]

The related proposition that density occasions external violence is also dubious. Many high-density countries lack the capabilities for effective expansion or external aggression. Whatever relationship exists is neither direct nor empirically evident. If at all causally connected, linkages between population and war are likely to be mediated by intervening effects of technological development and resource constraints.

This relationship is emphasized even more forcefully by Alfred Sauvy, past president of the United Nations Population Commission. The theory that "overpopulation causes wars is attractive at first sight: when men lack room they are held to feel the need to spread out and take the land and wealth of others." However, there are many highly populated countries that have not been expansionist and other less populated ones that have been highly belligerent. Sauvy is led to the conclusion that "wars are not due to unrest of compressed populations, but to differences in pressure."[19] Acutely overpopulated societies do not generally command the capabilities or resources for sustained military activity. Despite some prima facie evidence in this direction no one has yet demonstrated the direct link between population and war. This link, in fact, has been refuted in two large-scale, empirical studies of conflict and warfare.[20]

Conversely, the *interactive* effects of population growth, technological development, and resource constraints have, in several cases, contributed to the extension of national activities outside of territorial boundaries. For example, nineteenth-century colonial expansion was accompanied by considerable population growth in Europe in combination with increases in economic productivity and technological capabilities. Investigations by Robert North and myself have traced these dynamics to the outbreak of war in 1914 and to the subsequent re-

[17] Ibid.
[18] See, for example, Douglas Albert Hibbs, "Domestic Mass Violence: A Cross-National Causal Analysis" (Ph.D. diss., University of Wisconsin, 1971).
[19] Alfred Sauvy, *General Theory of Population* (New York: Basic Books, Publishers, 1969), p. 516.
[20] The Correlates of War Project, under the direction of J. David Singer, University of Michigan, and the Studies in International Conflict and Integration, under the direction of Robert C. North, Stanford University, both report this same absence of *direct* link between population (density) and war.

constitution of international politics during the interwar years.[21] Not unrelated are the official arguments presented by both the German and the Japanese leaderships in support of their positions and policies. *What is critical, therefore, is the nature of the population-resource-technology calculus.* Unless capabilities are available, unless a certain level of skills can be called upon, and unless certain resource needs or constraints are present, it is difficult to see how the population variable *alone* would provide important motivation for violence and warfare.

It is also frequently suggested that the widening gaps between affluent and poverty-stricken states will lead directly into war, the implication being that the starving millions will be goaded into violence by their misery. This is unlikely. The threat of international violence emerges less from such possibilities than from second- or higher-order effects linking competition and interactions between larger states to political considerations affecting poorer societies. When technological and resource variables are interjected into the equation, the calculus becomes one of mapping out linkages and transactions between technologically advanced and technologically deficient states, between resource-rich and resource-poor, and between high-energy and low-energy societies.

Not unrelated is the consideration that many of the resources vital to continuing growth and advanced industrial societies are located in poverty-stricken, low-energy, and low-technology societies. Their territories and accompanying resources supply the arena for potential conflicts and competition between more advanced states, and they themselves are likely to be under pressure to line up on one side or the other. Control and penetration by advanced industrial societies assures continuing flows of needed resources. The erosion of cold-war dynamics in no way militates against these processes. The use of trade, foreign aid, and other modes of transfer are rarely devoid of political pressures.

In these terms national propensities for expansion, conflict, and violence differ considerably depending upon the nature of the population-resource-technology calculus. States rating high on population, technology, and resources are likely to be associated with modes of international behavior markedly different from those associated with low population, low technology, and low resources—or variants thereof. Comparing states along these dimensions might highlight the political dimension. For example, the differences in modes of external

[21] Nazli Choucri and Robert C. North, "Dynamics of International Conflict: Some Policy Implications of Population, Resources and Technology," *World Politics*, supplementary issue on *Theory and Policy in International Relations*, forthcoming.

behavior throughout the past century between the Scandinavian countries and the major powers are illustrative of these interrelationships.[22]
The Scandinavians were inclined to rely upon trade rather than upon
colonial expansion for the satisfaction of needs and demands. There
were many reasons why this was the case. Not incidental is the fact
that the Scandinavians registered low on population, high on technology, and low on resources. Conversely, Germany and Japan, during the interwar period, were both high on population and technology
and low on resources.[23] China in 1912 could be viewed as high on
population, low on technology, and low on resources whereas today
the balance is much more on the high population, high technology,
and possibly even the high resources end of the continuum. To note
the differences in China's external orientation over the past century
may be to point to the obvious, but the differences are not unrelated
to changes in attributes and capabilities of which population, resources,
and technology are the most crucial.

Of course these comparisons are all relative, and what might be
viewed as high in one context may be considered low in another.
The intensely interdependent nature of these dynamics makes any
generalizations extremely hazardous. Nonetheless, several inferences
may be drawn from these sketchy comparisons: 1) Population alone
has no political implications, domestically or internationally; 2) a
state's population must be viewed in conjunction with its resources
and technological capabilities; 3) different combinations of population and capability allow for different internal and external policies
and behaviors; and 4) only through second-order effects do population variables assume any political importance.

In terms of *political* considerations the most critical international
implications of the population-resource-technology calculus are those
associated with conflict and violence. Elsewhere we have argued that
major wars often emerge by way of a two-step process: first in terms
of internally generated pressures toward expansion of interests that
are occasioned by growing needs and demands and then in terms of
reciprocal comparisons, rivalries, and conflicts for control over resources, valued goods, territory, or spheres of influence.[24] Each step
is closely related to the other, and each is intimately tied to the nature of the underlying population-resource-technology differential.

[22] Nazli Choucri, with the collaboration of Robert C. North, "In Search of
Peace Systems: Scandinavia and the Netherlands, 1870-1970," in *War, Peace
and Numbers,* ed. Bruce M. Russett, forthcoming.
[23] Richard P. Lagerstrom and Robert C. North, "Germany and Japan: A Comparative Application of a Model of Expansion" (Paper prepared for the Western
Political Science Association Meeting, April 8-10, 1971).
[24] Choucri and North, in *World Politics,* forthcoming. Also see Robert C. North
and Nazli Choucri, *Nations in Conflict: Prelude to World War I,* in preparation.

A major part of contemporary international complexities can be traced to the fact that the highly industrialized countries, which contain only a small portion of the world's population, consume a disproportionate share (on a per capita basis) of the world's supply of energy-producing fuels and mineral resources. About 6 percent of the world's population consumes close to 40 percent of the world's processed resources year by year.[25] The imbalances are equally pronounced in the raw materials sphere: Thirty percent of the global population lives in industrialized areas and consumes about 90 percent of the total world production of energy and mineral resources.[26] Additionally, increasing trends toward the establishment of processing plants in technologically deficient areas are associated with differentials in labor costs.

While it is indisputable that benefits accrue to developing societies in their transactions with industrialized states, it is not our purpose to clarify the cost-benefit calculus for the parties involved. We seek only to highlight various implications of these differentials—in resources and in technology—for contemporary international politics. The empirical data we bring to bear on this issue and the inferences which they allow pertain specifically to four major powers—Communist China, Japan, the Soviet Union, and the United States—and their relationships with other states and potential global repercussions. Our concerns are mainly with the international implications of national behavior, with specific emphasis upon potential conflict-producing dynamics.

IV. ENERGY DEMANDS: INTERACTIVE EFFECTS OF POPULATION AND TECHNOLOGY

The combined populations of Communist China, Japan, the Soviet Union, and the United States amount to 1.3 billion, growing at an average rate of 1.3 percent per year. This growth will undoubtedly continue to generate rapidly increasing demands for both the mineral and energy-producing resources that are so critical to industrial processes. There is considerable disagreement between scholars and policymakers concerning the precise loads to be expected on economically available energy sources. While it is apparent that the more technologically advanced countries enjoy a crucial advantage in obtaining resources that are difficult to reach or that require high levels of knowledge and skills and sophisticated machinery to process, less apparent

[25] Daddario, *Technology Review*, Vol. 73, No. 9, p. 20.
[26] M. King Hubbert, "Mineral Resources and Rates of Consumption," in *Proceedings of the World Population Conference, 1965*, Vol. III, p. 318.

are the potential repercussions of existing technological differentials among the various states of the world. These differentials are compounded further by the impressive postwar increases in the number of sovereign states in the international system. This proliferation has vastly complicated the process of international interaction, and this is further exacerbated by sharp differentials in populations, in access to resources, and in levels of technological development.

One key to defining the energy vector of the environmental crisis lies in the consideration that every advance in technology—every application, every invention, and every discovery—requires resources from the environment. Historically, technological developments have given rise to new energy and resource requirements without marked advances in energy-saving and energy-producing technologies, and there is every reason to believe that future developments in technology will occasion more extensive resource requirements. Today there is greater agreement between experts on variable estimates of the extent or nature of future requirements than on optimal modes of meeting those requirements. By necessity the development of guidelines for present resource allocations to meet expected future needs is central to any energy calculus and accompanying political and economic implications.

Because the industrialized countries consume most of the world's production of energy, forecasts of energy supply and demand are generally calculated in terms of one or more advanced countries and largely as a function of projected changes in standards of living and associated needs. When continued access to external sources of energy is assumed, the short-term outlook for more developed countries appears to be adequate, if not optimistic. In a 1966 study the Organisation for Economic Co-operation and Development (OECD) concluded that "ample supplies will be available for OECD countries at reasonable costs to support continued economic growth up to 1980 and beyond."[27] There is every reason to believe that this estimate can easily be extended to the year 2000. However, when the assumption of continued access to external sources is relaxed, or when individual domestic sources of energy are examined, assessments such as these emerge in a new light: It becomes apparent that new sources of commercially available energy are required and implications of increasing reliance upon energy imports must be critically evaluated and reassessed.

Present and future reliance upon imported energy varies extensively. Some countries import chiefly for economic advantage—when

[27] Organization for Economic Co-operation and Development, *Energy Policy: Problems and Objectives* (Paris, 1966), p. 143.

the costs of imported fuels are lower than the costs of domestic exploitation—and others import from economic necessity. In many cases the situation is such that domestic sources are simply not available or present levels of technology do not permit internal exploitation at other than prohibitive prices. Among developed states the situation looks as follows: Measured in terms of metric coal equivalents, most industrialized societies—including France, the Federal Republic of Germany (West Germany), Japan, the Netherlands, the Scandinavian countries, the United Kingdom, and the United States—are net energy importers. According to recent United Nations figures the United States produced an annual average of about 37.5 percent of the world's total production of energy between 1955 and 1968 while consuming a little over 39.8 percent.[28] The balance is on the inflow side. Japan produced 2.1 percent of the world's total and consumed over 3.3 percent. Again the balance is on inflow. The West European countries all consumed a larger share of world energy than their contribution in terms of domestic production. By contrast, of all the industrialized states only the Soviet Union is a net exporter, producing considerably more than is utilized domestically. Although the Soviet Union produces and consumes less than one-half of the total energy processed by the United States, the absolute levels involved are still extremely high. During the same period Communist China seems to have struck a balance, consuming approximately as much as was produced internally.

There is a strong, positive relationship between industrialization, energy consumption, and standard of living.[29] In the United States, for example, each person on the average consumes more than 3100 calories every day, a standard shared by less than 10 percent of the world's population.[30] It has been estimated that if present growth rates were to continue, 130 years would be required for some of the poorer countries to reach the level of per capita income which is now characteristic of the richer countries. Some may take less, others much longer. But by that time, at present growth rates, the population of the poorer countries would reach 130 billion persons.[31]

Implicit in differentials of income and capability are certain

[28] See United Nations Statistical Office, *World Energy Supplies* (UN Documents ST/STAT/Series J, Nos. 4-12) (New York, 1961-1969).

[29] Gerald Manners, *The Geography of Energy* (London: Hutchinson and Co., 1964). Because the correlation between energy consumption and economic activity is so close, one is often used to estimate the other.

[30] Harrison Brown, James Bonner, and John Weir, *The Next Hundred Years: Man's Natural and Technological Resources: A Discussion Prepared for Leaders of American Industry* (New York: Viking Press, 1963), p. 10.

[31] Harrison Brown, "Science, Technology and the Developing Countries," *Bulletin of the Atomic Scientists,* June 1971 (Vol. 27, No. 6), p. 11.

critical considerations. For example, rapid increases in world population impose severe burdens on efforts to raise standards of living: An annual population growth of one percent requires an annual growth of 4 percent in national income in order to maintain existing standards of living.[32] A world population of seven billion, living at the economic standard of the United States, would require from 200 to 400 times the present annual rates of mineral resources consumption (and commensurate magnitudes of energy fuels).[33] Implications of this nature raise serious questions concerning the dominant form of transaction between developed and developing societies: raw material exchanges for finished products or industrial goods. Undoubtedly, the encouragement of trade with developing societies enhances chances of industrialization and provides needed capital and other goods. But, at the same time, the prospect of rising prices for both fuel and mineral resources associated with impending constraints or local shortages (defined in economic terms) undoubtedly works to the disadvantage of those societies less capable of meeting prices.

The sometimes symbiotic relationship between a major industrialized state and a predominantly agrarian or commercial society leads to dependency relationships which are generally termed patron-client, colonial-colonized, or penetrating state—host country. The labels differ according to the degree of institutionalization in the relationships and the extent to which patterns of interaction, exchange of goods, and transference of services are legitimated by formal alliance relationships or by other authoritative means of control. This is nót to suggest that all relationships between unequal parties are exploitative in nature but rather that assistance and exploitation are sometimes closely related.

The political implications of transaction patterns are more clearly seen in the area of mineral resources than in the energy field. Critical to energy considerations is the fact that if all countries were to follow a path of industrialization charted by advanced societies, with accompanying patterns of consumption and demand, the problem of future supply would be vastly more critical than it is at present. Over the past twenty years demand for energy in the United States has increased at an average annual rate of 3.1 percent.[34] It is esti-

[32] Zdenek Vavra, "Projections of World Population (Distinguishing More Developed and Less Developed Areas at Present)," in *Proceedings of the World Population Conference, 1965*, Vol. 2: *Selected Papers and Summaries: Fertility, Family Planning, Mortality*, pp. 49-53.

[33] Statement by Preston E. Cloud, Jr., *The Effects of Population Growth, Hearings*, September 15, 1969, p. 6.

[34] United States Bureau of Mines, *Mineral Facts and Problems, 1970* (Washington: Government Printing Office, 1970), p. 13. The 1970 edition of this volume places great emphasis on prediction and forecasting. In view of the

mated that the absolute consumption of electric power in the United States alone is doubling every ten years and, on a per capita basis, every twelve years.

The demand for energy for the rest of the world has been growing at rates nearly double those of the United States, with the largest growth in the industrialized countries of Asia and Africa. Energy consumption for commercial purposes is also growing faster in the less developed countries. Despite variabilities in philosophical perspectives—whether malthusian, nonmalthusian, or marxist—it is difficult to see how resultant levels of energy demand can be met with known sources of fuel. For this reason the critical imperatives in the energy field include: 1) increasing the efficiency of present energy systems; 2) improving production methods to minimize environmental resistance; and 3) developing new energy systems.[35]

But will present reserves of fossil fuel be sufficient to meet rising demands until the commercial development of alternative sources of energy? Throughout human history more than three-quarters of the world's total energy consumption has depended upon fossil fuels. By current calculations, however, fuel shortages are expected in the foreseeable future (at least in economic terms), but much in dispute is the question of whether the lifetime of fossil fuel reserves is in fact 30 or 300 years. A general consensus seems to emerge that in the short run—from now until the turn of the century—known fuel reserves are adequate to meet expected rises in demands. Beyond this the situation remains uncertain.[36] *The primary danger, however, is not one of fuel depletion but of rising costs of energy processing: dollar costs, real costs, and costs to the environment occasioned by*

interdependence between economic, technological, and other factors it has been deemed necessary to develop alternative predictions based on contingency forecasting techniques. See pages 9-11 of the 1970 edition for a description of method, assumptions, and caveats. For each mineral resource the Bureau of Mines presents a "high," "median," and "low" prediction of demand and supply in 2000. Contingencies and caveats are clearly spelled out. The 1965 edition relies on more inflexible trend extrapolation techniques.

[35] Ibid., p. 19.

[36] Between now and whenever the new technologies achieve effective output there will be a difficult period during which the countries of the world will be relying heavily upon oil, coal, and other traditional resources. Thus, in a technical sense the energy crisis is not imminent. Yet many social and political implications are already manifest, and many more can be foreseen in decades to come. The eventual technological capability to build fast breeder reactors is not in question despite uncertainties concerning their timing for commercial purposes. Once breeders do become operational on a large scale, they would supply a large part of the world's energy demands for several centuries to come. At efficient rates of uranium usages it is estimated that the date of depletion of the energy stock would be prolonged to at least a millenium. See Hans Thirring, *Energy for Man: Windmills to Nuclear Power* (Bloomington: Indiana University Press, 1958).

extraction. The development of alternative forms of energy is seen as a means of offsetting inevitable increases in the costs of processing fossil fuels. But uncertainties involving the timetable for the commercial development of nuclear energy, of thermonuclear fusion, or, even more remotely, of solar energy make it difficult to assess prospects beyond the year 2000.[37]

In terms of political implications only giant industrial states will be able to afford or even possess the capabilities for developing the new technologies. States that succeed in reducing the costs of energy before others will thus be able to gain important advantages in the world market and strengthen their industrial capability and leverage for influence in the less developed world. This will almost certainly create or perpetuate dependency relationships and competition between industrialized states for influence in less developed regions. Although the problem of energy distribution internationally is more likely to be alleviated by the development of cheap nuclear power, from this perspective, at least, differentials in costs will undoubtedly render inequalities of wealth even more salient than they are today.

The farther one projects into the future, the more dependent forecasts are upon continued technological and social development to sustain and support emerging technologies. On balance it appears that in the field of energy supply and demand, in which the long-range outlook is almost wholly dependent upon new technologies, speculating beyond the year 2000 is less fraught with difficulties on the demand side than on the supply side. In terms of the larger environmental crisis, however, it is difficult to appreciate the full implications of the resource vector without a parallel perspective on minerals.

V. RESOURCE CONSTRAINTS: MINERAL DISTRIBUTIONS AND INTERNATIONAL IMPLICATIONS

The critical issues for mineral resources involve demand and

---

[37] These comparisons are, strictly speaking, not exactly comparable. But as one expert puts it:

> Unless we find a lot more uranium, or pay a lot more money for it, or get a functioning complete breeder reactor or contained nuclear fusion within ten or fifteen years, the energy picture will be far from bright. There is good reason to hope that the breeder will come, and after it contained fusion, *if* the U^{235} and helium hold out—but there is no room for complacency.

(Preston E. Cloud, Jr., "Realities of Mineral Distribution," in *The Effects of Population Growth, Hearings,* p. 225, reprinted from *Texas Quarterly,* Summer 1968 [Vol. 2, No. 2], pp. 103-126.) Estimates and calculations are wildly approximate and are complicated even further by the factor of delay between discovery and exploitation of deposits. There is also the possibility that if poorer ores are usable, as they presumably would be with breeders, the supply of uranium should not be an immediate constraint.

depletion, costs and distribution. The magnitude of consumption in the United States alone during the past 30 years has exceeded all known previous consumption aggregated over the history of mankind. The costs of many minerals are rising faster than the growth of the economy and, for many minerals, the rates of discovery and development of new reserves have been declining over the past twenty years. From a global perspective, therefore, the main cause for alarm seems to be the exponential rise in rates of extraction and usage. The major international repercussion of such trends is that most industrialized states are becoming increasingly dependent upon external sources for satisfaction of domestic needs.[38]

As with other vectors of the environmental crisis, the evidence is sufficiently ambiguous to occasion radically different assessments of problems and prospects. Added complications are occasioned by methods of projections: Frequently used contingency techniques are primarily based upon projection of rates of population growth and economic performance, thereby compounding uncertainties. In many cases assessments of future supply and demand of mineral resources portray a bleak situation in view of the rising extraction and consumption rates in conjunction with the projected rates of population growth. Rarely included in the same analyses are projections of future supplies or possible substitutes. Pessimistic views regarding the future adequacy of raw materials tend to overlook the fact that both reserves and demands are functions of time: The amount of resources available tends to increase with new discoveries, new substitution possibilities, and new technological developments. The pattern of copper, whose reserves in the United States have remained relatively constant over the past 30 years, or iron ore, whose worldwide reserves are considered to have doubled over the past decade largely due to technological improvements in extraction and processing, illustrate two cases in point. Nonetheless, the interactive effects of technological development and increasing substitution possibilities raise serious questions concerning the validity of the more pessimistic assessments.

Conversely, once the cost factor is included in this calculus, the situation looks much different. A major contention between optimists, who foresee mineral plenty, and pessimists, who project unavoidable shortages, is whether cost increases of a dislocating nature can, in fact, be averted. Magnitudes of costs and not absolute depletions are at issue, costs which could impose severe strains on industrial economies if not large-scale disruptions of the underlying substructure.

In those terms optimism regarding mineral resources is predi-

---

[38] *Minerals, Facts and Problems, 1970*, pp. 2-5.

cated on the development of low-cost, energy-intensive modes of extracting progressively lower grades of ores at only gradually increasing prices. The basis for this position is the observed relationship between the concentration of a mineral and its abundance. But the arithmetic-geometric ratio, whereby the amount of mineral increases exponentially as its concentration decreases arithmetically, is applicable only to certain minerals. For some minerals the arithmetic-geometric ratio is simply not applicable; for others the difference between the concentration of ore in presently mined ore bodies and the concentration in much lower but more abundant grades is prohibitively large. Such is the case with tin, nickel, molybdenum, manganese, cobalt, industrial diamonds, lead, and zinc.[39] The concentration of these minerals is very high in known mining locations and very low in all other rock. This situation, in effect, buttresses more pessimistic assessments of future resource supplies. It also undercuts the basic rationale underlying more optimistic assessments which are based on inferences drawn from the arithmetic-geometric ratio in cases in which it is simply not applicable.

Still unclear, however, is the ability of industrial society to develop economically viable substitutes for all critical minerals that are scarce as well as to increase significantly the possibilities of recycling, often called secondary production. Comparatively little recycling is presently undertaken in the United States or elsewhere, largely because of the geographic dispersion of recyclable substances. The problem here is one of organization and not of technological feasibility (although they are highly interdependent).[40]

In sum, while there is little consensus about the severity of mineral depletion, there is general agreement concerning the definition of the relevant factors. Both optimists and pessimists view technology as the most crucial variable. Cheap energy, energy-intensive extraction of low-grade ores, and substitutions of more plentiful raw materials for minerals facing shortages are held as keys to the problem, but the actual feasibility of these solutions is much disputed. More complex and still unclear, however, are the political—especially international—implications of the resource situation in the present and immediate future. Although resources may be located in less developed countries, in terms of applying known technology the developed countries are clearly at an advantage. This, coupled with their increasing dependence upon external resources, raises important questions concerning future trends in international policies although

---

[39] Preston E. Cloud, Jr., "Realities of Mineral Distribution," *Texas Quarterly,* Summer 1968 (Vol. 2, No. 2), pp. 103-126.

[40] In this regard see *Minerals, Facts and Problems, 1970.*

relations between developed societies are no less crucial in a world of potential mineral scarcity.

In the introduction to a volume on the international minerals situation, *Mineral Facts and Problems: 1970*, the United States Bureau of Mines notes that an increasing reliance by industrial countries upon external resources in recent years has been coupled with decreasing reliance on any one source. As a step toward mapping out some of the political implications of these developments for Communist China, Japan, the Soviet Union, and the United States the author has sought to determine the extent of their reliance upon foreign sources for 37 mineral resources critical to industrial processes by computing a dependency index based upon the latest available data. The index, defined as imports-exports/consumption, allows for a comparative assessment of reliance upon external sources mineral by mineral across countries.[41] This index, of course, is influenced by the specific definition of imports, exports, and consumption as presented by the Bureau of Mines. It is also influenced by variability in data accuracies and estimates. Allowing for a margin of measurement error for cross-national comparisons, the appendix to this article summarizes the dependency trends in these four countries, discussed more extensively below.

According to computations based upon governmental data the United States is highly reliant upon external sources for manganese, nickel, platinum, tin, zinc, bauxite, beryllium, chromium, cobalt, and fluorspar, and it is moderately reliant upon imports of mercury, titanium, iron ore, copper, and aluminum.[42] Manganese is essential to steel production, and, in view of the source countries—Brazil (26 percent) and Gabon (31 percent)—it may be the most likely mineral constraint for the United States in this century. Major exporters for other essential minerals are Belgium-Luxembourg, Canada, Mexico,

[41] See the appendix for discussion of the dependency index measure and for problems and caveats. See Nazli Choucri and Dennis L. Meadows, with the research assistance of Michael Laird and James P. Bennett, "International Implications of Technological Development and Population Growth: A Simulation Model of International Conflict" (Cambridge, Mass: Department of Political Science and Alfred P. Sloan School of Management, Massachusetts Institute of Technology, September 1971), for an earlier, briefer version of this comparative discussion of mineral resources in four states. The dependency index measure ranges from $+1$ to -1 in cases in which stockpiles are excluded; otherwise the measure may exceed $+1$. A quotient closer to $+1$ signifies greater reliance on external sources; conversely, one closer to -1 signifies greater dependence on internal sources. See the appendix for sources of data cited below and the period over which computations are based.

[42] Conversely, the United States is a net exporter of molybdenum, tungsten, vanadium, coal, gold, helium, sulfur, and magnesium. For other key minerals, such as iron ore, copper, petroleum, and natural gas, there has been no trend toward increasing United States reliance on foreign sources since 1958.

the Philippines, the Republic of South Africa, Spain, Thailand, and the United Kingdom. With few exceptions *exporting countries are either allied directly to the United States or lie within the American sphere of influence.*

In the case of the Soviet Union the situation is almost the reverse. It is demonstrably less reliant upon external sources. There are only two industrial minerals for which net imports exceed 20 percent of current consumption. One is bauxite, imported from Greece (40 percent) and the Socialist Federal Republic of Yugoslavia (60 percent). To date the Soviet Union has preferred to import bauxite from closer (and presumably more secure) sources despite lower quality rather than to acquire higher quality bauxite from more extensive deposits in Jamaica and Surinam (both of which are leading exporters to the United States). The second mineral is tin, imported from Malaysia (30 percent) and the United Kingdom (68 percent). However, since cheap substitutes do exist for tin, this metal cannot be considered militarily or industrially crucial.

Differences between the United States and the Soviet Union in terms of reliance upon external sources is even more forcefully portrayed in a recent study noting that of 36 minerals crucial to industrial processes the Soviet Union is self-sufficient in 26 and the United States is self-sufficient in only seven.[43] To some extent these divergent trends have resulted from consciously pursued policies. The United States has generally permitted individual firms to pursue short-term profit maximization and limited its support for domestic extraction industries to exploration and depletion subsidies. In addition, the United States has stockpiled minerals thought, at some point, to have been strategically important (and, in many cases, continues to do so despite changing situations). Soviet policies, in contrast, have generally been directed toward achieving industrial as well as short-term military independence of foreign sources for most crucial minerals. Foreign trade has always been subservient to the requirements of central planning: Economic and political considerations have customarily molded Soviet trade patterns.[44] In those terms at least the United States is considerably more vulnerable to dislocations occasioned by discontinuities in mineral flow.[45]

By these computations Communist China is almost totally self-

[43] Dr. Raymond Ewell, "U.S. will Lag U.S.S.R. in Raw Materials," *Chemical and Engineering News,* August 24, 1970 (Vol. 48), pp. 42-46.

[44] Charles K. Wilbur, *The Soviet Model and Underdeveloped Countries* (Chapel Hill: University of North Carolina Press, 1969).

[45] Several earlier studies have uncovered the same basic trend noted here. See Ewell, *Chemical and Engineering News,* Vol. 48, pp. 42-46; G. A. Rousch, *Strategic Mineral Supplies* (New York: McGraw-Hill Book Co., 1939); and

sufficient in mineral resources. With the exception of titanium (used mainly in high-speed aircraft and other military applications) it produces practically all of the minerals and fossil resources it needs for consumption. We have calculated the dependency index for 1966 and again for 1968, and the same general patterns emerge. Of course, uncertainties concerning the accuracy of Communist Chinese data make these inferences tentative, but the emerging trends are unmistakable.

By contrast Japan is almost totally dependent upon external sources for key minerals. There are thirteen important minerals for which imports equal or exceed 80 percent of consumption. These include both fuel and industrial resources. Of all of the technologically advanced powers Japan is confronted with no alternative other than reliance upon uninterrupted international trade to sustain its economy. In this case the issue is not whether resources might be acquired more cheaply elsewhere but that they are simply not available in Japan. Unlike the United States or the Soviet Union cost considerations are not as directly relevant.

Reliance on external sources raises the dual questions of security and continuity of relations with exporting states, be they developed or developing. In the case of the United States the leading mineral exporters are Canada and Mexico. Although, in those two cases at least, serious disruptions of resource flow are unlikely, the situation is more uncertain with respect to Brazil and Gabon (magnesium), or to Malaysia and Thailand (tin), or to Jamaica (bauxite), or to the Republic of South Africa and the Philippines (chromium), among others.[46] Because the political scene is highly fluid, it is increasingly difficult to forecast future outcomes on the basis of linear extrapolations from the past. Thus, in assessing future resource needs for any state political and economic factors become inevitably intertwined. It is therefore important to examine the availability issue in a wider environmental context.

In view of the interdependencies between determinant variables the comparative importance of individual minerals for each state can be evaluated on a two-dimensional field.[47] One axis measures the centrality of the mineral to a state's economy; the other measures

Charles F. Park, Jr., *Affluence in Jeopardy* (San Francisco, Calif: Freeman, Cooper and Co., 1968). A fourth study rated eleven states according to self-sufficiency regarding 26 industrial minerals; see C. K. Leith, I. W. Furness, and Cleona Lewis, *World Minerals and World Peace* (Washington: Brookings Institution, 1943). A table comparing the eleven countries according to degrees of self-sufficiency is presented on page 45.

[46] By contrast the Soviet Union is a major exporter of chromium to the United States.

[47] I am grateful to James P. Bennett for assisting in formalizing these distinctions.

the overall availability, including political and economic factors, roughly as in figure 1.

FIGURE 1. COMPARATIVE IMPORTANCE OF MINERALS

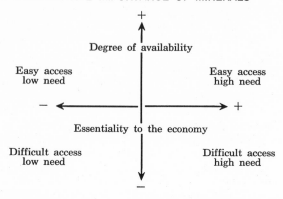

This crude perspective might highlight the relative cruciality of key minerals while allowing for cross-national comparisons. The most serious difficulty with such assessments—across minerals and across states—is their static nature. Technological innovations, changes in tastes, interaction between prices and availability, and changes in consumption patterns all interject highly variable effects, the implications of which are difficult to gauge. In addition changes in the position of one mineral in the field are inextricably bound with changes in the position of all other minerals. In this context substitutions, recycling, and new discoveries assume critical importance.

The centrality of a mineral depends, among other factors, on the type of economy in question. However, with respect to availability political considerations are paramount. For all states, especially the United States and the Soviet Union, the major questions in this regard pertain to the political orientation of the exporters, their geographic proximity and political volatility, and the degree of international competition for key world resources. Those considerations have become critical to any calculus of future mineral availability and accessibility. Clearly the greatest uncertainties pertain to lower income countries. Rapid industrialization will undoubtedly create additional demands on known reserves and exert pressures for readjustments of present modes of exchange.

The issue is not whether the major powers are exploiting or assisting developing countries—although this is clearly an important question—but that rapid industrialization in low-income countries, coupled with growing populations, will place additional burdens upon national governments and upon the existing resource base. Their national governments in turn—if the past several decades provide ready analogies for the unfolding situation—will undoubtedly express dissatisfaction with the industrialized-power–host-state relationship and demand readjustments. To the extent that major powers are willing to modify patterns of interaction and relationships the imbalances may be resolved by peaceful means. If the costs of readjustments are perceived as being too high, or if crucial national interests are at stake, probabilities are high that the industrialized powers will exert additional pressure, and nonmilitary means of control might give way before direct military coercion.

We realize that the more conflict-related aspects of the environmental crisis have been stressed so far. But we find it difficult to appreciate potential integrative forces in light of political considerations with clear implications for conflict. Conflict-producing dynamics become even more relevant when viewed from a combined population-resource-technology perspective. The synergistic and interactive environmental effects of these three vectors are most apparent in advanced industrial societies although the dynamics in question are emerging increasingly in rapidly developing low-income countries.

VI. CORRELATES OF GROWTH: ENVIRONMENTAL PROBLEMS AND ORGANIZATIONAL IMPERATIVES

The advanced industrial societies have been developing with little serious thought as to how their development—economic, technological, and scientific—may affect their own ecologies and the world environment. Today the global correlates of industrial growth are demonstrable: Much of what is termed production involves, in fact, extraction which depletes resources and occasions increasing environmental pollution. Pollution and depletion are two different manifestations of man's impact on his environment. The former is essentially a by-product of inadequate—but sometimes unavoidable—disposal systems resulting in the corruption of air, water, soil, and other aspects of the environment by human beings as a function of their technology. The latter emerges from the overuse of a given resource or of the more readily available deposits. In these terms pollution and depletion are direct correlates of growth and of man's unwillingness to modify the conditions that aggravate environmental problems. This situation is reinforced by the nature of our social organizations which place little formal value upon minimizing environmental dislocations occasioned by industrial processes and by the increasing numbers of people exposed to, and drawing upon, advancing technology.

By its very nature technological growth generates a vicious cycle: Increasing technology implies greater energy consumption, which implies increasing industrialization, which then generates further demands for material goods and services, which in turn results in greater consumption of more readily available resources, creating greater environmental problems and dislocations. The production, conversion, transfer, and consumption of energy are also responsible for a large part of our environmental problems. But this is only one side of the issue. The other is a materials disposal problem: Increasing technological growth has not given rise to a commensurate concern for the development of optimal modes of material disposal—optimal in both economic and environmental contexts. Thus, water pollution, air pollution, soil dislocation, and the like are different manifestations of our disregard for materials rejected in the course of industrial production. Some methods of disposal place greater loads on the environment than others, and some modes are less costly than others. So far we have opted for minimizing short-range economic costs at the expense of costs generated by longer range effects. Now we are confronted with cumulative environmental effects produced over long periods of time. We need to clean up the mess, and we need to develop preventive guidelines for the future. In each case we have been moving too slowly. That experts disagree as to the actual severity, magnitude, or extent of environmental dislocation should not be construed as a sign of optimism regarding our present predicament: The existence of serious environmental dislocations is not at issue, only their extent.

To place sole responsibility for our environmental crisis on the dynamics of growth would be incomplete and inaccurate. The present situation is further exacerbated by our economic and social systems— whether capitalist, socialist, or a mix thereof—which actively encourage environmental problems, thus rendering the implications of industrialization and population increase even more critical than might otherwise be the case. For example, the exclusion of negative outcomes incurred in the course of production from a price system designed to capture the costs of production encourages disregard for pollution control or for the development of materials disposal systems with minimal negative environmental implications. The transference and use of public goods, such as air and water, at zero cost provides little incentive for active environmental concern. Indeed, the costs of production are minimized by a disregard for effects occasioned by externalities.

By treating the environment as a free public good individuals in a society escape short-range costs, but, in the long run, the costs to the environment are cumulative and cannot be avoided by means other than direct confrontation. We have now begun to realize both the long- and short-range implications of our economic systems. If specific monetary costs were attached to environmental property, the effect would be to introduce cost-benefit criteria into the manipulation of goods that so far have been considered to be essentially free. However, any moves in this direction would involve large-scale organizational changes, a consideration few societies are willing to envisage on a scale which might provide a degree of effectiveness. In these terms advanced socialist societies demonstrate a remarkable similarity of view with their counterparts in the West.

Environmental problems are not confined to industrialized states. Rapidly developing low-income countries are beginning to incur the same kinds of problems. The overuse of soil capacity is not uncommon, and evidence of air and water pollution is becoming increasingly apparent. Unless other countries bear, or at least share, the costs, the political implications of any direct attempts to minimize the environmental side effects of industrialization must, by necessity, involve some explicit control of both pace and extent of growth. In those terms, at least, it is unlikely that developing societies would adopt self-imposed constraints on growth. Concern for the nature of the environment might appear as a luxury that only developed societies can afford. Quality-of-life issues pale in comparison to sustenance of life.

Even more complex is the development of international guidelines for environmental control: The gaps between developed and less developed societies might appear too great to allow for active cooperation in the development of control processes. It must be recognized that aside from political difficulties, the imposition of limits upon industrialization involves severe additional, built-in difficulties which make self-imposed constraints almost impossible. One means of controlling negative environmental outcomes would involve the explicit allocation of national resources for clean-up purposes or for the development of preventive measures in anticipation of environmental problems caused by industrial processes. In light of the scarcity calculus, however, diverting resources to objectives other than those associated directly with the maximizing of productivity is not a practical suggestion.

The important point is that many of our environmental problems are exacerbated—if not directly occasioned—by our social and economic systems. Appropriate organizational changes might make it possible to avert outcomes more serious than those presently apparent. Negative environmental effects are not necessarily correlates of industrial growth. Thy become so only to the extent that explicit provisions for regulation and control of technological externalities are not incorporated into and planned for in the growth calculus. In this context the application of band-aid technology or incremental piecemeal solutions is not likely to make an appreciable dent in the problem at hand. Nor are isolated programs designed to alleviate air or water pollution likely to improve the situation significantly.[48] If national environmental control programs are envisaged, to some extent these might need to be developed along congruent international lines and based upon globally articulated preferences and priorities.[49] The formulation of blueprints is a major undertaking the magnitude of which is dwarfed only by the potential worldwide implications if such efforts are not undertaken in the immediate future. Even more critical is the need to modify our economic systems so as to render them congruent with whatever measures of environmental control are devised. By addressing ourselves only to the clearest manifestations of the environmental crisis, such as air or water pollution, we may be doing future generations a disservice which they might find impossible to rectify. Unfortunately, melodramatic overtones of prevailing doomsday philosophies have resulted in a lessening of our appreciation of present predicaments.

Aside from cost factors various manifestations of the environmental crisis suggest that in the world of the late twentieth century various forms of ecological factors rank with population, technology, and resources as critical variables requiring measurement and regulation. In view of diverse environmental effects of industrialization, even if the poorer societies were capable of developing at rapid rates in relation to their population growth, a global population living at a standard equivalent to that of the United States would almost certainly create more rather than fewer disturbances in the physical environment, and accompanying patterns of consumption and production would only aggravate the political problems noted above. In those terms population control is not sufficient, nor is control over patterns of consumption in highly industrialized countries, nor the development of international guidelines for projected growth in technology-deficient areas. Such guidelines cannot be adequately developed without our willingness to undertake large-scale reassessments of our values, social and economic systems, and dominant modes of exchange.

The ultimate goal of rapid industrialization pursued by so many lower income countries is loaded with problems and uncertainties the

[48] In this connection see Frank P. Grad, George W. Rathjens, and Albert J. Rosenthal, *Environmental Control: Priorities, Policies and the Law* (New York: Columbia University Press, 1971).

[49] At this point it is difficult to say whether the congruence thesis has much validity; considerable research is still to be done.

magnitudes of which necessitate serious reassessments of the goal itself. Dominant international values emphasize the merit of technological advance. We must no longer accept sustained economic growth as a primary international objective. However, given the imperatives imposed by large and growing populations, it is difficult not to appreciate the necessity for technological advance. We must not accept too readily the assumption that technological innovation per se will alleviate our current problems, just as we must not accept the suggestion that population control per se will alleviate the present environmental crisis. What should be done is difficult, if not impossible, to say with any degree of precision. But we must be willing to reassess even the most hallowed political, social, and economic assumptions and value preferences. Beyond that the merits of alternative solutions or policies can be assessed only in light of the assumptions, data, and modes of analysis upon which they rest.

VII. FUTURE PERSPECTIVES: RESEARCH IMPERATIVES AND POLICY ALTERNATIVES

The global implications of our present predicament can be fully appreciated only in the dual contexts of costs and feasibilities: what needs to be done and what the costs are likely to be. In political terms the major issues of the future concern the control, allocation, and distribution of resources and technology. How this comes about, who develops the guidelines, and what control mechanisms are to be imposed upon the controllers are all crucial questions which pertain directly to whatever type of international institutions might be developed for such purposes. However indispensable many of them may be, present international institutions are scarcely adequate for regulating the critical variables at the core of present environmental problems. Related obstacles involve existing discontinuities in national and international preferences and priorities and accompanying authority structures and processes. In those terms, at least, the evolution of congruent national, regional, and global priorities amounts to a major challenge.

A compelling difficulty emerges from the fact that the dynamics of our present predicament are not fully understood nor are the long-range implications of proposed remedial action. Policies adopted to alleviate one kind of problem all too often produce unexpected consequences. More than ever before it has become necessary to undertake long-range investigations of potential effects occasioned by alternative courses of action. In view of these uncertainties it is important that we develop, refine, and apply methodologies *now* for analyzing relationships and interdependencies involving social organization and habit structure, acquisition of resources, pricing systems, economic and social underpinnings, population dynamics, technological growth, and resulting environmental resistance.

But research and analysis is only one side of the coin. The other, and more critical, imperative is to communicate the results of research to policymakers. The too frequent gap between academic and policy-oriented discourse is a luxury that can no longer be afforded. The academic task is twofold: 1) to specify and compile required data and 2) to analyze the data in a critical fashion. It is necessary to develop priorities for the compilation of data on different aspects of the environmental crisis. In many cases data is indeed available and needs only to be transferred to a format useful for analysis.[50] But this is not always the case. Indeed, we often do not know what it is that we ought to be asking. But in many cases the problem is one of gathering data in primary form.

The situation with respect to analysis is more encouraging. A number of useful and extremely promising methodologies are now available for undertaking concerted analyses of long-range dynamics. But it is necessary to explore ways of communicating their policy-relevant implications to others outside of the academic community. In general the imperatives at hand necessitate less the development of novel modes of analysis than the application of existing modes to problems of concern. The actual choice of method or research technique depends largely upon the specific problem encountered, on intellectual preferences, and on assessments of potential payoffs.

By way of illustrating critical linkages between 1) long-range scientific research, 2) analysis of implications for policymaking, and 3) translation from academic to operational contexts we draw upon three distinct though complementary modes of analysis, each representing different manifestations of policy-oriented methodologies and designed to clarify different aspects of any one issue.

The first of these, system dynamics, is both a philosophical orientation and a specific methodology for analyzing long-range implications of policies and decisions in complex, nonlinear, multiloop systems of which social systems are the most complex. This type of analysis simulates the behavior of systems over a long period, sometimes going as far as 100 years into the future.[51] The kinds of data

---

[50] The extensive body of statistical data compiled by the United Nations since its inception is only one case in point.

[51] See Jay W. Forrester, "Counterintuitive Behavior of Social Systems," *Technology Review,* January 1971 (Vol. 73, No. 3), pp. 52-68; Jay W. Forrester, *Principles of Systems* (Cambridge, Mass: Wright-Allen Press, 1968); and Dennis L. Meadows et al., "The Limits of Growth: A Global Challenge" (Cambridge, Mass: Alfred P. Sloan School of Management, Massachusetts Institute of Technology, July 9, 1971). (Mimeographed.)

needed to analyze long-range dynamics associated with environmental issues involve observations on population levels, economic performance, resource allocation and utilization, patterns of consumption, technological advances, and so forth. Indeed, considerable analysis of such data is already underway.

A major capability of system dynamics as a research tool lies in the isolation of sensitive points in the system as well as those points which contribute little to future outcomes. The policy relevance of such information is obvious: If we can identify long-range implications of short-range decisions, it might be possible to ground our planning efforts on stronger footing, avoiding actions which appear to occasion benefits in the short term but in fact produce negative outcomes in the long run.

The second research approach, decision analysis, based on bayesian statistics, represents an alternative to classic statistics and is designed to trace the probabilities associated with various outcomes occasioned by alternative decisions at key points. In the context of environmental issues the data requirements involve information on national preferences and priorities, alternative policies and programs, and so forth. This form assesses the probabilities attached to a range of proposed policies thereby allowing for a critical evaluation of feasibilities.[52] However, as is also the case with system dynamics, the cost factor is neither directly nor explicitly introduced into the analysis, a drawback that is not to be minimized for purposes of research.

The third of these research approaches, policy analysis of alternative allocations, deals specifically with cost considerations. It is addressed to different budgets based upon alternative preference structures and priorities. The data needed pertains to budgetary distributions as they relate to environmental issues. What emerges from this approach is the cost calculus attached to alternative modes of resource allocations.[53] The main advantage, therefore, is direct and explicit assessment of the cost-benefit equation which provides crucial information about the cost implications of proposed policies or, alternatively, sets up competing policies and observes their costs and feasibilities.[54]

Obviously, these three modes of research into present environmental predicaments differ considerably in terms of abstraction from

[52] See Howard Raiffa, *Decision Analysis: Introductory Lectures on Choices under Uncertainty* (Reading, Mass: Addison-Wesley Publishing Co., 1968).

[53] See Charles L. Schultze et al., *Setting National Priorities: The 1972 Budget* (Washington: Brookings Institution, 1971).

[54] In this connection it becomes imperative to broaden our concept of cost to incorporate other than direct monetary considerations. For persuasive arguments see Alice M. Rivlin, *Systematic Thinking for Social Action* (Washington: Brookings Institution, 1971).

reality. Of the three, system dynamics is the most comprehensive, yet it is also the most removed from concrete day-to-day decisions that face policymaking communities. Decision analysis and bayesian statistics represent one step in the direction of political realism by providing probabilities attached to alternative paths and outcomes. Analysis of budgeting and resource allocations are the most specific, and they are also closely related to the stuff of politics and most directly concerned with linkages between national resources and national priorities.

To date, each of these methods has been applied in discrete fashion with little consideration for the possibilities of bringing these different scientific procedures to bear upon the development of policy alternatives, domestic or international, and even less consideration for systematic analysis of long-range implications. Through the judicious use of such methods for the analysis of appropriate data it is now possible to construct in a laboratory setting realistic models of social systems which allow for experimentation with hypothetical situations and alternative futures. Drawing upon empirical data on population dynamics, resource constraints, and technological development, these techniques allow us to alter various values for key variables subject to different policy decisions and allow us to observe now the changes that would take place over future time. In addition we can begin to identify the manipulables of a situation, as well as the cost of manipulation.

Systematic research is no substitute for immediate and specific action. But, at the same time an incremental, piecemeal, or band-aid approach to global problems is no substitute for judicious investigation and systematic analysis. The lines of investigation described in the following essay of this volume are illustrative of what must be done before we can estimate variable long-range implications of different policy alternatives.

Currently underway at the Massachusetts Institute of Technology is a series of computer-based simulations of the longer range political and economic implications of population growth, technological developments, and resource constraints.[55] A primary emphasis is on potentials for conflict and warfare. On the assumption that conflict might be avoided if the preventive action is undertaken early enough these investigations have begun to raise a series of "what if" questions pertaining to alternative futures, costs, and feasibilities. For example, what would be the long-range implications for the Uni-

---

[55] See Choucri and Meadows, "International Implications of Technological Development and Population Growth."

ted States (or other states) if population growth were curtailed significantly, or, alternatively, if consumption per capita were reduced, or if the costs of controlling external sources of raw materials and energy-producing fuels become too high, or if competition for resources becomes too intense?

Reports of these investigations are presented elsewhere. Let it suffice here to reiterate that appropriate technical skills and accompanying methodologies in addition to a certain amount of empirical data are *presently* available for undertaking extensive investigations of alternative futures and implications and consequences, both domestic and international. The transference of computer-based results from the academic community to the real world may be effectively undertaken through the application of bayesian statistics in conjunction with policy analysis. The bayesian paradigm would allow for the assessment of probabilities associated with different paths or policies that states might pursue in seeking, for example, to assure continued resource availability or to minimize conflict-laden avenues of international behavior. The practical costs involved in adopting one policy over another can then be assessed in the context of overall national preferences and priorities by a judicious application of policy analysis. The most sophisticated and useful of such modes is alternative budgeting analysis in the United States case as undertaken by the Brookings Institution.[56] In this context the political and economic costs and consequences attached to the "what if" or "if . . . , then . . ." questions can be identified and evaluated accordingly. Equally possible are systematic assessments of the political costs and feasibilities of modifying national priorities and habits, expectations and institutions. The situation becomes considerably more complex when one views the world as a whole and assesses the viability of alternative international policies and institutions and their accompanying implications for relations between states.[57]

In sum, research imperatives for the present and immediate future are fourfold: 1) to examine systematically and objectively the longer range implications of short-term actions and decisions; 2) to develop a whole series of alternative policies and alternative futures and examine their implications in laboratory and simulation settings; 3) to translate results into terms that are amenable to analysis of accompanying costs and feasibilities, economic as well as political; and 4) to devise means of disseminating information on methods,

[56] Schultze et al.
[57] For a discussion of these issues from a United States perspective see North and Choucri, "Population and the International System: Some Implications for United States Policy and Planning."

procedures, findings, and implications to national leaders and citizens alike in ways that are objective, valid, comprehensible, and believable. The major concern is to keep the information truthful and accurate.

APPENDIX: DEPENDENCE ON EXTERNAL SOURCES: MINERAL RESOURCES IN COMPARATIVE PERSPECTIVE

This appendix presents in summary form our computations and findings concerning the relative dependence (or reliance) of China, Japan, the Soviet Union, and the United States on external sources for mineral resource requirements. The dependency index has been defined as imports-exports/consumption; or (M-X)/C. As noted in the text above, the index assumes values between $+1$ and -1. The higher the value or the closer it is to $+1$, the higher is a state's reliance on external sources for the particular mineral in question. Our computations are presented most extensively for the United States, for which the data are most accurate and available. We note those minerals for which the United States is highly dependent on external sources, those for which it is moderately dependent, and those for which it is only marginally dependent as well as those for which the United States is a net exporter.

DEPENDENCY INDICES: UNITED STATES

Summary

For key minerals, such as iron ore, coal, copper, petroleum, and natural gas, there has since 1958 been no trend toward increasing United States dependence on foreign sources. For minerals for which the United States is and has been for some time highly dependent on foreign sources, over this same time period, no conclusive trend toward greater dependence on foreign supplies appears: The dependency index, (M-X)/C, has increased for some while it has decreased for others.

Two minerals for which the United States is dependent on foreign sources and whose sources of supply are likely to be the most insecure politically are manganese and chromium. Because manganese is essential to steel production, it could be considered the most likely mineral constraint for the United States in this century (see below).

TABLE 1. HIGH DEPENDENCE: DEPENDENCY INDEX IS GREATER THAN .5, OR MORE THAN ONE-HALF OF CONSUMPTION IS (NET) IMPORTED

Mineral	Dependency Index (Average 1966-1970)	Major Sources 1966-1969 (as Percentage of United States Imports)	Trend in Dependency Index 1958-1970
Manganese	.9	Gabon (31 percent) Brazil (26 percent)	Large decrease[a]
Nickel	.7	Canada (90 percent)	Large increase[b]
Platinum group	.7	United Kingdom (43 percent) Soviet Union (26 percent)	Slight decrease
Tin	.6	Malaysia (66 percent) Thailand (27 percent)	Large increase[b]
Zinc	.6	Canada (51 percent) Mexico (18 percent)	Large increase[b]
Asbestos	.8	Canada (92 percent)	(Not computed)
Bauxite	.9	Jamaica (59 percent) Surinam (26 percent)	Unchanged
Beryllium	.7	Brazil (36 percent) India (27 percent)	Erratic, no trend
Chromium	.8	Republic of South Africa (40 percent) Soviet Union (24 percent) Philippines (17 percent)	Slight decrease[a]
Cobalt	.7	Congo (Kinshasa) (43 percent) Belgium-Luxembourg (30 percent)	(Not computed)
Fluorspar	.8	Mexico (75 percent) Spain (14 percent)	Unchanged[c]

[a] Holding United States stocks and stockpiles constant would improve this measure but greatly change the direction of the dependency index trend only in the case of chromium and manganese, where the dependency index, if stocks were held constant, would possibly increase over the period 1958-1970.

[b] 1964-1970 only; for 1958-1964 the trend was downward.

[c] 1959-1970.

TABLE 2. MEDIUM DEPENDENCE: DEPENDENCY INDEX IS LESS THAN
          .5 BUT GREATER THAN .2, OR 20-50 PERCENT OF
          CONSUMPTION IS (NET) IMPORTS

Mineral	Dependency Index (Average 1966-1970)	Major Sources 1966-1969 (as Percentage of United States Imports)	Trend in Dependency Index 1958-1970
Mercury	.3	Spain (31 percent) Italy (21 percent) Canada (19 percent)	Slight decrease
Potash	.3	Canada (89 percent)	
Titanium[a]	.3	Australia (92 percent)	Slight increase
Antimony	.4	Republic of South Africa (44 percent) Mexico (26 percent) Bolivia (24 percent)[b]	
Industrial diamonds	.3	Ireland (47 percent) Republic of South Africa (15 percent)	
Iron ore	.3	Canada (53 percent) Venezuela (28 percent)	Unchanged
Lead	.3	Peru (21 percent) Canada (21 percent) Australia (17 percent)	

[a] Rutile only.
[b] Ore and concentrates only.

TABLE 3. LOW DEPENDENCE: DEPENDENCY INDEX IS POSITIVE
          BUT LESS THAN .2, OR LESS THAN 20 PERCENT OF
          CONSUMPTION IS (NET) IMPORTS

Mineral	Dependency Index (Average 1966-1970)	Major Sources 1966-1969 (as Percentage of United States Imports)	Trend in Dependency Index 1950-1970
Natural gas	<.1	Canada (92 percent) Mexico (8 percent)	
Natural gas liquids	~0	Principally Canada	
Petroleum	.1	Canada (35 percent) Venezuela (28 percent)	Unchanged
Rare earths	.1	Australia (64 percent) Malaysia (31 percent)[a]	
Aluminum	<.1	Canada (69 percent)	
Copper	.1	Chile (29 percent) Canada (23 percent) Peru (20 percent)	Unchanged

[a] Monazite only.

TABLE 4. MINERALS OF WHICH THE UNITED STATES IS A NET
EXPORTER: DEPENDENCY INDEX IS NEGATIVE, OR
EXPORTS ARE LARGER THAN IMPORTS

Mineral	Dependency Index (Average 1966-1970)	Major Sources 1966-1969 (as Percentage of United States Imports)
Molybdenum	—.7	Canada (100 percent)
Phosphate rock	—.4	Netherlands Antilles (80 percent)
Silver[a]	—.1	Canada (50 percent), Peru (15 percent)
Sulfur	— 0	Canada (56 percent), Mexico (44 percent)
Tungsten	—.3	Canada (39 percent), Peru (19 percent)
Vanadium	—.1	Canada and Netherlands Antilles
Coal	—.1	Canada and West Germany (1967 only)
Gold	—1.5	Canada (49 percent)
Helium	—1.0	None
Iron and steel scrap	—.1	Canada (95 percent)
Magnesium	—1.8	Canada (50 percent), Norway (28 percent)
(?) Uranium	(?)	Republic of South Africa (79 percent), Canada (17 percent)

[a] Excludes coinage.

DEPENDENCY INDICES: COMMUNIST CHINA, JAPAN, THE
SOVIET UNION

Soviet Union 1967	Japan 1968		Communist China 1966	Communist China 1968
Dependency index greater than 0.5				
None	Antimony	1.0	Titanium ?	Titanium ?
	Asbestos	0.9		
	Bauxite	1.0		
	Copper	>1.0		
	Petroleum	1.0		
	Platinum	1.0		
	Tin	0.9[a]		
	Tungsten	0.8		
	Zinc	>1.0		
	Fluorspar	0.9		
	Titanium	1.0		
	Lead	0.8		
	Mercury	0.8		
Dependency index less than 0.5 but greater than 0.2				
Bauxite	Silver		Copper	Aluminum metal
Tin	Iron ore ?			
Dependency index less than 0.2 but greater than 0				
Cadmium	Coal		Iron ore	Copper
Fluorspar	Coke		Nickel ?	Lead
Mercury	Nickel			Silver
Tungsten				Aluminum metal
Zinc				Zinc
Dependency index apparently equal to zero				
			Antimony ?	Antimony ?
			Asbestos ?	Asbestos ?
			Fluorspar ?	Fluorspar ?
			Petroleum	Petroleum
			Magnesium	Magnesium
			Phosphate rock	Phosphate rock[b]
			Coal	Sulfur
			Iron ore	Coal
Dependency index less than zero				
Antimony	Cadmium		Bauxite	Bauxite
Asbestos	Magnesium		Coke	Coke
Chromium	Sulfur		Tin	Iron ore
Coal			Manganese	Manganese
Coke			Tungsten	Mercury
Copper			Mercury	Tin
Iron ore			Molybdenum	Tungsten
Lead				
Magnesium				
Natural gas				
Nickel				
Petroleum				
Sulfur				

[a] Excludes secondary consumption, the effect of whose inclusion would be to reduce the dependency index (probably not below 0.6 or 0.7).

[b] However, Communist China is a large net importer of fertilizer (see *Mineral Facts and Problems, 1965*, pp. 14, 157).

ADDING THE TIME DIMENSION TO ENVIRONMENTAL POLICY

Dennis L. Meadows and Jorgen Randers

DENNIS L. MEADOWS is an assistant professor in the Alfred P. Sloan School of Management, Massachusetts Institute of Technology, Cambridge, Massachusetts. JORGEN RANDERS is a graduate student at the Sloan school. This research is supported by a grant from the Volkswagen Foundation.

I. INTRODUCTION

The vast majority of the decisions made in our global society are responses to problems in which cause and effect are closely related in time and in space. When a problem becomes important, its source is usually obvious, and any appropriate response usually becomes effective in time to eliminate the difficulty. For this class of phenomena it is satisfactory to react after a problem is already apparent. Thus, the institutions involved need only monitor the current status of the system; they need not maintain a long planning horizon. It is important to realize that most environmental problems do not fit into this category. The delays associated with most environmental processes will require us to add an explicit consideration of the time dimension in formulating environmental policy.

Four attributes of environmental deterioration introduce significant delays. First, the fundamental source of deterioration is the complex socioeconomic system causing population and economic growth in our finite world. This system has tremendous inertia. Actions taken now may not significantly decrease pollution for a decade or more.[1] Second, the physical, chemical, and biological processes which govern pollutant flows through the environment introduce significant time delays between the generation of a material and its appearance in some distant part of the ecosystem. Third, the time elapsing between exposure to a pollutant and the first appearance of adverse symptoms in man or other species may often approximate the lifetime

---

[1] An excellent example is provided by the attempts to alleviate air pollution in the United States. Although new technologies have been developed and new laws have been enacted to drastically reduce the amount of pollution emitted by many sources, population and production are growing rapidly enough that total air pollution continues to worsen. (See *Environmental Quality: The Second Annual Report of the Council on Environmental Quality, together with the Message of the President to the Congress* [Washington: Government Printing Office, August 1971], pp. 212-217.)

of the affected individual. Fourth, the response to environmental pollution generally involves not only new technology but also changes in social values and institutions. Although technology may adapt quickly, society typically does not. Thus, environmental pollution is not a momentary problem with an instantaneous solution.

Many characteristics of our public and private institutions impart to them a planning horizon far shorter than that required to deal effectively with environmental pollution. Industrial organizations severely discount the future costs and benefits of current actions, assigning little importance to implications more than ten years in the future. Decisionmakers, overloaded with work, naturally respond to those problems with the closest deadlines. Corporate and public decisionmakers, seeking rapid promotion or reelection, implement first those policies which promise immediate results. Finally, even in democratic elections no vote is given to most of those who must bear, for the next 50 years or more, the future costs of current actions.

It is not surprising that this mismatch exists between the time-span of environmental problems and the time-horizons of institutions designed to deal with those problems. Mankind has never had an effective way of understanding, much less controlling, complex processes whose outcomes are revealed decades after they have been set in motion. The future, beyond a few years from now, has been considered unimaginable, and therefore it has been left out of policy considerations. Human society has been ingenious in designing institutions and laws to deal with problems that span several national boundaries, but it has not yet learned to deal effectively with problems that extend over several decades.

Engineers wishing to change the behavior of mechanical or electrical systems have long recognized that they must first understand the time-variant characteristics of a process before they can design appropriate mechanisms to control it. For example, an effective heating and cooling system can only be designed after one has a clear understanding of the laws of thermodynamics, the range of temperatures to which the system is likely to be exposed, and the delay between detection of a temperature discrepancy and the activation of the heating or cooling mechanism.

Similarly, to design environmental controls we must understand the time-variant, or dynamic, characteristics of those processes which generate pollution and delay pollution's passage through the physical and biological systems of the globe. If we do not develop and use methods that let us explicitly consider the time dimension in our analysis of environmental problems, we will surely replicate organizational forms which already exist instead of creating new ones with the planning horizons we actually need.

The information available today on environmental processes typically is incomplete and inaccurate. The tools necessary for the analysis of complex socioeconomic systems are still undergoing refinement. Nevertheless, it is necessary to use available tools now to gain as much understanding as possible from the body of information that does exist. Since environmental degradation is already taking place and since the policies which will determine future rates of degradation are currently being formulated, it is not possible to wait until complete knowledge is available.

Fortunately, systems-analysis tools have reached a level of sophistication at which they can be extremely useful in bringing together the pieces of information that do exist about environmental processes and in assessing the dynamic implications of that information so that they can be used as inputs to long-term policy considerations. This article presents two of those information-ordering studies of environmental deterioration. These two studies, of DDT and solid waste flows, are part of a continuing program to understand the dynamics of environmental deterioration. They provide information on environmental time delays and at the same time illustrate the use of system dynamics as a general approach for analyzing the consequences of environmental control policies over time.[2]

While the studies summarized here do not offer detailed specifications for the new institutions we need, they suggest several requirements which must be met by any successful response to environmental deterioration. Thus, at the end of the article several design criteria are listed which can help to bring the time dimension into environmental management, thereby ensuring more effective control arrangements.

II. SYSTEM DYNAMICS

It is clear that social, economic, political, physical, and biological factors are all involved in the processes which govern man's impact on his natural surroundings. While we can perceive the individual elements of this complex system, the analysis of their interactions is

[2] The system dynamics methodology was developed by Jay W. Forrester of the Massachusetts Institute of Technology during his study of corporate problems. The field is widely known as industrial dynamics, after Forrester's book by that name, but the title is no longer appropriate. Fourteen books and over 100 articles published by the System Dynamics Group at MIT have illustrated the application of the approach to problems including internal body disease, urban decay, commodity price fluctuations, and population growth in traditional societies. The basic elements of the approach are described in Jay W. Forrester, *Industrial Dynamics* (Cambridge, Mass: M.I.T. Press, 1961); by the same author, *Principles of Systems* (Cambridge, Mass: Wright-Allen Press, 1969); and A. L. Pugh, *DYNAMO II User's Manual* (Cambridge, Mass: M.I.T. Press, 1970).

beyond the capabilities of man's unaided mind. Formal system analysis tools are required to trace the long-term implications of all factors involved in pollution and to evaluate alternative control programs. System dynamics is a theory of system structure which permits an analyst to represent, graphically and mathematically, the interactions which govern the long-term behavior of complex socioeconomic systems. It is a simulation method, and so it is useful both in understanding the causes of present problems and in testing the effectiveness of alternative policies.

No system analysis tool can provide new empirical data on individual components of the system. The amount of mercury released into the environment for each ton of oil which is burnt, the precise magnitude of the various coefficients which determine the movement of polychlorobiphenyls (PCBs) through the ecosystem, and the biological implications of various pesticide concentrations in plant or animal species are all examples of information which must be obtained through direct measurements on the system. System analysis tools first become useful in integrating this diverse data to obtain a comprehensive picture of the system and to understand its probable response to alternative policies. Fortunately, in many cases we already have enough information to formulate improved policies.

Information about the determinants of environmental deterioration varies greatly in its comprehension and accuracy. The spectrum

FIGURE 1. THE QUALITY SPECTRUM OF INFORMATION

Source	Intuitive judgment	Summary statistics	Controlled physical measurement
Quality	Low		High

of information available is shown diagramatically in figure 1. About some aspects of the environment we have only the inituitive judgment of experts. In other cases we have fairly complete physical measurements made under carefully controlled conditions. Often we have only statistical information, gathered under a wide variety of conditions, from which it is possible, through formal statistical techniques, to infer the underlying relationships.

The language employed by system dynamics to express system relationships can incorporate any level of information. Of course the lower the quality of the inputs the less the reliance that can be placed on the results. However, the absence of uniformly good data need not deter analysis. When decisions cannot wait, it is important to base them on the best data available even if it is not perfect. Even intuitive judgment and statistics are better inputs to urgent decisions than no information at all.

Fortunately, improved long-term policies can often be designed, even in the absence of precise data, as long as the underlying structure of the system—the complicated network of causal relationships— is generally understood. It is this basic structure which determines a system's basic behavior modes, not the exact numerical values of its components. While individual coefficients will change over time, the underlying structure typically does not. Since informed judgment is a good source of information on structure, it is possible to understand the probable behavior modes of a system over extended periods of time. This point is critical to the design of effective environmental policies, and it will be illustrated here through brief descriptions of the DDT and solid waste studies. The analysis of DDT focuses on the delays arising only through the interactions of physical and biological factors. The study of solid waste generation also incorporates several social, economic, and technological determinants of environmental deterioration.

III. CASE ONE: THE DELAYED APPEARANCE OF DDT IN THE BIOSPHERE

For the broad class of environmental problems related to material pollutants the objective of policy is to alter the concentration of the material at specific places in the ecosystem over time. This may be done by changing the location or the quantity of the emission or by removing the material from the ecosystem after it is released. Selection of the best policy depends on a comprehensive understanding of the relation between alternative patterns of emission and the consequent concentration in the ecosystem over time. The relationship between the use of DDT and its ultimate concentration in various animal species illustrates the control problems engendered by long time delays.

In another article we have surveyed the literature on the individual physical attributes of DDT's movement through the environment.[3] Empirical data on DDT is incomplete and, in places, contradictory. Enough is known, however, to identify the structure of DDT flows. The principal flows of DDT in the environment are those shown in the diagram in figure 2. As in most complex systems, the overall behavior depends primarily on this set of interactions between the constituent elements. Thus, identification of the DDT flow structure

---

[3] Jorgen Randers and Dennis Meadows, "System Simulation to Test Environmental Policy: A Sample Study of DDT Movement in the Environment" (Unpublished working paper, System Dynamics Group, Alfred P. Sloan School of Management, MIT, Cambridge, Mass., 1971).

FIGURE 2. STRUCTURE OF DDT FLOWS THROUGH THE ENVIRONMENT

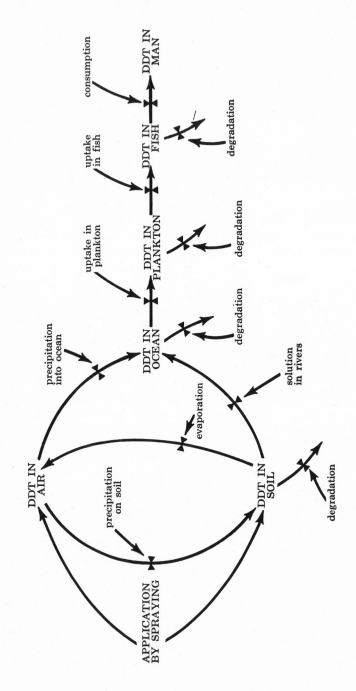

permits us to determine with some confidence the time delay inherent in the flow of DDT through the environment. It is this delay which will govern the change in DDT levels after effective abatement programs are enacted.

When DDT is applied, only part of it reaches the ground. The remainder is suspended in the atmosphere. Much of the DDT reaching the ground also finds its way into the atmosphere by evaporating eventually from the soil. Once in the air, the pesticide can be carried long distances by atmospheric movements before it finally falls back on the soil or into the ocean. DDT may also be washed from fields and carried downstream in watersheds.

Some of the DDT in the oceans is taken up by plankton and other organisms. As the plankton is eaten by fish and the fish are consumed by birds or man, the DDT finally enters these higher animals. As the chemical moves up the food chain, it is concentrated biologically. Some DDT also returns to the oceans when excreted by live fish or when released from the tissues of dead fish. DDT molecules survive this long journey because of their great stability. The only important way in which DDT is removed from the environment is through slow degradation in the soil, in the oceans, and in living matter.

There is reasonable consensus in the literature about the structural relationships portrayed in figure 2. The professional disagreement on DDT concerns the relative importance of DDT transportation in rivers, of sedimentation of DDT in the oceans, of the uptake of DDT in plants, and of regional differences in DDT concentration. For instance there is still uncertainty over how fast DDT degrades, how much of it sediments, at what rate it evaporates, by what factor it concentrates in fish.[4] These questions are less important to decision-makers than they may appear. The overall behavior of the DDT system is determined much more by the structure of the pollutant flows than by the precise value of specific coefficients. Once the structure is known, policymakers may employ simulation analyses of the model to test the sensitivity of their conclusions to much higher and lower assumed values for each doubtful or controversial parameter in the model. To illustrate this approach we have expressed the flows shown in figure 2 mathematically, employing the best available data on flow rates, degradation half-lives, etc. This mathematical model was then analyzed through computer simulations. The resulting runs, presented in graphical form, indicate the probable future concentra-

[4] The most serious uncertainty does not involve the various paths of DDT movement but rather the biological implications of its presence at various concentrations in different species. That important issue does not concern us in this analysis of DDT transmission delays though it is important in evaluating the relative costs and benefits of alternative policies.

tions which could result from various control policies initiated in 1970. The aggregation of the model makes it of little use in predicting *precise* future DDT concentrations at any specific geographical point or at any given time. Its main use is in portraying the relative delays inherent in the system's response to alternative policies.

The Implications of Alternative DDT Policies

The historical application rate of DDT from 1940 to 1970, estimated in *SCEP*, was taken as a fixed input to the analysis (see table 1).

Table 1. ESTIMATED DDT APPLICATION RATES: 1940-1970 (PRODUCTION OF DDT IN UNITS OF 10^3 METRIC TONS/YEAR — UNITED STATES ONLY)[a]

Year	DDT	Year	DDT
1944	4.4	1957	56.6
1945	15.1	1958	66.0
1946	20.7	1959	71.2
1947	22.5	1960	74.6
1948	9.2	1961	77.9
1949	17.2	1962	75.9
1950	35.5	1963	81.3
1951	48.2	1964	56.2
1952	45.4	1965	64.0
1953	38.4	1966	64.2
1954	44.2	1967	47.0
1955	59.0	1968	63.4
1956	62.6	Total	1,220.0

[a] From *Chemical Economics Handbook: 1969* (Stanford, Calif: Chemical Economics Service, Department of Business and Industrial Economics, Stanford Research Institute, 1969), reprinted in *Man's Impact on the Global Environment: Assessment and Recommendations for Action* (Report of the Study of Critical Environment Problems) (Cambridge, Mass: M.I.T. Press, 1970), p. 132.

Four alternative policies governing the global application rate between 1970 and 2000 were tested through simulation: 1) continuing to increase the application of DDT globally at the same average rate as that observed during the past decade; 2) holding DDT application between 1970 and 2000 constant at the level observed in 1970; 3) decreasing the application gradually from its current level to zero in the year 2000; and 4) dropping DDT application around the world to zero immediately in 1970. As an index of the relative timing and levels of DDT concentration which could result from each of these policies we determined through simulation the average concentration of DDT in marine fish which would result in each of the four situations.

Run 1 of figure 3 shows a typical output from a simulation analysis of the model. In this analysis it is assumed that DDT application grows through the year 2000 at its average rate over the past two decades. Time in years is shown across the horizontal axis from

1940 to 2000. The variation over time of several important variables is shown on the graph. Each curve is drawn to a different vertical scale. DDT application rate (tons/year), DDT levels in soil (tons), and DDT in marine fish (tons) are indicated. The curves shown in the figure are conditional projections. Implicit in the analysis are assumptions about the structure and coefficients governing the pollutant flow and about the future policy of mankind in generating the pollution. Since there are undoubtedly errors in each assumption, the simulation can never serve as a precise prediction. However, because the analysis is based on the best information currently available and because the study explicitly includes the time dimension a model in this form, even with all its imperfections, is much superior to the intuitive impressions which are currently the basis of pollution control policies.

Run 1 projects future DDT levels assuming there is no change in the current policy governing DDT application. The application rate of DDT thus continues to rise indefinitely. The levels of DDT in soil and in fish lag behind the application rate because of the time delays inherent in the DDT distribution processes. Both levels increase rapidly, however, eventually running off the scale of the graph. With this pattern of DDT application the level of DDT in fish doubles between 1970 and 1980 and reaches four times the 1970 level by 1990.

What will happen if the world decides now to level off the application rate of DDT, holding it constant at about the present rate? The probable results of this policy are illustrated in run 2 of figure 3. The amount of DDT in soil levels off nearly as quickly as the application rate, but the DDT in fish continues to rise for more than 50 years after the application rate becomes constant. The final equilibrium value of DDT in fish is more than twice the 1970 value.

In run 3 the result of a world decision to phase out use of DDT is depicted. It is assumed in this simulation that the application rate begins to decrease in 1970 and reaches zero by the year 2000. However, because of the delays inherent in the numerous pathways DDT takes through the environment the level in fish goes on rising for more than a decade after DDT usage reaches its peak. DDT in fish does not come back down to the 1970 level until 1995—25 years after the decision to decrease the application rate was made.

Although our social and economic institutions could never move so quickly, with the computer we can analyze the probable implications of a policy which stops the use of DDT completely next year, all around the world. The result would be similar to that shown in run 4. The level of DDT in soil would drop almost immediately. The level in fish would rise slightly for a few years and then gradually decrease. Even after 50 years there would still be a measurable amount

FIGURE 3. THE RESULTING AMOUNTS OF DDT IN SOIL (S, IN TONS) AND IN FISH (F, IN TONS) FOR DIFFERENT FUTURE APPLICATION RATES (R, IN TONS/YEAR).

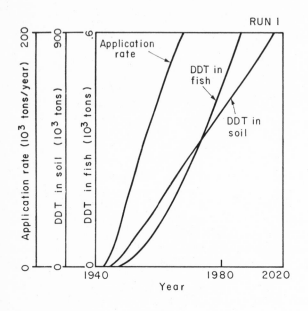

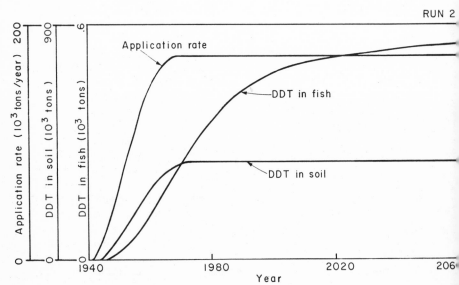

FIGURE 3 (continued)

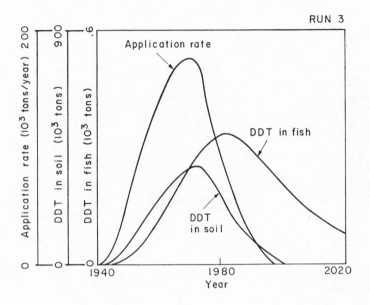

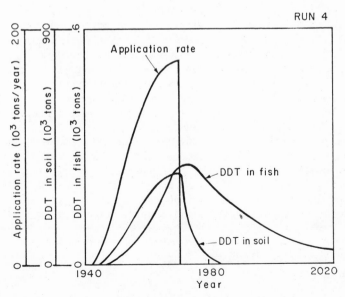

of DDT in fish as the last long-lived molecules circulate through the natural distribution processes and into the food chain.

To test the implications of errors in our estimates of the parameter values the simulations above were repeated twice with substantial changes in the entire set of parameter values. First, all parameters (partition coefficients, degradation half-lives, etc.) were changed by a factor of two to five to present the most "optimistic" picture of DDT dispersal that is still consistent with known data. To alter the model consistently so that delays would be decreased some parameters were increased and others were decreased to as little as one-fifth their original value. The policy shown in run 3 of figure 3—lowering DDT application rates to zero by the year 2000—was then tested on the revised model. Peak concentrations in fish and soil were much lower. However, DDT concentrations in marine fish still did not decrease below 1970 levels until sixteen years after the implementation of the abatement policy.

As a second test all parameters in the DDT structure were altered in a way which would increase the time required for DDT levels to respond to policy: The most "pessimistic" parameter values were chosen. In this run even when DDT usage was reduced to zero by the year 2000, DDT levels in fish remained above 1970 levels beyond the year 2020. Two other system studies of DDT flows have found delays of approximately the same magnitude as those shown in this set of studies.[5]

DDT plays a useful role in the environment only when present on the surfaces of plants or buildings which may harbor insect pests. Its value is zero or negative at all other points in the environment. Since the chemical evaporates quickly, effective pest control requires reapplication as often as every six months. In contrast we have just shown that after DDT is last used it may be found for up to 50 years in the tissues of fish. While the contrast between the duration of benefits and costs is seldom as extreme as in the case of DDT and related chemicals, other pollutants do exhibit the same general delayed response. To base pollution control policies on a comparison of *current* costs versus *current* benefits seriously underestimates the time dimension appropriate to our current actions. Yet current institutions are generally designed to employ only that comparison.

Once it is released into the environment, the concentration of DDT over time is primarily the result of physical and biological factors. For most other pollutants social and economic delays are also im-

---

[5] H. L. Harrison et al., "Systems Studies of DDT Transport," *Science,* October 30, 1970 (Vol. 170, No. 3957), pp. 503-508; G. M. Woodwell et al., "DDT in the Biosphere: Where Does It Go?," *Science,* December 10, 1971, (Vol. 174, No. 4014), pp. 1101-1110.

portant in determining the effectiveness of alternative policies. A study of solid waste generation illustrates the importance of these influences on the delayed response of pollutants to control policies.

IV. CASE TWO: THE DELAYED RESPONSE OF SOLID WASTE GENERATION

Many physical, social, and economic factors interact to determine the rate at which a society generates solid waste materials. The important physical elements and policies are portrayed graphically in figure 4. The representation is a general one and holds for any nonrenewable resource which can be recycled. Copper, iron, mercury, and lead are all examples. In this case many different human policies influence the flow of materials. In the DDT example only the application rate was a discretionary variable. Here extraction, production, discarding, recycling, and, to some extent, dispersion may be deliberately altered by policy. No attempt will be made here to explain the model in detail or to defend its individual assumptions. Both

FIGURE 4. THE FLOWS OF MATERIAL RESOURCES THROUGH THE ENVIRONMENT

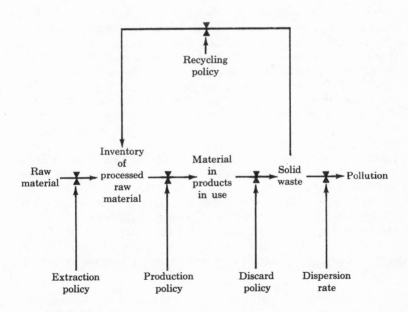

these functions are fulfilled by the technical report on the study.[6]

Again, however, there is no disagreement on the aggregated structure of the pollutant's flow. Raw materials are extracted and added to resource inventories. From there the resource flows into products in use. As products containing the material are discarded, the material becomes solid waste. Few elements are atomically destroyed in use; thus resources are not lost from the global system. However, solid waste materials may become so dispersed, inaccessible, or intermixed that they can no longer be economically exploited. Then they are termed pollution.

The structure above interrelates ten elements characteristic of all nonrenewable, recyclable materials. The precise values of parameters involved would change depending on the material under consideration, but the general behavior of the structure is similar in each case. For example, we have carried out computer simulations of this structure, using numerical coefficients characteristic of the metal copper. With the copper model it was then possible to test the relative impact of alternative policies. A study of this sort does not focus explicitly on the form of the institutions which would actually implement the policies. Instead, it attempts to understand how the system governing the generation and transmission of pollution flows would have to be changed to attain the desired ends. When the most desirable set of changes has been identified, it becomes appropriate to consider what form of institution could actually implement the necessary changes.

The DDT study examined only the cost aspects of the material flows, not the benefits. Generally it is desirable to include in system dynamics analyses both the costs and the benefits associated with the movement of a material through the global system. In the solid waste study the products in use are related directly to the material standard of living of society. The levels of pollution and solid waste are measures of the environmental costs which must be borne to attain the use of the material in products. One policy objective in this system might be to hold products in use at some acceptably high level while decreasing the depletion of resources, the accumulation of solid waste, and the level of pollution.

Among the policies which have been proposed for attaining this objective are: 1) developing new recycling technologies; 2) taxing the extractive industries; 3) subsidizing the recycling of solid waste; 4) imposing a solid waste tax on the user; and 5) increasing the products' average lifetime by technical changes in product design, im-

[6] Jorgen Randers, "The Dynamics of Solid Waste Generation" (Unpublished working paper, System Dynamics Group, Alfred P. Sloan School of Management, MIT, Cambridge, Mass., 1971). An abridged version of the paper is presented in *Technology Review*, April 1972 (forthcoming).

provements in the service and repair facilities, and changes in the consumers' usage patterns. As a whole our society attempts technical and economic solutions first, while assuming that the social factors, such as changes in consumer usage patterns, are beyond control. With an approach like system dynamics it is possible to evaluate the relative effectiveness of these alternatives.

The Implications of Alternative Solid Waste Policies

One important policy alternative is to maintain the status quo. The probable implications of that policy for the flow of a typical material through the global ecosystem are shown in run 1 of figure 5. Here it is assumed that there is no recycling. Thus, the natural resource is gradually depleted. Solid waste grows at first and then peaks and declines as the increasing cost of the resource diminishes the flow of the material through the system. The standard of living provided by products incorporating this material is maintained for about 30 years and then declines. This decline is caused by the diminishing extraction rate which no longer can keep up with the discard rate— even though the latter decreases as a consequence of the increased product lifetime. This increase in product lifetime is caused by the increase in the market price of raw material which occurs when the natural resource becomes more scarce.

Obviously society would not let pollution mount as shown in run 1 without strenuous efforts to develop new controls. A combination of economic, social, technical, and geological factors is involved in the generation of solid waste and the ultimate decline of the products in use. Thus, it would appear that a combination of social, economic, and technical policies should be employed to improve the behavior of the system.

Many alternative policy sets can be tested in the general model. One combination of policies found to be particularly effective for the copper parameters we used was: 1) a 25 percent tax on extraction; 2) a 25 percent subsidy to users of recycled material; 3) an increase in the product lifetime by 50 percent through changes in consumer usage patterns and improved service and repair facilities; 4) a doubling of the maximum recycling fraction through improved solid waste disposal and new recycling technology; and 5) a reduction of the raw material per product in such a way that the ratio (weight of product/ product lifetime) decreases 10 percent.

In combination these changes give us the situation shown in run 2. In response to these policies the peak value of solid waste is reduced to two-thirds its initial value, pollution rises to only three-fourths its former level, and the services from products in use are substantially increased. Because the study employs merely an aggregated represen-

tation of a generic resource precise relative weights of the policies
analyzed in run 2 are not significant. Nor would the simulation run
be an appropriate basis for long-term predictions of precise pollution
levels. Both the degrees of emphasis on various policies and the precise
future values of important system elements are sensitive to reasonable changes in the coefficient values of the solid waste structure.
The general directions indicated by the policy set (tax on extraction,
subsidy of recycling, etc.), however, are certainly valid.

We saw in the DDT study that DDT concentrations continue to
rise for several decades after effective abatement policies have been
implemented. That means, clearly, that if we wait until DDT concentrations in the environment are the cause of unacceptable damage,
we will experience those concentrations and the damage they engender
for at least several decades after control policies are implemented.
The solid waste system behaves in an analogous fashion.

FIGURE 5. THE RESPONSE OF SOLID WASTE FLOWS AND PRODUCTS
IN USE TO ALTERNATIVE POLICIES

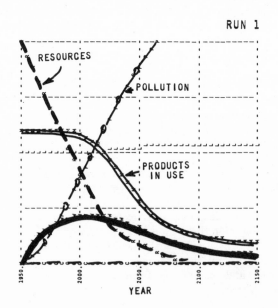

FIGURE 5 (continued)

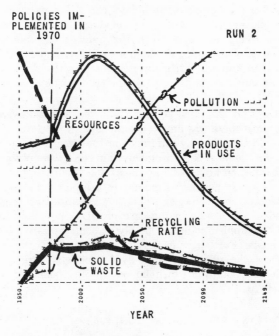

POLICIES IM-
PLEMENTED IN
1970

RUN 2

POLLUTION

RESOURCES

PRODUCTS
IN USE

RECYCLING
RATE

SOLID
WASTE

YEAR

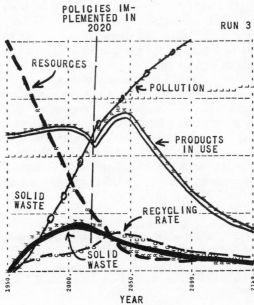

POLICIES IM-
PLEMENTED IN
2020

RUN 3

RESOURCES

POLLUTION

PRODUCTS
IN USE

SOLID
WASTE

RECYCLING
RATE

SOLID
WASTE

YEAR

The successful policies in run 2 of figure 5 were implemented in 1970, well before pollution levels had reached significant levels in the model and before there was any obvious decline in the material standard of living associated with the number of products in use. The costs of implementing the program employed in run 2 would be high, and there would be little obvious payoff in the short run. Thus, most of our current institutions would tend to delay imposition of such policies.

Suppose that the same policies employed in run 2 were not implemented until there was an obvious decline in the level of products in use. Would there be any difference in the effectiveness of the policies? In run 3 the same policies employed in run 2 were postponed until 2020. The delay in imposition produces a substantial decrease in the effectiveness of the policies. Products in use barely recover the level attained before the decline, and pollution rises to much higher levels than it did in run 2. As in the case of DDT, policies implemented only after the problem is unmistakably present typically do not avoid sustained costs. Further, it is clear from the analysis that under any circumstances the relatively short-lived products leave a legacy of solid waste and pollution which far outlive any benefit derived from the products' use.

V. TIME DELAYS AND POLLUTION CONTROL

In both the DDT and the solid waste problems we found two characteristics: The costs of pollution must be borne for periods much longer than the period of benefit derived from the polluting activity; and there may be a delay of ten years or more between the implementation of a policy and its first obvious benefits. If corrective action is postponed until the actual costs of pollution are unacceptable, there may no longer be an opportunity to avoid sustained penalties. Both of these characteristics are the result of long delays in the processes which govern the transfer of materials through the environment. It seems reasonable to expect that delays of the magnitude found in the above studies are inherent in the transfer and impact of many materials causing environmental deterioration. For example, more recent system dynamics studies suggest that eutrophication and mercury pollution also exhibit these attributes.[7]

[7] A. A. Anderson and J. M. Anderson, "System Simulation to Test Environmental Policy III: The Global Distribution of Mercury" (Unpublished working paper, System Dynamics Group, Alfred P. Sloan School of Management, MIT, Cambridge, Mass., 1972); and J. M. Anderson, "System Simulation to Test Environmental Policy III: The Eutrophication of Lakes" (Unpublished working paper, System Dynamics Group, Alfred P. Sloan School of Management, MIT, Cambridge, Mass., 1972).

What are the implications of these two dynamic characteristics for the institutions we might form to control the deterioration of our natural environment? They mean very simply that long-term improvements in our natural surroundings will seldom result from a comparison of short-term costs versus short-term benefits of polluting activity. Clearly, society must seek in its new environmental institutions a measure of foresight and resolve not often visible in our current national and international institutions. At the very least control decisions must be based on the anticipated consequences of current action rather than on the perceived costs of past actions.

Basing control decisions on anticipation rather than reaction implies new technical capabilities and new institutional values. The technical implications are clear. Institutions must develop the capabilities to: monitor pollution release rates as well as absolute levels in the environment; develop and employ models which can relate current pollutant release rates and alternative future abatement policies to the levels of environmental pollution they will produce in the future; and devise biological testing procedures and ecological experiments *well in advance* to provide the factual basis for relating projected pollution levels to the future biological damage they will produce. The need for technical changes has been recognized, and useful work is underway to develop the necessary models. However, even very sophisticated forecasting capabilities will be of little use until political change is also achieved. In the introduction we briefly mentioned those attributes of current organizations which yield a short planning time horizon. If we structure our environmental institutions so that they are subject to the same short-term pressures as most current institutions, they cannot be expected to succeed in stopping environmental deterioration.

The long time delays in the DDT and the solid waste pollution studies force immediate consideration of a fundamental issue. What obligation do the people who currently inhabit the globe owe those who will live on it twenty or 100 years from now? No formal modeling studies can provide the answer to that question. But we are unlikely to halt the continued degradation of our environment unless a specific commitment is made to the future. Over the past century we could rationalize the damage done to our natural systems in the belief that our technological and economic progress more than compensated posterity for the degraded environment and the diminished natural resource base left to future generations. Today many people doubt that belief.

The recent concern over environmental deterioration is a necessary precedent to establishing effective international institutions of the sort sought in the 1972 United Nations Conference on the Human Environment. However, intense interest is not alone sufficient. We must also assess realistically the total nature of the pollution problem and determine the most effective forms for the organizations and programs which will control it. Implicit in many of our current environmental programs are the assumptions that pollution control requires only slight extensions in our technical capabilities and minor shifts in the magnitude and area of capital investment. Probably neither of these assumptions is correct for most pollutants. The inherent dynamics of ecological processes demand a planning horizon of 50 years or more. Institutions or international agreements based on short-term considerations are likely to fall far short of their goals.

PART III

INTERNATIONAL INSTITUTIONS:
THEIR PRESENT AND POTENTIAL ROLES

THE ROLE OF THE UN IN ENVIRONMENTAL PROBLEMS

Richard N. Gardner

RICHARD N. GARDNER is the Henry L. Moses Professor of Law and International Organization at Columbia University. He has served as a consultant to the secretary-general of the Stockholm Conference on the Human Environment on the international organizational implications of action proposals.

During the first quarter century of the United Nations its nonpolitical work was dominated by one subject — the economic development of the less developed countries. In this period "progress" tended to be measured in terms of gross national product (GNP), and "cooperation" usually meant what the rich countries could do for the poor through aid, trade, and technical assistance.

The major landmarks in the growth of UN development activities were the launching of the Expanded Program of Technical Assistance (EPTA) in 1953, the UN Special Fund in 1958, the first UN Development Decade in 1961, the UN Conference on Trade and Development (UNCTAD) in 1964, the UN Development Program (UNDP) in 1965, the UN Industrial Development Organization (UNIDO) in 1966, and the International Development Strategy for the Second UN Development Decade (DD II) in 1970. The original focus of UN specialized agencies as instruments for standard-setting, technical exchange, research, and intellectual cooperation was soon submerged by their new responsibilities for assisting the developing countries.

In the early 1960s, however, a new element was added. The world organization began to consider the problems of population growth and science and technology. To be sure, this was still in the context of helping the developing countries. But in the summer of 1968 the Swedish government placed on the agenda of the Economic and Social Council (ECOSOC) an item on the "human environment." When, as a result of this initiative, the General Assembly decided to convene a conference on this subject at Stockholm in 1972, it added a new dimension to UN activities. Henceforth, and increasingly in the 1970s, the world organization in its nonpolitical work will be concerned with "quality of life" issues as well as GNP — and with problems of developed as well as less developed countries.

I. WHY THE UNITED NATIONS?

"Getting action in the United Nations," a diplomat once com-
plained, "is like the mating of elephants. It takes place at a very high
level, with an enormous amount of huffing and puffing, raises a tremendous amount of dust, and nothing happens for at least 23 months."
Many of those who see the urgent need for action on environmental
problems are skeptical of entrusting responsibilities to the United
Nations, whose more than 130 members are so deeply divided by
national, racial, and ideological antagonisms and differ so greatly in
their perception of environmental problems and in the ability to contribute to their solution. Anxieties about the UN as a repository of
environmental responsibilities are heightened by the organization's
precarious financial condition, the uneven quality of its Secretariat,
and the problems that have often arisen in promoting effective action
through its family of largely independent specialized agencies.

Why, then, assign a major role to the United Nations in environmental matters? Instead of looking to the UN would it not be better
to assign primary responsibility to a new global organization with
"real teeth?" or to a high-level group of scientists? or to a purely
"Western" organization of noncommunist industrialized countries?
or to an East-West body including all industrialized countries but
leaving out the developing countries of the world? Some may think
these questions became academic once the decision was made to call
a UN Conference on the Human Environment. But such questions
continue to be asked and will undoubtedly be looked at again by
key governments should UN efforts at Stockholm or thereafter prove
unsuccessful.

The basic answer to the questions posed above is that while there
are problems in using the UN for environmental action, the problems
in bypassing it in favor of other institutions would be more serious
still. Governments are simply not ready to surrender environmental
decisionmaking to a supranational body with legislative and enforcement powers. As to independent scientific "wise men," they can be
useful in an advisory capacity, but what is required now is action by
governments. So we are forced to employ some method of intergovernmental cooperation.

It goes without saying that the primary responsibility for dealing with environmental problems rests with each state. It is also
obvious that regional cooperation is appropriate when countries share
particular environmental problems because of geography or the nature
of their economic systems. But regional organizations cannot act
effectively on environmental problems which are global in extent, like
pollution of the oceans or the release of carbon dioxide and particulate
matter into the world's atmosphere. Since all countries are contribu-

tors in some degree to these phenomena and all are in turn threatened by them, all ought to be involved in some manner in dealing with them.

The UN is the only framework available for cooperation on both an East-West and a North-South basis. While environmental cooperation through forums like the North Atlantic Treaty Organization (NATO) and the Organisation for Economic Co-operation and Development (OECD) can be a useful supplement to UN efforts, it is no substitute for them. Recent discussions have shown that the Union of Soviet Socialist Republics is no less concerned than other states with problems of air and water pollution and with the need for exchanges of technology and information on pollution control. The communist countries of Eastern Europe have participated actively in the environmental programs of the Economic Commission for Europe (ECE). The People's Republic of China (Communist China) has indicated that it is ready for environmental diplomacy no less than ping-pong diplomacy. It is evident that environmental cooperation between communist countries and the industrialized noncommunist world can serve the environmental and political objectives of both. What is somewhat less obvious is that the meeting of communist and noncommunist environmental experts in UN forums to work out programs can give them added leverage in pressing environmental interests within their respective national bureaucracies. This could be particularly important for the scientists of communist countries who cannot look to powerful nongovernmental groups at home to reinforce their efforts.

The case for North-South cooperation on environmental problems is no less compelling. Observers like George F. Kennan, it is true, have proposed to bypass the United Nations in favor of an environmental agency run by the developed countries of the world.[1] But the Kennan approach ignores the importance of involving the developing countries from the outset in global environmental efforts. The industrialized countries of the world control less than half of the world's land area. They have no authority to legislate for the territory controlled by others or for the oceans and polar regions that are beyond national jurisdiction. The notion that decisions taken on the global environment by a "club" of developed countries would carry sufficient legitimacy to determine the actions of the rest of the world is wholly unrealistic.

Although most of the world's pollution is now caused by the advanced countries, the actions of the less developed countries can have serious effects on the global environment. As they press forward

---

[1] George F. Kennan, "To Prevent a World Wasteland: A Proposal," *Foreign Affairs,* April 1970 (Vol. 48, No. 3), pp. 401-413.

with their own plans for development, it is vital to the general welfare as well as their own that they not make all the same mistakes that the advanced countries have made. Rich and poor states alike, for example, must be concerned if Middle Eastern countries permit oil pollution from drilling off their coasts or if African countries permit the wanton destruction of their wildlife and natural resources.

Moreover, experience in the United Nations has indicated that the difficulties of involving the developing countries in environmental cooperation have been greatly overstated. With the notable exception of Brazil, which purports to see in international discussions of environment a sinister plot against its national development, the developing countries in general have supported the preparations for Stockholm. Obviously, they will resist any environmental actions which prejudice their development, but most of them recognize that successful development must take account of environmental factors, and most want international assistance to help them cope with environmental problems. As Maurice F. Strong, secretary-general of the Stockholm conference, has remarked:

> In my recent travels in the developing countries, I have found that while the word "environment" has not yet acquired the magic it has in the more industrialized countries, the issues it embraces are of real and growing concern to them: polluted water supplies, degradation of agricultural lands, depletion of wildlife and fisheries, and, perhaps most urgent, the problem of cities which are growing at rates unprecedented in human history. Some of these cities face the prospect of water contamination and health hazards which will make them unfit for human habitation within the next decade or so. Indeed, the "eco-catastrophes" of which we hear so much are much more likely to occur in the developing world than in the wealthier countries which have the resources to deal with these problems.[2]

If North-South as well as East-West cooperation is needed to preserve the world environment, it would be foolish not to try for such cooperation within the United Nations. The UN is the only worldwide forum available. Its various agencies are already doing valuable work on different parts of the environmental problem. Moreover, there is another consideration for using the United Nations that has nothing to do with the environment at all. At a time when the United Nations is undergoing a severe crisis of confidence a success in the field of environment could bring the organization an increased

---

[2] Institute on Man and Science, *International Organization and the Human Environment: Proceedings of an International Conference, Rensselaerville, N.Y., May 1971*, p. 21.

measure of public support, particularly in developed countries like the United States in which such support is badly needed. The "spaceship earth" mentality encouraged by environmental cooperation may even, in the long run, reinforce the UN's efforts in peacekeeping and peacemaking.

II. THE STOCKHOLM PROCESS

Marshall McLuhan is famous for the observation that "the medium is the message." Strong is the originator of another phrase, "the process is the policy." Its relevance to the UN is evident. While public attention has focused on the Stockholm conference, the process of getting to Stockholm may have even greater long-term significance than the conference itself.

It is doubtful if any UN meeting has been so thoroughly prepared in advance as the Stockholm conference. The 27-state Preparatory Committee for the United Nations Conference on the Human Environment, appointed by the General Assembly to supervise preparations, held four meetings in New York and Geneva between the fall of 1970 and the spring of 1972. It set a broad agenda for the Stockholm meeting to include:

1) planning and management of the environmental quality of human settlements;

2) environmental aspects of natural resource management (defined broadly to include animal, botanical, and mineral resources);

3) identification and control of environmental pollutants and nuisances of broad significance;

4) educational, informational, social, and cultural aspects of environmental issues;

5) economic development and the environment (including environmental policies as a component of comprehensive planning in developing countries); and

6) international organizational implications of proposals for action.

Detailed work on specific proposals went forward in intergovernmental working groups concerned with marine pollution, conservation, monitoring, and a draft declaration on the human environment. International nongovernmental organizations also took a major role. The International Union for Conservation of Nature and Natural Resources (IUCN) took the main responsibility for the drafting of four conventions relating to conservation, one of them providing for a world heritage foundation to preserve natural and cultural areas of great importance to humanity. The International Council of Scientific Unions (ICSU), through its Scientific Committee on Problems of the Environment (SCOPE), provided a major channel for advice from the scientific community on a number of problems, notably environmental monitoring. A number of privately sponsored conferences, such as the Massachusetts Institute of Technology Study of Critical Environmental Problems (SCEP) and its international successor, the Study of Man's Impact on Climate (SMIC), provided further inputs for Stockholm.

Special efforts were made to assure meaningful participation from the developing world. The broad concept of environmental problems reflected in the agenda items outlined above helped to reassure developing countries that environment was not just a concern of the rich. The relation between development and environment was explored in June 1971 in an experts meeting at Founex, Switzerland.[3] Following the Founex meeting, regional seminars were held in Bangkok, Addis Ababa, Mexico City, and Beirut to examine the environmental problems of the major developing regions and help the countries of these regions develop action proposals in the light of their own interests.

Another significant step in the preparatory process was the handling of contributions from the specialized agencies. Before the appointment of Strong a subgroup of the Administrative Committee on Coordination (ACC) had parceled out responsibility for preparing basic papers for Stockholm to the various specialized agencies — not only papers on technical subjects of concern to these agencies but also papers on broader issues such as international organizational arrangements (assigned to the Food and Agriculture Organization [FAO]). One of Strong's first decisions after his appointment was to cancel these arrangements and provide that basic papers for Stockholm would be produced by his own specially recruited secretariat with the help of part-time consultants from different countries. The specialized agencies thus made their contributions to Strong's secretariat rather than directly to the Stockholm conference. In this way Stockholm was launched with a strong unifying perspective and without the self-serving parochialism so characteristic of UN activities in other areas.

Preparation of the sixth agenda item concerned with organizational arrangements presented a special problem. Everyone recognized that this was, in a way, the most important item on the agenda since effective arrangements of a continuing character would be necessary to carry forward a program of work approved at Stockholm. The Stockholm conference, lasting only two weeks, would not have

---

[3] See *Development and Environment,* Report submitted by a panel of experts convened by the secretary-general of the United Nations Conference on the Human Environment, Founex, Switz., June 4-12, 1971. (Mimeographed.)

time to approve such arrangements unless their main outlines were pretty well agreed. Yet there were obvious difficulties in an international secretariat telling governments what organizational arrangements they should undertake.

The answer to this dilemma was a flexible process of consultation between the secretariat, governments, and private scholars. A three-day meeting under the auspices of the Institute on Man and Science and the Aspen Institute for Humanistic Studies in May 1971 helped initiate this process.[4] An international workshop in Aspen during the summer of 1971 produced a set of general institutional recommendations.[5] About the same time a more detailed paper outlining specific institutional choices was prepared by this author and discussed in Geneva by a group of governmental delegates, secretariat officials, and scholars. Aided by this discussion and by the Aspen paper, another consultant produced a second draft on which comments were solicited from representatives of governments and UN agencies. The final secretariat paper on the organization item was then completed at the end of 1971 and sent to governments for their formal consideration. The paper was scheduled for detailed consideration at the final meeting of the Preparatory Committee in March 1972.

Clearly, the Stockholm preparatory process has stimulated a significant pattern of cooperation — with developing countries, with nongovernmental groups, and with different parts of the United Nations system. It now remains to be seen what specific organizational proposals of a continuing character can best promote the general interest in effective environmental action.

III. BASIC ORGANIZATIONAL PRINCIPLES

Out of this process of informal consultation a broad consensus was achieved well before the Stockholm conference on general principles for international organization. At its third session in September 1971 the Preparatory Committee endorsed the following "general criteria" proposed by Strong:

(a) Any organizational arrangements should be based first on agreement about what needs to be done. Until this is reached, no firm decision can be made on the ways and means to be adopted;

(b) All functions that can best be performed by existing organizations should be assigned to those organizations, both international and national, most capable of carrying them out

---

[4] *International Organization and the Human Environment.*
[5] International Institute for Environmental Affairs, *The Human Environment: Science and International Decision-Making* (1971).

effectively. No unnecessary new machinery should be created;

(c) It is more logical to consider a network of national, international, functional and sectoral organizations with appropriate linkages and "switchboard" mechanisms, whereby international organizations supplement and complement national organizations, than to think in terms of a global "super agency";

(d) Any action envisaged should allow for the preliminary state of knowledge and understanding of environmental problems, and should be flexible and evolutionary;

(e) Governments will want to attach highest priority to the need for co-ordination and rationalization of the activities and programmes of the various international organizations active in the environmental field. This is essential in order to avoid overlap and duplication and to assure most effective use of scarce resources of money and manpower;

(f) Any policy centre that is expected to influence and co-ordinate the activities of other agencies should not itself have operational functions which in any way compete with the organizations over which it expects to exercise such influence;

(g) In the establishment of any additional or new machinery it is essential to provide strong capability at the regional level;

(h) The United Nations should be the principal centre for international environmental co-operation;

(i) The organization of environmental activities within the United Nations should be so designed as to strengthen and reinforce the entire United Nations system.[6]

Another way of summarizing the consensus would be as follows. First, the key international environmental institutions should be intergovernmental in character. Governments are not prepared to surrender authority to a supranational agency that could bind them to act against their will. Governments may, however, be willing to delegate authority to international entities to act in carefully prescribed areas under norms and policies already agreed upon. Since effective environmental action in most cases will require action by governments, private scientific groups cannot be given the major responsibility for international cooperation though they can make a most valuable contribution in an advisory capacity.

Second, the central machinery for environmental cooperation should be within the framework of the United Nations. Since environmental problems are global as well as regional and local, they must be dealt with in global as well as regional and local institutions. Organizations of limited membership based on political alliances, re-

---

[6] *Report of the Secretary-General to the Preparatory Committee for the United Nations Conference on the Human Environment* (UN Document A/CONF. 48/PC. 11), paragraph 222.

gional contiguity, or levels of development cannot act effectively on environmental problems in the territories of nonmembers nor in areas outside of national jurisdiction like the oceans where all states have rights and responsibilities. The United Nations system represents the only comprehensive system of global cooperation in existence and has already acquired much experience in environmental cooperation. To bypass it now would not only be wasteful from the point of view of environmental action but would deal a heavy blow to the position of the United Nations as the central world institution for global cooperation.

Third, it would be undesirable to create a UN specialized agency to deal with environmental problems. Environment covers a broad range of subjects already being dealt with within the functional responsibilities of existing specialized agencies: atmospheric pollution in the World Meteorological Organization (WMO), environmental health in the World Health Organization (WHO), conservation of soil, forest, and animal resources in the FAO, etc. Environmental matters are also being dealt with in the UN regional economic commissions. A specialized agency for the environment would result in duplication of activities and would compound already serious problems of coordination.

Fourth, any new organizations established to deal with environmental problems should be capable of growth and adaptation in response to growth in mankind's knowledge and appreciation of environmental questions. Governments may be willing to make commitments for environmental cooperation tomorrow that they are not willing to undertake today. Thus any new institutions established at Stockholm should have built into them some procedures for periodic review and appraisal of their effectiveness with an opportunity for institutional revision.

Fifth, there is need for some central intergovernmental machinery in the UN to perform the function of "policy review and coordination." In other words some institutions will be needed to identify important issues requiring the attention of governments and international agencies, to suggest priorities for further international action with respect to these issues, and to review existing programs in relation to environmental goals. A vital part of this function will be to achieve an efficient and integrated set of programs by international agencies either by influencing these agencies directly or by influencing them indirectly by influencing the policies of their member governments.

IV. THE ORGANIZATIONAL CHOICES

Within this broad but rather vague consensus some difficult institutional choices remain to be made. Some of these choices will be made at Stockholm, at least provisionally; others may be postponed to the future. In either case they are likely to be a subject of concern to UN members for some years to come. The following are among the most important.

The Environmental Secretariat

One of the basic instruments for "policy review and coordination" will be a new environmental secretariat: a central environmental "brain" to identify what needs to be done and how to do it through international agencies and national action. Among other things it could provide a forum for the exchange of views between governments and scientists; serve as an environmental reference service for governments and international agencies; provide advisory services not available elsewhere; conduct informational and educational activities; and keep under continual review the adequacy of the world's environmental activities both in information gathering and environmental regulation. The secretariat could issue an annual "Report on the State of the World Environment," and it could organize meetings in particular countries and regions to gather information and focus attention on particular problems.

In considering the precise organizational arrangements for a new secretariat two potentially conflicting considerations are involved. One is to give special status and visibility to the new secretariat, providing it with sufficient administrative autonomy so that it may hire a greater proportion of senior personnel under fixed-term contracts for its specialized tasks than is possible in the present UN Secretariat. The other consideration is to assure effective coordination of activities specifically concerned with the environment with other, related UN activities and to maintain some consistency in staffing patterns within different parts of the secretariat. The organizational choice is between making the new secretariat 1) a part of the Department of Economic and Social Affairs of the UN Secretariat (headed perhaps by a commissioner for the environment); 2) a regular department of the UN Secretariat headed by an undersecretary-general; or 3) a semiautonomous body within the UN similar to the secretariats of UNCTAD and UNIDO. Given the emphasis that has been given to status, visibility, and autonomy in pre-Stockholm discussions, a solution of the third type seems a likely outcome.

A further question is just what units of the existing UN Secretariat, if any, should be incorporated within the new one. Within the existing Department of Economic and Social Affairs the Resources and Transport Division, the Center for Housing, Building, and Planning, and portions of several other units are currently concerned with environmental problems as these are defined on the Stockholm agenda. Such units are "operational" in the sense that they plan and execute projects. Transfer of these units to the new secretariat would violate the principle cited earlier that the new secretariat should not be operational. On the other hand, if the new secretariat confines itself to planning functions, as now seems likely, careful attention will have to be given to the question of how it can influence the operational units located elsewhere.

The Intergovernmental Arrangements

The second basic instrument for "policy review and coordination" will be some kind of intergovernmental body to review the work of the new secretariat and make recommendations for action by governments and international agencies. One of the most difficult questions in this regard is whether or not to locate this body within the framework of ECOSOC.

The argument for an ECOSOC solution is that environment falls within the responsibilities of ECOSOC as defined in the Charter of the United Nations and that the interrelated issues of development and environment should be dealt with in the same and not different bodies. Institutional fragmentation could lead to conceptional fragmentation; separate bodies dealing with development and environment might produce conflicting resolutions reflecting limited and contradictory perspectives.

At its 51st session in July 1971 ECOSOC approved a comprehensive program to reform and revitalize its work. It recommended to the General Assembly that its membership be doubled to 54, and it created three 54-member committees to deal with coordination, science and technology, and review and appraisal of the Second UN Development Decade. A charter amendment enlarging the council was approved by the 26th session of the General Assembly.

If the enlargement of ECOSOC and its new committee structure produce the hoped-for increase in ECOSOC's prestige and effectiveness, then environment could well be an additional component of ECOSOC's expanded role. Indeed, some have argued that environment must be put into ECOSOC since to locate it under the General Assembly would encourage pressures to give the General Assembly responsibility for review and appraisal and science and technology, thus undercutting the new reforms.

But would an environment committee under ECOSOC have the necessary status and visibility? Would it be likely to attract environment ministers or senior environmental advisers? Probably not. ECOSOC could, of course, establish a commission on environment, equivalent in status to the Commission on Human Rights, the Commission for Social Development, and the Commission on the Status of Women. That solution might have more visibility and status, but it would defeat the objective of integrating environmental problems with ECOSOC's other work.

Perhaps the only solution to this dilemma — and it may well be the best solution for ECOSOC in the long run — would be to have the council adopt the practice of organizations like the OECD and the European Community in which responsible ministers or senior decisionmakers are regularly brought from capitals to take decisions in specialized areas. If this pattern was followed, ECOSOC could hold special meetings each year at the ministerial or senior decisionmaker level devoted to trade and development, science and technology, environment, and perhaps also population. These meetings could be carefully prepared in advance by specialized ECOSOC committees on these subjects.

The problem with such an ambitious solution is whether ECOSOC could ever be strengthened to a point at which it could attract ministers and senior decisionmakers on a regular basis to deal with the environment or anything else. When ministers meet in the European Community or in the OECD, they include representatives of all the members of those organizations, and they meet as a supreme decisionmaking body capable of adopting budgetary and other decisions without review by a superior organ. By contrast, even an enlarged ECOSOC will represent less than half of the UN membership; under the charter all of its policy decisions can be reviewed and altered by the assembly, and only the assembly can take binding financial decisions. These factors, coupled with the steady decline in the council's effectiveness in recent years, have led many delegations concerned with the environment to doubt whether ECOSOC is a strong enough repository for environmental functions. As one UN expert has put it: "Why try to graft a live function onto a dead organ?"

The alternative to an ECOSOC solution is to set up a separate intergovernmental body concerned with environment. This could, of course, be done by an amendment to the charter creating a new environmental council, but very little support for such an approach has materialized among delegations which prefer the simpler and well-worn method of creating new intergovernmental bodies as subsidiary organs of the General Assembly under article 22 of the charter. If the Stockholm conference follows this approach, the 27th session of the General Assembly could launch the new environmental body without delay with powers and procedures specially adapted to the environmental challenge. The question of consolidating such a body into a strengthened ECOSOC could be postponed for consideration at a later stage.

Whether an ECOSOC or General Assembly formula is followed, it is clearly essential that the new intergovernmental body be composed of highly qualified senior officials with responsibility for environmental policy. One of the difficulties with both the assembly and ECOSOC is that when dealing with specialized economic and technical subjects they tend to be composed of second- and third-string diplomats reading instructions from capitals. If the new environmental body is to work, the institutional arrangements should specify — as has been done in some UN specialized agencies — that governments should send highly qualified persons who have responsibility for taking decisions in their respective governments.

Another major question about the intergovernmental arrangement is whether there should be periodic "Stockholm conferences" every three or four years to enable the world community as a whole to consider environmental questions and review the operation of the new institutions. Since it is agreed that any institutional arrangements made in Stockholm will be provisional and since it is obvious that governments at Stockholm will be prepared to take but a small fraction of the important decisions necessary to save the world environment, a decision to hold "Stockholm II" in three or four years has much to be said for it. On the other hand, the experience with UNCTAD suggests that huge conferences trying to deal with a broad range of subjects may not always be the most effective approach.

A superior alternative to a series of Stockholm conferences might be a periodic review of environmental issues in the General Assembly, perhaps in a new committee created to deal with scientific and environmental questions and composed of qualified experts. Under this more modest approach the basic institutional arrangements adopted at Stockholm could be kept under review by a small committee of the intergovernmental body and brought to the General Assembly when revisions seemed ripe for adoption. The adequacy of international arrangements in particular environmental problem areas could also be reviewed by the intergovernmental body which could recommend the calling of conferences when a consensus developed on new measures appropriate for international agreement.

Arrangements to Broaden the Knowledge Base

There is general agreement that new institutions are needed to assist in the advance and exchange of environmental knowledge. The functions to be performed by such institutions include monitoring (the collection, storage, and communication of data on what is happening to the physical environment and what effects this is having on man); evaluation (the transformation of data into scientific judgments about environmental hazards and trends); research (into both the causes and remedies of environmental problems); and the exchange of national experience (not merely with different scientific and technical approaches but also with institutions and policies). The documentation prepared for Stockholm revealed that these functions are already being performed to a much greater extent than is generally recognized by UN specialized agencies and regional commissions as well as by intergovernmental and nongovernmental organizations outside the UN. Nevertheless, there is an obvious need for a central mechanism or mechanisms to coordinate the processes of information exchange, bring together the information coming from different sectoral and regional networks, and provide a coherent scientific perspective on major environmental problems.

Three main approaches are available to achieve this end. The most ambitious is the proposal for an International Center for the Environment (ICE) which developed out of discussions in SCOPE. This proposal envisages a large group of scientists working together in a permanent facility under the direction of the scientific community. Despite the obvious attractiveness of such an ambitious idea there is widespread doubt that the necessary financial resources could be found in the near future or that the scientific community is willing and able to take on the responsibility for such a vast enterprise. In the communist countries and in many other UN members the scientific groups that would be participating in such a center would be arms of their governments. They might encounter difficulty if the center rendered opinions on behalf of the world's scientific community with which their governments could not concur. Even with regard to those countries whose scientists are independent from government it has to be recognized that objective scientific "truth" on most environmental matters simply does not exist, that judgments involve the balancing of many relevant factors, and that a center might have great difficulty in speaking with one voice. In any event the scientific community was not able to reach agreement on the ICE proposal in time for action in Stockholm; if such an ambitious plan is to be adopted, we must await agreement at a later stage.

A less ambitious alternative to the ICE would be to create some kind of scientific advisory group to assist the new secretariat and intergovernmental body. This advisory group could be composed of eminent scientists serving in their individual capacities. It could establish subgroups to deal with specific environmental problems.

A third, even less structured possibility would be simply to convene panels of independent scientists when necessary to consider particular environmental problems. After all, SCOPE and the IUCN already exist; they could continue to work informally with the new environmental institutions just as they have cooperated in the preparation of the Stockholm conference. A formal committee might well get in the way of more flexible arrangements. Given the highly varied character of environment issues, it might be best to rely on existing nongovernmental groups and simply bring together those scientists best qualified to deal with a particular problem when there is a demonstrated need to do so.

Funding Arrangements

New international environmental activities will cost money. One basic question is whether the money should come exclusively from the regular budgets of the UN and its specialized agencies and existing voluntary funds or at least in part from a new "environmental fund" financed from voluntary contributions. Clearly, the basic costs of the new secretariat and intergovernmental body should come from the regular budget. A new fund would cover the costs of monitoring, research, and technical assistance when these various costs cannot be borne by developing countries.

One of the major advantages of a special environmental fund would be in helping to coordinate the activities of the different parts of the UN system. It would also help assure that the funds would be used to support activities that clearly rate priority from an environmental point of view rather than from the point of view of the narrower interests and activities of individual agencies whose primary concern is not with environment. A central fund could be used to support individual projects whose primary objective is environmental restoration or preventative action.

An environmental fund might have advantages from the point of view of both industrialized countries and developing countries. Industrialized countries could be clearly assured that their funds would be used for environmental purposes rather than simply be added to existing funds. In some cases, such as that of the United States, this might make it easier to get public and legislative support for additional contributions to international agencies. At the same time developing countries concerned that the added costs of environmental measures should not come out of existing funds would be able to identify the environmental funds as clearly separate and additional to funds available to them from normal sources.

On the other hand, many governments may not be willing to contribute to a separate "environmental fund." They may feel that any additional funds to support environmental projects should be channeled through existing agencies without being segregated from normal contributions so that the agencies would be free to use their total resources without restriction in the light of their own decisions and priorities. It can also be argued that environmental and development policies should be mutually reinforcing elements of a single national development plan: Separate sources of funding could hinder achievement of this objective.

The Prevention and Settlement of Disputes

Governments are always reluctant to accept restraints on their freedom of action. Yet without some restraints in the field of environment states cannot be protected against damage from their neighbors, and the seas and atmosphere cannot be preserved. If restraints are accepted by states and embodied in international agreements, there is the difficult question of how to resolve differences that may arise in interpretation of the agreements and how to secure compliance with them. In areas in which no international agreements have been concluded there may be a need for some mechanism to define customary rules of international law or achieve ad hoc settlements in the common interest.

One possibility is to make greater use of the International Court of Justice (ICJ) in settling environmental disputes. The court could, without amendment of its statute, arrange to sit in special chambers and make use of scientific advisors or "assessors" to inform itself of the facts. But nonjudicial procedures like negotiation, fact-finding, mediation, and conciliation seem preferable in most environmental disputes to permit a more flexible adjustment of interests through mutual accommodation.

Preventive environmental diplomacy would be assisted if UN members could agree to report to the new environmental secretariat on all national activities (private as well as public) that might affect the environment of others and to consult in good faith with other members and international agencies when questions or objections were raised. In the event of a disagreement the proposed intergovernmental body on the environment, with the aid of a specially constituted scientific advisory panel, could report on the facts and make recommendations to the parties concerned. A nongovernmental organization like the IUCN could be asked to serve in appropriate cases as an "expert witness." Obviously the members of the UN are not ready to accept an "environmental veto" by international agencies, much less an environmental "police force." But an international review process, particularly if it involves recognized scientific authorities, could have great influence.

Institutions to Deal with Marine Pollution

There is general agreement on the fragmentary and inadequate character of the institutional framework in this area. Marine pollution from maritime commerce is being dealt with in the Inter-governmental Maritime Consultative Organization (IMCO). Marine pollution from offshore oil installations will be dealt with at the law of the sea conference now being planned by the General Assembly Committee on the Peaceful Uses of the Seabed and the Ocean Floor beyond the Limits of National Jurisdiction. Marine pollution from ocean dumping — the transportation by ships of waste materials to the oceans from land — has been the subject of negotiation in the Intergovernmental Working Group on Marine Pollution established by the Preparatory Committee for the Stockholm conference.

Pollutants reaching the oceans from rivers, from pipelines, from land runoff of agricultural, industrial, and municipal wastes, and from the atmosphere are the most important sources of marine pollu-tion. Yet they are totally unregulated except for International Atomic Energy Agency (IAEA) standards on the disposal of radioactive wastes. These sources will have to be dealt with through international cooperation if the health of the oceans is to be protected. Interna-tional action could take the form of monitoring pollution from these sources, setting standards of water quality for different parts of the marine environment, and eventually setting limits on the dis-charge of pollutants.

A general obligation to protect the health of the marine environ-ment is contained in article 25 of the 1958 Convention on the High Seas which obliges states to "co-operate with the competent inter-national organizations in taking measures for the prevention of pollu-tion of the seas or air space above, resulting from any activities with radio-active materials or other harmful agents." In the absence of an organization of general competence in this area, however, this obligation has not yet had much significance.

There are various possibilities for international institutions to cope with marine pollution problems. One proposal is to transform IMCO into an international regulatory agency with jurisdiction over all types of marine pollution and to transform the WMO into an atmosphere and oceans authority with responsibility for monitoring and scientific research. Another approach is to confine IMCO and the WMO to their existing activities, strengthen the research work of the Intergovernmental Oceanographic Commission (IOC), and give responsibility for the regulation of oil drilling on the continental shelf, ocean dumping, and marine pollution from land-based sources to whatever new institution emerges from the law of the sea conference. Still another approach is to give IMCO responsibility for ocean dump-ing and offshore oil pollution problems pending the conclusion of the law of the sea conference, which may be many years away, but to deal with land-based sources of marine pollution through other arrangements. It is doubtful if these difficult questions can be resolved at Stockholm; they will be with us for many years to come.

V. CONCLUSION

Whatever institutions are created at Stockholm, their vitality will obviously depend on the behavior of governments. Will the members of the UN devote the necessary resources to national and international environmental efforts? Will they accept limitations on their traditional freedom of action in the interest of preserving the common biosphere? Many leaders now use the rhetoric of "spaceship earth," but are they really prepared to accept the political and economic costs of self-denial that this rhetoric implies?

If, as seems likely, Stockholm yields no clear answers to these questions, it will be particularly important to preserve a role for the nongovernmental organizations. The ICSU and the IUCN can play an indispensable role as environmental "ombudsmen" in the post-Stockholm period. These centers of scientific excellence and environmental expertise can raise questions about governmental policies even in the absence of formal intergovernmental procedures, and they can prepare public opinion for bolder measures than governments are now prepared to accept.

The institutional decisions which governments take at Stockholm and after will have the most profound consequences not only on the quality of environmental cooperation but also more broadly on the whole system of international relations. Failure to devise a workable pattern of cooperation to cope with urgent environmental issues could lead to international disputes and a poisoning of political relations. On the other hand, success in environmental cooperation could help humanity deal with other pressing problems.

A record of successful achievement in this area would demonstrate the UN's capacity to adjust its institutional habits and deal efficiently with major threats to the survival of mankind. It could show the way to new approaches in the economic and political areas. Perhaps, in the long run, it could stimulate new perceptions of interdependence and strengthen the political commitment of governments to a stronger United Nations.

THE UNITED NATIONS' INSTITUTIONAL RESPONSE TO STOCKHOLM: A CASE STUDY IN THE INTERNATIONAL POLITICS OF INSTITUTIONAL CHANGE

Brian Johnson

BRIAN JOHNSON is a senior fellow at the Institute for the Study of International Organization, University of Sussex, Brighton, England.

I. THE FOCUS OF STOCKHOLM

The imminence of the first intergovernmental conference on the whole human environment has provided a focus for discussion of the new environmental tasks that may fall to international institutions. In fact this is now a major question for intergovernmental decision. Governments must decide in the coming months what part they want the world organization, with all its political and administrative tensions and frustrations, to play in mastering a crisis in the management of the entire human household.

The forthcoming United Nations Conference on the Human Environment has this institutional problem on its agenda. Subject area 6 of the Stockholm conference agenda, entitled "The International Organizational Implications of Action Proposals," invites governments to discuss, and at Stockholm to agree upon, institutional arrangements within the United Nations context to deal with environmental matters. It is not surprising that this agenda item has tended to occupy the center of attention among those governmental and international officials directly concerned with preparations for the conference. Equally, it is inevitable that full deliberation of this (last) agenda item should have been deferred until the fourth (and final) meeting of the Preparatory Committee for the Conference on the Human Environment. Nevertheless, a great deal of discussion has taken place and a number of private, semi-official, and official views have been expressed. The process through which these discussions have taken place marks a potentially significant break with traditions of United Nations institutional diplomacy. Indeed it is possible that this change may itself exert some influence on the outcome of negotiations. One observer has described these deliberations as a "rolling debate." But what has been significant about it is not so much its continuing intensity as the fact that this "rolling debate" has not been confined to intergovernmental institutions, foundations, and universities.[1] The fact that the secretariat of the Stockholm conference was authorized by governments to encourage and participate in such a many-sided dialogue represents a degree of intergovernmental acknowledgement of the deep interest of professional, local, and private groups in environmental questions and of the extent to which such groups have so far been important in stimulating official environmental action.

The evident political potency of peoples' anxiety over their environment has attracted interest groups and institutions of many persuasions. Naturally, supporters of action through the United Nations have been actively involved in such campaigning and have made a vigorous case for establishing the United Nations in a paramount position in international environmental activities. Furthermore, the organizations that make up the United Nations system are themselves actively engaged in staking their claims to environmental responsibilities, authority, and resources. It is not the purpose of this article to argue the merits or demerits of one or other international organization for this or that environmental task. My purpose here is twofold. First, I attempt some clarification of the present distribution of environmental responsibilities among the major international organizations. Second, I discuss certain principles and possible approaches to the problem of organizing the world's environmental monitoring and protection activities which have been put forward in the course of international consultation on this question and which governments will be considering in the context of the forthcoming Stockholm conference.

[1] Meetings convened in 1971 to discuss institutional implications of action proposals envisaged for the Stockholm conference include: International Organization and the Human Environment, cosponsored by the Institute on Man and Science and the Aspen Institute for Humanistic Studies, held at Rensselaerville, New York, May 21-23, 1971; The Crisis of the Human Environment and International Action, sponsored by the International Studies Program, University of Toronto, held at Toronto, Canada, May 25-27, 1971; Sixth Conference on the United Nations of the Next Decade, sponsored by the Stanley Foundation, held at Sinaia, Romania, June 20-26, 1971; First International Environmental Workshop, cosponsored by the International Institute for Environmental Affairs and the Aspen Institute for Humanistic Studies, held at Aspen, Colorado, June 20-August 6, 1971; Panel of Experts on International Organizational Implications, convened by the secretary-general of the United Nations Conference on the Human Environment, held at Geneva, Switzerland, July 8-9, 1971; International Legal and Institutional Responses to the Problems of the Global Environment, cosponsored by the Carnegie Endowment for International Peace and the American Society of International Law, held at Harriman, New York, September 25-October 1, 1971; and The UN System and the Human Environment, sponsored by the Institute for the Study of International Organization, University of Sussex, held at Brighton, England, November 1-4, 1971.

II. CURRENT ENVIRONMENTAL ACTIVITIES OF INTERNATIONAL ORGANIZATIONS

It is not possible for governments to prepare and create new international arrangements *ab initio*. Over the past few years an uncoordinated multiplicity of international bodies, both intergovernmental and nongovernmental, have launched a variety of programs of research and cooperation. Environmental activities of existing international organizations may be classified under six main headings: atmospheric pollution; marine pollution; water pollution and water resources development; land use and conservation of natural resources; urban environmental problems; and control of selected pollutants. The table in appendix 1 lists 45 specific activities grouped under those headings. It shows that activities under all these headings are being carried out by about two dozen intergovernmental organizations, most of which are part of the United Nations system.[2] This table illustrates the haphazard way in which environmental interests and responsibilities are scattered under present arrangements.

Some of these activities are functionally defined by the purpose of the agency carrying them out. For example, the World Meteorological Organization (WMO) is currently monitoring air pollution of global significance and working on the standardization of national data; the World Health Organization (WHO) is starting a decade of studies on the effects of environmental pollution on human health; the *Codex Alimentarius* Commission established by the Food and Agriculture Organization (FAO) is working on international standards for food, including acceptable levels of additives and pesticide residues; the Intergovernmental Maritime Consultative Organization (IMCO) has done considerable work on oil pollution and is currently conducting studies on other forms of marine pollution in preparation for an international conference on marine pollution in 1973; the International Civil Aviation Organization (ICAO) has held a conference at which the development of international standards and recommended practices for aircraft noise abatement and the study and measurement of sonic booms were discussed.

Other environmental activities have been undertaken on a regional basis by the United Nations Economic Commission for Europe

[2] Nongovernmental international organizations concerned with the environment are at least as numerous. Outstanding among these are the International Council of Scientific Unions (ICSU), which has established a Scientific Committee on Problems of the Environment (SCOPE), and the International Union for the Conservation of Nature and Natural Resources (IUCN). At least twenty specialized international scientific organizations are concerned with advancement of research related to preservation of the environment. Many of them are affiliated with the ICSU.

(ECE), including examination of standards for motor exhaust emissions and the effects of water pollution by European iron and steel industries. Regional bodies, outside the United Nations system, such as the Council of Europe, the European Community, and the Committee on the Challenges of Modern Society (CCMS) set up by the North Atlantic Treaty Organization (NATO) have also undertaken research, data collection, and pilot studies on environmental problems while the Organisation for Economic Co-operation and Development (OECD) is engaged in environmental studies which include the management of air and water resources, noise, and pesticides. In addition, nongovernmental bodies are examining problems ranging from the identification of research efforts necessary for solving international environmental problems (ICSU) to the conservation of rare species and natural habitats (IUCN) and the promotion of integrated national case studies of environmental problems (the Commonwealth Human Ecology Council).

This complex and impressive picture of multiple efforts is deceptive and tends to conceal several obvious dangers. It is deceptive because institutions and agreements which on paper look impressive often yield very little in terms of positive results. One conspicuous example may be cited: The 1954 Brussels Convention (and annex) for the Prevention of Pollution of the Sea by Oil was signed by 36 countries. In 1962 the same governments agreed to several amendments to that convention, and in 1969-1970 they signed a further International Convention relating to Intervention on the High Seas in Cases of Oil Pollution Casualties. Yet a recent report by a group of experts to the United Nations secretary-general observed that ocean dumping of oil may have reached the level of 10 million tons a year and today threatens to destroy organic life in many parts of the ocean.[3]

In addition to the problem of lack of enforcement and inadequate surveillance of existing agreements there are innumerable problems of jurisdictional vacuum and overlap. Governments are increasingly finding themselves technically bound to the decisions of bodies that not only contradict the requirements of other intergovernmental organizations but are themselves inadequate for the scale of the problem involved. All this duplication leads, of course, to a considerable wastage of scarce technical expertise, as well as wasted time in official representation and other governmental resources. Much more important, however, is the clear inadequacy of the scope of present measures in the face of rapidly increasing environmental pressures.

[3] See UN Document E/5003 ("Report of a Group of Experts to the Secretary-General").

III. INTERNATIONAL INSTITUTIONAL ATTITUDES OF THE INDUSTRIALIZED COUNTRIES

The marked diffusion of responsibilities for environmental action among a number of United Nations and non-UN agencies indicates the extent to which the industrial countries of the West have so far proceeded on an ad hoc basis in agreeing on intergovernmental action. Until the Stockholm initiative there was no official attempt at a comprehensive or global view. No one has denied that the dangers arising from man-induced changes of the environment defy not only national political boundaries but also regional political groupings. But the enthusiasm of industrial countries for action through existing regional or interregional organizations has been conspicuously faint when the organization's membership presented political problems of cooperation.

Governmental Attitudes

The international institutional interest of the governments of industrial countries has generally been limited to considerations of environmental pollution, especially of air and water. National policy is generally worked out between two branches of government. The first is national environment departments, offices (or their equivalents) which project the regional ramifications of domestic pollution problems, assess the domestic impact of other regional polluters, and, especially in the case of the leading maritime countries, add a general view of national interests in relation to prospective pressures for shipping regulations. Scientific and international organization sections of external affairs departments make up the other major branch of governments involved in these decisions. These tend to concern themselves with pollution questions only insofar as they infringe on the national economic interest as traditionally conceived. On wider environmental issues their policy views consist largely of reactions to proposals offered by international organizations or, exceptionally, another government.

The interplay of these interests tends to reinforce the view that all international environmental problems are problems of pollution. From this view stems the belief that the problems really only concern the industrialized — and polluting — countries. Two additional factors encourage governments of industrial countries to maintain this type of attitude. One is their belief that pollution is the only aspect of the environmental crisis that interests their publics. The other, related to this belief, is the general dislike, shared by public officials with most politicians, of getting involved in the business of projecting trends, whether in air or water pollution, possible climatic change due to industrialization, population growth, or consumption of scarce natural resources. A certain suspicion among governments at proposals for international machinery with the resources or authority to undertake major predictive studies follows from this distrust of projecting trends. Proposals for international inspection or policing authorities have also generally met with strong reactions. There is also considerable opposition to proposals that national governmental departments should draw upon the findings of research bodies beyond national control for their information and guidance.

Attitudes of the Scientific Community

Understandably, the scientific communities of the industrial countries share little of this official caution as regards the political embarrassments of projecting trends. Nor are they notoriously concerned about budgets or concessions concerning sovereignty. In most problem areas, however, scientific opinion is widely, and often sharply, divided between those who believe that there is a most urgent need for action — or restraint of action — and those whose assessment of the evidence leads them to the conclusion that because current knowledge or information is inadequate or inconclusive a great deal more data collection, research, and monitoring work must be done before any major action is merited.

This division of views may in many cases result more from differences in personal temperament or philosophy than from differences in knowledge of, or confidence in, the evidence. It is, for instance, noticeable that the members of the scientific community more concerned with urgency for action are generally the ones who see environmental problems — and solutions — in an integrated or systematic framework: For instance, they link population growth projections with figures on raw material scarcities and the realities of political division which militate against ideal technical solutions. This group generally tends not only to greater pessimism as to the degree of environmental crisis that the world faces but also to a more radical view of the need for coordination of scientific and political policies and philosophies to match what they know of the delicacy and complexity of interrelationships in natural systems.

The other, or "reductionist" group, on the other hand, tends to see environmental problems in more traditional or compartmented terms. The response of these scientists tends to be programmatic rather than systematic, calling for further research by specialists to examine a particular phenomenon or the development of a technology designed to solve a specific problem. Neither group would disagree as to the need for vastly more research in all fields of human impact on the environment. But sharp differences do occur between them as to the necessary design and priorities of research facilities and their relations to operational environmental programs.

Attitudes of the General Public

Among that growing section of the public in the major industrial countries that is aware of and concerned about environmental issues international institutional arrangements are probably of only the most marginal interest. The environmental awareness of most citizens in industrialized countries has so far moved little or no further than the effluent in the local river or the risks of mercury poisoning in tuna fish. The United States is perhaps the single exception. There is some evidence[4] that both Congress and the executive are feeling the pressure of environmental interests to take a lead in international institutional arrangements.

It must be remembered, however, that in both the United States and Europe private environmental activists tend to divide more or less clearly into two groups. One group believes in the efficacy of governmental action and would therefore support intergovernmental action in protection of the environment through the United Nations or through some other machinery. The other, more radical, and generally younger group is also active and vocal and tends toward cynicism at all governmental programs whether at the national or the international level. This group would discount the value of any international institutional machinery as being subject to the overwhelming exploitative and developmental pressures which it is busy opposing at the local level. Although this latter group is so far of insignificant electoral influence (except, perhaps, on established politicians' speeches at election time) its ideas tend to correlate with those of more radically oriented biologists and other scientists. A result of this like-mindedness may well be a steady increase in these scientists' influence in proposing to the wider pubic the pasqualian proposition that in environmental matters caution should get the benefit of the doubt or, as George Kennan has put it: "The principle should be that one exploits what a careful regard of the needs of conservation leaves to be exploited, not that one conserves what a liberal indulgence of the impulse to development leaves to be conserved."[5]

With this profile of specialist and public concern in mind hesitancy on the part of governments in industrial countries over intensive technical and diplomatic efforts in institutions with politically awkward or unsympathetic memberships is understandable.

[4] See, for example, the April 1971 *Newsletter* of the Conservation Foundation, Washington, devoted to preparations for the Stockholm conference. See also U.S. Congress, Subcommittee on Energy, Natural Resources, and Environment of the Committee on Commerce, *Hearings on S 3575*, 91st. Cong., 2nd sess.

[5] George F. Kennan, "To Prevent a World Wasteland: A Proposal," *Foreign Affairs*, April 1970 (Vol. 48, No. 3), p. 408.

IV. INDUSTRIAL COUNTRIES' INTERNATIONAL INSTITUTIONAL ALTERNATIVES

The same hesitancy has also occurred in contemplating cooperative activities through institutions whose memberships appear inappropriate geographically. European reactions to the United States initiative of proposing the creation of the NATO Committee on the Challenges of Modern Society, in a speech of Henry Kissinger in March 1969, have been a good deal less than enthusiastic. The CCMS was duly established in December 1969. But officials of most NATO countries openly concede that the primary motive behind its creation was the desire to present a public image of the organization as a useful and effective body with interests and responsibilities beyond its military function.

Clearly, NATO's membership covers a geographical region (or regions) that makes no sense in environmental terms. Yet the United States has been insistent that NATO be given specific responsibilities in areas of environmental research and action. Other NATO members have accepted this development with reluctance. In fact, however, the activities of NATO's CCMS need not prove a great problem in achieving coordination with other international organizations' mandates or spheres of activity. This is because the committee has been set up to operate by licensing the "pilot" projects of member states, whose findings are eventually "approved" by NATO's membership as a whole. These pilot projects are conceived and executed entirely by individual member countries. Indeed, in practice most of them are projects which member governments were carrying out, or would have carried out, in any case, the NATO label having been added later for political reasons. This is not to deny the usefulness of some of the work done under these auspices. An American pilot project, for example, on engine emissions and automobile safety will be valuable to European and other manufacturers in assessing the standards for which they must prepare in designing for the American market. Similarly, a British pilot project on job satisfaction in industry may produce important findings for other countries. But it is difficult to see why the findings of these studies could not have been disseminated and discussed in another forum, for example, the OECD.

It has also been suggested that any attempt by industrial countries to use international organizations whose membership includes a substantial number of less developed countries is inevitably doomed to futility and political impasse.[6] The vast majority of the United Nations' membership, it is argued, accords environmental considerations a low priority while a small minority gives them a relatively

---

[6] See, for example, Kennan, *Foreign Affairs*, Vol. 48, No. 3, pp. 407-408.

high priority. However, this minority is directly responsible for most of the problem. It may be seen, therefore, as highly unlikely that a body governed by the United Nations' entire 129-country membership would be able to act with sufficient speed and decisiveness to meet the need for international research, coordination, standards setting, and surveillance of environmental problems.

Thinking along these lines has led governmental officials, chief executives of heavy industry, and representatives of various international organizations from Western Europe, North America, and Japan to discuss the creation of international consultation, negotiation, and research machinery for limitation of environmental pollution among the major trading and industrial countries of the West.[7] In particular, two institutional recommendations have been put forward, which have since been presented to senior officials of the Commission of the European Community, NATO's CCMS, the General Agreement on Tariffs and Trade (GATT), the OECD, the ECE, the United Nations Conference on Trade and Development (UNCTAD), and the United Nations Institute for Training and Research (UNITAR).

The first of these recommendations was for an international environmental institute in which representatives of industry and government could meet at a technical level to suggest jointly agreed standards and norms which would be socially and economically feasible and effective in producing environmental improvement. The institute would produce recommendations (standards, controls, tax incentives, etc.) on, for example, pollution control, which could subsequently be embodied in national legislation and international agreements. The other proposal involved the establishment, either through GATT or the OECD, of intergovernmental negotiations on the general application of the costs of environmental controls and standards to processes and products in order to avoid distortion of trade and of free market decisionmaking over the rational international distribution of the factors of production.

Not surprisingly, the two proposals have increasingly been seen as being necessarily linked. The process of negotiation over environmental protection measures will almost certainly call for centralized technical analysis and research. The relative suitability of various intergovernmental organizations both for research and negotiation of Western industrial countries is, at the time of writing, being discussed in several forums.

One school of thought favors the machinery of GATT for this activity. Others point out that any extension of the ongoing GATT

---

[7] For example, at an international conference convened by the Atlantic Council of the United States in Washington in January 1971 on Goals and Strategy for Environmental Quality Improvement in the 1970s.

negotiations on nontariff barriers into this realm suffers from two practical disadvantages. The first is that technical discussions are, in the case of GATT, currently confined to the governmental level. National governmental experts naturally consult experts from their national industries, but there is no provision for such contacts between industry and GATT officials. The second is that there are emergent problems as regards who the negotiating participants should be. If the very slow pace of GATT progress in nontariff negotiations is maintained, there is a real danger that groupings of GATT members may have in the meantime worked out joint negotiating procedures which would thus probably bring the progress of nontariff environmental negotiations to a standstill.[8]

It has therefore been argued that the OECD, with its much more limited membership and its established machinery for cooperation on technical issues in which industry and the scientific community participate, would provide a forum in which much more rapid progress could be made, perhaps sufficiently rapid to avoid the sort of "bloc" negotiation on environmental questions which is likely to present such formidable problems once a community position has been forged within the context of an enlarged European Community.

As regards the establishment of an international environmental institute within the Western industrialized country context, once again the desirability of prompt action to take into account a wide range of trading interests is being stressed.[9] Altiero Spinelli, a member of the Commission of the European Community, has recently proposed such an institute for an enlarged community. The transatlantic response to this proposal was that is should be widened from the ten prospective members of the enlarged community to include all of the OECD's membership and possibly also Australia.[10] It has more recently been proposed that the purpose of the newly established International Institute for the Management of Technology in Milan (to which the Federal Republic of Germany [West Germany], Italy, the Netherlands, and the United Kingdom have thus far agreed to make governmental contributions, three other OECD members having also

[8] At the present time the Commission of the European Community is gearing itself to negotiate nontariff barriers (explicitly standards of health, safety, etc.) among the ten members of an enlarged community in addition to progressing toward objectives of new systems of fiscal standardization, trade preferences etc. Before GATT negotiations on environmental aspects of trade came to fruition, the ten members of the enlarged community would almost certainly be acting as a unit. Agreement between such a group, the United States government acting on guidelines approved by the Congress, and the developing country membership would seem to be a flat impossibility unless radically different attitudes toward environmental threats become manifest.

[9] Unpublished paper by the Atlantic Council of the United States, June 1971.
[10] Ibid.

given indications of their willingness to contribute) should be expanded from the current one of training in science and technology management to embrace environmental research and training functions. The Milan institute could then, perhaps, relate its research and technical assistance capacities, supplemented presumably by United States–financed environmental research, to the technical requirements of both the European Community and the OECD.

The early establishment of a broad-membership environmental research institution might help to counteract the alternative tendency of industrial countries to use environmental cooperation as cement for emergent regional political alliances, rather as the environmental activities of NATO were promoted by the United States. The argument for prompt action in this direction is likely to be strengthened, especially in American minds, by the current evidence of fragmentation of the post–World War II international trading and investment system. At the same time it must be recognized that research, technical cooperation, and negotiation arrangements on industrial pollution problems in the context of international trade between Western industrial countries fail completely to recognize, let alone approach, the environmental hazards to which careless industrial development in any part of the world may expose mankind as a whole. Authoritative warnings have been given of the dangers that projected rates of oceanic and atmospheric pollution may begin to affect the capacity of the earth to support life by the end of this century. Clearly, no regionally defined research, technical assistance, or negotiating machinery can hope to define or resolve these wider problems.

It was this realization that elicited Kennan's proposal that a powerful international environmental agency, having East-West membership and consisting notionally of the ten leading industrial states "with the Scandinavians and perhaps with the Benelux countries as a bloc," should be established for the triple purpose of: 1) information collection, storage, and retrieval; 2) coordination of research and operational activities in the international field; and 3) establishment of international standards and provision of technical help to governments in meeting them.[11] This authority would have to be entirely separate from the United Nations for, according to Kennan, its membership, as well as its constituent agencies, must inevitably tend to give developmental considerations priority over those of environmental conservation, and hence the organization should not be trusted with the guardianship of the biosphere.

It seems fairly clear that no government could subscribe to Kennan's analysis of the need to subordinate all developmental de-

[11] Kennan, *Foreign Affairs,* Vol. 48, No. 3, pp. 410-411.

cisions to a predominating conservationist body. Nevertheless, one aspect of the Kennan proposals is likely to appeal to the institutional preferences of scientific communities and also to ecologically concerned nongovernmental organizations and informed Western publics generally. Kennan advocates that each government should delegate the handling of its relations with the international environmental agency to a major national scientific institution; these scientific bodies would then collectively take over the responsibility of staffing the international agency and supervising its operations. It is thus possible that such an approach, especially if its chief emphasis was on collaboration on such topics as research into climatic change, might elicit collaboration from the Union of Soviet Socialist Republics. This at least was the impression of some leading American scientists who accompanied a group of American public figures on a recent visit to Moscow.[12] In their view scientists holding high positions in the administration of Soviet science appear prepared to make a strong case with their government for the need for international cooperation for vital global environmental research, especially on changes in world climate. This American group also noted, during its Moscow visit, that Soviet scientists expressed the view that international cooperation was urgently needed for a number of other common goals for long-term environmental research. There are, however, indications that Soviet scientists are considerably less concerned than their counterparts in Western industrial countries with the environmental problems of the less developed countries.

If stripped of authority in the matter of standards setting and restricted entirely to the collection, evaluation, and dissemination of research and information, something along the lines of Kennan's proposals might appeal to a number of governments of developed countries. However, the clearly global nature of the agency's purview would make it virtually impossible both on political and technical grounds to exclude representation from less developed countries.

V. THE DEVELOPING COUNTRY PERSPECTIVE

There was a tendency, especially evident in the first two meetings of the 27-state Preparatory Committee for the Stockholm conference, for Western governments generally to react negatively to an understandable caution and suspicion on the part of the poorer coun-

---

[12] Verbal statement at the international critique panel of the First International Environmental Workshop, Aspen, Colorado, July 1971, by Thomas Malone, chairman of the ICSU, who visited Moscow together with other American scientists and advisers to Senator Frank Church, David Rockefeller, Charles Yost, and General James Gavin, who led this unofficial group in July 1971.

tries as to how the industrialized countries' preoccupation with the international environment issue would affect the third-world's priority task of feeding, sheltering, employing, educating, and caring for the health of its peoples. Within the United Nations system the third-world majority is understandably determined that those whose industrial technology has produced the major part of today's pollution should assume the cost of cleaning it up. But, at the same time, there is a growing recognition — in both developed and developing countries — that there is much more to the environmental crisis than industrial pollution. In fact, the environmental problems of poverty may be represented as being even more acute and more widespread than the environmental problems of affluence. This fact has been widely and publicly recognized by the leaders of industrialized countries with responsibility for environmental matters. Peter Walker, the British secretary of state for the environment, wrote recently that "for many people in Britain, the environment begins and ends with the four squalid walls of the room in which they and their families live. . . . The Department of the Environment is just as much concerned with our historic slums as it is with our historic buildings."[13] If applied by industrialized country governments to the global environment, inclusive definitions of environmental problems, such as Walker's, will certainly help to reassure third-world leaders.

Inevitably, the poor stand to gain most from the protection and improvement of their environment as they have fewer resources to spare to escape their surroundings, repair costly mistakes, or take remedial action. This is true of the ghetto areas of the rich West's cities, which suffer most from atmospheric pollution, noise, and the bite of highway development. It is equally true of the poor in the rapidly growing pattern of third-world urban agglomerations. Nor are developing countries' environmental problems restricted to urban life. Many parts of Asia are losing as much land annually through soil erosion, waterlogging, and salination as they are reclaiming for new cultivation. The devastating and largely unforeseen side effects of the Aswan and Kariba dams have received widespread publicity.[14] What is less appreciated is that in many, if not most, developing countries their irreplaceable base of natural capital, the very foundation of their development, is being eroded by wrong use.

It would thus be only the shortest view of their interests that would cause industrialized countries to assume that the Stockholm meeting must necessarily turn into a sort of UNCTAD, a session of

[13] Peter Walker, in "The Way We Live Now," *The Times* (London), June 22, 1971, p. 1.
[14] See, for example, a report by Claire Sterling in the *Sunday Times* (London), February 21, 1971, p. 21.

confrontation politics in which the poor states demand vast financial
or trading concessions in return for assent to the establishment of
international procedures and machinery to take the globe's pulse and
to heal some of its rich-man–inflicted sores and ills. Undoubtedly,
it could turn out this way. But most developing countries are well
aware of the temptations which industrial countries may feel to cooperate together through international institutions over which the
third world could have no influence and in whose work their inseparable environmental and developmental interests could go largely ig-
nored.

It is not surprising, however, that developing countries have
approached the question of institutional arrangements with particular reserve. To some extent this caution parallels that of industrial
country governments: Third-world countries are, for example, as unenthusiastic as rich countries about the abdication of sovereignty to
regional or interregional bodies. Initially, too, this lack of institutional interest stemmed from the general lack of appreciation of the
degree to which environmental concern was relevant to developing
countries' overriding domestic preoccupation with combating poverty
through economic development. But the process of preparation for
the Stockholm conference has changed these attitudes to a remarkable
extent.

So far developing country views on institutional needs have been
confined to general assent to two propositions.[15] The first is that the
predominant form of international institutional arrangement for environmental protective action should be regional and focused around
a specific problem or ecological system, e.g., a river basin. The second is that international resources and organization to be devoted to
environmental matters should concentrate on the implications for
developing countries of industrial country environmental action, principally in the areas of trade, investment, and technological transfer,
and on ensuring that the net level of resource flow from rich to poor
countries for developmental purposes was not reduced or diverted to
environmental considerations which were not held by the developing
country concerned to merit priority over general developmental objectives.

The report of a panel of 27 experts convened at Founex, Switzerland, by the secretary-general of the Stockholm conference to discuss
the interrelationship of development and environment questions as

[15] The author has used, for his sample of developing country opinion, the
work of a panel of experts on development and environment which he attended
at Founex, Switzerland, June 4-12, 1971, and also the view of third-world representatives who participated in the First Environmental Workshop at Aspen,
Colorado (June-August 1971).

they affect third-world countries identifies a number of existing and potential problem areas in rich-poor country relations in which the interests of the developing countries must be "articulated clearly, analysed objectively and provided for in any international arrangements which are made."[16] The panel also called for:

> Action to cushion the disruptive effects of such [environmental] measures on the trade of the developing countries through a system of prior consultation and warnings by the developed countries of environmental actions contemplated by them. . . . Conflicts of trade interests arising in this area should be resolved through existing and evolving arrangements and procedures. In this connection, the existing GATT framework — under which most of the industrialised countries have assumed specific rights and obligations — should be further used to mitigate such problems so as to reduce the fears of the developing countries that a desire for a better environment may lead to an increase in protectionism.[17]

Institutional responsibilities were also suggested for research and data accumulation on further possible trade disruption:

> First, a comprehensive study should be made, possibly by UNCTAD, of the major threats that may arise to the exports of the developing countries, the character and severity of such threats, and the corrective action that may be possible. Second, the FAO should continue its present useful work on food standards considerations, including contamination, and seek to establish agreed environmental standards and guidelines for the export of foodstuffs. Third, the GATT should undertake to monitor the rise of non-tariff barriers on grounds of environmental concern and bring out pointedly any such trends in its Annual Reports.[18]

On the subject of the implications of environmental action by the industrialized countries for the transfer of technology the panel proposed that further research be undertaken, preferably under the auspices of the United Nations Advisory Committee on the Application of Science and Technology to Development (UNCSAT). At the same time, however, the need to build ecological study and analysis into development planning and preinvestment work and to promote ecological balance in the course of future investment was also recog-

[16] "Development and Environment" (UN Document GE. 71-13319), p. 21.
[17] Ibid., p. 22.
[18] Ibid., p. 23.

nized to have important institutional implications.[19] However, it seemed clear that these must take the form of changes in the structure and procedures of the various multilateral aid agencies (discussed below) rather than be the activity of any separate environmental agency.

The attitude of leaders in developing countries to institutional arrangements following Stockholm has perhaps been summed up best in language of the report of the group of experts on development and environment which presents priorities which are the polar opposite to those of Kennan:

> The environment problem has to be placed in its proper perspective both in the developed and the developing countries. It should not be presented as a pollution problem in the developed world and a poverty problem in the developing countries; instead it should be treated as *a problem of the most efficient synthesis of developmental and environmental concerns at different stages of social transitions.*[20]

VI. THE PRACTICAL INSTITUTIONAL ALTERNATIVES

The Case for Laissez Faire

Probably no one involved in the "rolling debate" on how to gear United Nations machinery to handle environmental problems would suggest that present arrangements and programs will be adequate if the United Nations system is to undertake a larger role in this field. In the case of some industrialized country governments, however, a caution which is based on previous experience with institution building in the context of United Nations diplomacy has been their predominant theme in discussing institutional proposals. Indeed, their hesitancy over greater use of the United Nations system has sometimes led to the not unfamiliar syndrome of greatest optimism as to the effectiveness of present UN system executive and coordinative arrangements being expressed by those with the least confidence in them in the hope of diverting international initiative to other, more favorable forums.

A corollary of this posture has been the considerable optimism shown by governments over their own capacity to coordinate policy both internally and in relation to each other. A position taken by

---

[19] It has been stressed at these and other meetings that ecological caution in the course of investment is not by any means always a negative matter of restraining or avoiding action. One example of environmentally creative development is the farming for both conservation and food purposes of rare species of game animals in East Africa.

[20] "Development and Environment," p. 25. (Author's italics.)

officials of certain developed countries faced with these institutional problems is that the basic principle for international environmental action should be for an intergovernmental body (with a small supporting secretariat) to designate a "lead agency" for a specific environmental problem. This agency would be responsible for initiating work in the given area and for coordinating the work of other agencies on the same problem. The British government, which at an early stage in the Stockholm preparations circulated a paper along these lines, clearly had in mind that the central governmental body should be within the United Nations and that intergovernmental coordination of most, if not all, international action to protect the environment should be within the framework of the UN. Thus, if there is an appropriate United Nations specialized agency covering an environmental problem, it should take over the setting and monitoring of world standards in its particular area. When an environmental problem is clearly regional, like that of pollution of the Baltic Sea, responsibility should go to the ECE, which spans Eastern and Western Europe. The OECD, a nonregional grouping of the rich industrialized Western countries and Japan, should, in several governments' view, restrict its activities to research into ways of handling the economic problems associated with tackling industrial pollution. The Science and Technological Research Committee of the European Community (Aigrain Group) would promote international cooperation in development of antipollution technology. The Council of Europe, which has already taken a lead in nature conservation, should continue to handle that matter in the context of Western Europe but should be restricted to this role. The United Nations Educational, Scientific and Cultural Organization (UNESCO) should have world responsibility for public education on environmental matters. And so on.

Given the ineffectiveness of intra-United Nations coordination between the specialized agencies[21] and the absence of any wider coordinating arrangements between other institutional bodies with environmental programs, such a principle throws all coordination and priority-setting responsibilities back to the coordinators of national governments' policies as pursued in various international organizations. Yet the absence of any effective means of producing such coordination is as conspicuous in national capitals as it is in New York and Geneva. Indeed, to many national governmental officials any

[21] The ineffectiveness of the General Assembly, the Economic and Social Council (ECOSOC), and the Administrative Committee on Coordination (ACC) in this area have been widely acknowledged. See, for example, *A Study of the Capacity of the United Nations Development System* (Jackson report) (UN Document DP/5) (2 vols.; Geneva: United Nations, 1969).

quest for such central priority setting is seen as futile, or worse, as reflecting a passion for order and symmetry in organizational affairs which would inhibit flexibility of response to changing events and is completely impractical anyway. In this view which, perhaps not surprisingly, has been shared, and indeed promoted, by representatives of the specialized agencies duplication and overlapping of jurisdictions are seen as regrettable but inevitable and in any event as a relatively small price to pay for the flexibility and institutional humanity that goes with the present haphazard "scatter-gun" approach. Some even argue that a lack of clarity in division of responsibility is positively desirable in the international organization field and that sharper divisions and clearer authority simply breed sharper and more heated conflicts.

It appears, at the time of writing, that despite its obvious appeal both to the "line" departments of governments and to their corresponding specialized agencies the *laissez faire* approach outlined above will be rejected by governments as being inappropriate to the multidisciplinary, multisectoral nature of the environmental problems. Alternative proposals have, instead, focused on a perceived need for a central intergovernmental body supported by a small but highly qualified secretariat with both the authority and the power (through the administration of funds for new environmental activities) to develop, via the specialized agencies but also any other institutional or national bodies of appropriate competence, a complete and integrated system of knowledge collection and assessment on international environmental problems. The institutional issue has in fact, since the third Preparatory Committee meeting for Stockholm in September 1971, turned largely around the location and status of this intergovernmental body and of its secretariat.

Proposals for a Major New Intergovernmental Council on the Environment

A United Nations council on the environment, separate from and of equal status with ECOSOC, has been quite widely canvassed, at least in the United States and Sweden, as a means of improving coordination of existing environmental programs. One proposal is that the Trusteeship Council, having now fulfilled its mandate, should be given a new mandate for environmental protection. Advocates of a separate environmental council feel that any body of lesser status, such as a special commission or committee of ECOSOC, would have insufficient influence over the programs of the various agencies.

Such a radical innovation among the various intergovernmental bodies would, however, require amendment of the Charter of the

United Nations. The precedent of the establishment of the United Nations Children's Fund (UNICEF), the United Nations Development Program (UNDP), the United Nations Industrial Development Organization (UNIDO), and UNITAR by General Assembly resolutions under article 59 of the charter is not sufficient, for a change would clearly modify the basic structure of legal authority between the various United Nations agencies. The General Assembly could, of course, create, by resolution, an environmental body comparable in legal status to UNCTAD (which is a permanent organ of the General Assembly), but only the creation of a council of equal status to ECOSOC (in addition to the interests of ECOSOC itself) would give the new intergovernmental body clear legal authority over the specialized agencies.

As regards charter revision, two opposed schools of thought exist. One school would welcome an opportunity for revision and would advocate creation of an environmental council as only one of several major changes. These "revisionists" point out that, despite great doubts expressed in many quarters, it proved possible eventually to get ratification by the major powers called for in article 108 of the charter for amendment of the articles of the charter relating to the composition of the Security Council and ECOSOC. The other school looks with distrust on the whole prospect of charter revision, fearing that the cure might prove worse than the disease. If a charter revision was to prove agreeable to governments, there is no shortage of suggestions as to what form it should take. There have been pleas for a council composed of representatives of the various international organizations (both within the United Nations and outside it). The principal objection to this is that prevention of jurisdictional "poaching" might become the major activity of the council and the resultant approach of "negative coordination" become institutionalized. Alternatively, there have been calls for appointment of environmental experts to such a council, the experts to be chosen either by governments or by the secretary-general; but such a solution would meet serious resistance from most states if the council were to have proscriptive as well as prescriptive authority. The most likely course of agreement would be for a situation similar to the present election process for ECOSOC, i.e., representation of a number of countries elected by the General Assembly.

The possibilities and the advocates are numerous. Yet for the reasons set forth above consensus on the need for such a major constitutional change has so far been shown to be lacking.

Coordination of Environmental Activities through Modification of
Existing United Nations Institutions

Apart from the specialized agencies themselves, which appear to
prefer responsibility for interagency coordination to be left in the
hands of the ACC, a majority of observers feel that some form of
budgeting control over the agencies is essential if an integrated program of environmental activity is really the objective. Some observers
have been attracted to the idea of building on the potential of the
UNDP's central financing role which the Jackson report stressed
as vital at the country level and using this not only at the country
but also at the regional and global levels to coordinate the specialized
agencies' environmental activities.

Placing environmental responsibilities within the UNDP might,
it is argued, help to ensure that environmental considerations are included in development projects from their inception (i.e., from the
preinvestment survey or institution-building project). Certainly, this
is the logical and desirable place to examine such considerations
rather than after a training institute's curriculum has been set or a
feasibility study for a road or dam completed. It seems desirable that
additional funds should be made available to developing countries
to ensure that such environmental considerations are taken into
account at the planning stage of projects. But the case for control
of separate funding by a development-financing institution for a
purpose which may be at odds with the institution's traditional developmental interest seems doubtful to a number of governments
as well as nongovernmental observers. Nevertheless, this problem of
institutional arrangements to ensure the optimum of environmental
concern in development aid is an important one and is discussed below.

The creation of the United Nations Fund for Population Activities in 1969 does provide a precedent for such an approach. Moreover,
the parallel has a certain relevance. A number of United Nations
agencies, including the WHO, the FAO, UNESCO, UNICEF, and the
United Nations' own Population Division, had undertaken various
activities and research related to population limitation policies and
family planning. But governments felt that the situation had not
resulted in sufficient priority being given to the subject by any agency as in each organization established priorities held sway. The solution adopted in this instance was to establish a population unit, with
its own separate source of voluntarily contributed funds, within the
UNDP. The resulting United Nations Fund for Population Activities was to develop projects both with United Nations agencies and
also directly with governmental and nongovernmental institutions
such as the Population Council and International Planned Parent-
hood Federation. Its close relationship with other bureaus of the

UNDP and its control by the UNDP's 37-member Governing Council represented a new and centralized approach to the complex problems associated with limiting population for social and economic objectives.

It seems inevitable that the same logic that produced the intergovernmental initiative of the United Nations Fund for Population Activities will be applied by some to giving coordination and direction to environmental research monitoring and action programs within the United Nations system. Moreover, if a similar set of rules as applies to the Fund for Population Activities were drawn up for a parallel environmental fund, this new addition to UNDP would also be enabled to fund and coordinate the activities of national and international institutions, public and private, outside the United Nations system. Such an arrangement could be elaborated to include a more formal governing body for the United Nations environmental fund, possibly to be composed of a committee of ECOSOC with non-voting but permanent seats occupied by the heads of the United Nations specialized agencies and perhaps certain nongovernmental bodies, such as the ICSU and the IUCN.

Yet, while some commentators have seen this course as logical and practical, a greater number are more concerned by its drawbacks. There is considerable uncertainty as to the advisability of applying the approach of the Fund for Population Activities to a very different set of problems. The field of environmental protection is vastly wider and more complex than that of population; it also calls for a stronger emphasis on regional cooperation; it demands a wider range of specialists and a great variety of technical research capabilities; it has very complex legal implications; most important of all is the fact that environment cannot be treated as another "specialist" subject like food production, health, or population limitation as environmental protection inevitably embraces all of these subjects. At the same time many have seen incongruity or even real danger in adding environmental protection responsibilities to an agency whose management has economic development as its primary competence and interest. Moreover, even if this objection is discounted, it remains true that the UNDP has not yet demonstrated its ability to wield the power of the purse over the United Nations' specialist arms. Though it is too early to make any firm judgment on the matter, there is evidence that the Fund for Population Activities may already be tending to operate quite separately from the rest of the UNDP. The UNDP undoubtedly has the potential to emerge gradually as a policy-setting and -controlling body for the whole United Nations developmental system by becoming its cabinet office as well as its finance ministry. But that situation is still a long way off. Flexibility is important in arrangements for a central environmental institution or institutions part-

ly because it may be desirable for a central environmental secretariat
and the central developmental secretariat to be merged at some point
in the future if a real synthesis of developmental and environmental
interest occurs.

It seems, therefore, that with a consensus emerging on the need
for a strong secretariat administering a central fund and continuing
skepticism as to the advisability of embarking on charter revision, a
central environmental secretariat will be established either under an
environmental committee or commission of ECOSOC or under an
environmental organ of the General Assembly. Innumerable arguments, mostly of a housekeeping nature, may be mounted pro and
con either of these two solutions, as, for example, the problem of the
relationship of environment to the established divisions of the Department of Economic and Social Affairs, such as resources and transport,
housing, building, and planning, population, etc., if it is placed in
ECOSOC. Logically, again, environment should subsume all other
economic and social activities, but this, if only for political reasons
which symbolize the difference between the UN's national constituency and the domestic constituency of an environmentally aware industrialized country, is most unlikely to prove acceptable.

Unquestionably, ECOSOC is the most logical and the constitu-
tionally designated focus for coordinating activities in the realm of
the environment. The fact that it is in the throes of a major self-
reform and expansion of membership from 27 to 52 (for reasons only
partly based on greater effectiveness) has encouraged constitutional-
ists to see the environment as a potential field for its revival. However, the record of this body in coordination of the specialized agencies
has been so dismal in the past that many fear that the new coordinative concept of "environment" may suffer fatally from being placed
in an arena which, under token obeisance to the need for unity of
approach, yearly endorses by its default the reign of separatism and
specialization.

An environmental body, on the other hand, that sat as a permanent organ of the General Assembly could — like UNCTAD —
evolve its own shape and character. Equally important, its deliberations would be likely to receive far more attention than those of an
ECOSOC commission or committee competing for attention both
within the council and with the world's press with commissions ranging from statistics to narcotic drugs and the status of women. Indeed, there can be little doubt that *pace* the sense of propriety of the
pundits of international constitutional law, the environmentally concerned publics of the main contributing countries to the United Nations will almost inevitably be inclined to believe that governments
had given the environment the international brush-off unless some-

thing like the conversion of the Trusteeship Council (and committee of the General Assembly) or the creation of a new council takes place as a result of Stockholm. The solution favored by the Stockholm secretariat meets this concern, and it is to be hoped that it will prevail. The secretariat's paper for governments on this subject proposes an intergovernmental body that is a subsidiary organ of the General Assembly but that — like the UNDP Governing Council — reports to the General Assembly *through ECOSOC*, thus preserving the possibility of maintaining ECOSOC's statutory coordinating role.

At a practical level, however, it is arguable that it matters very little where or even at what level the intergovernmental body is located, provided that the secretariat, and especially its chief executive, is given sufficient status, visibility, and at least a measure of leverage through the control of funds. The first two of these elements seem assured. The degree of leverage depends, clearly, on the scale of the funds envisaged. This is of course the crucial joker in the pack of questions surrounding the institutional issue. What are the likely reactions of donor governments to yet another United Nations fund? Does the environment have the international electoral appeal of, say, population?[22] The answer appears to be that it may in certain countries, notably the United States, Japan, and possibly Sweden and Canada, whose electoral concern with environmental questions is clearly great. But it is unlikely to receive more than token contributions from most of the other traditional major donors to UN funds. Nevertheless, even with this limited range of support there is evidence to suggest that at least the bottom end of Maurice Strong's wide-bracket estimate of $15 million to $25 million a year for initial operations may be met. It seems likely, too, from past experience with comparable beginnings of voluntary UN funds, that this sum will steadily grow as the more skeptical donors become exposed by domestic pressure groups to invidious comparison.

Such a starting sum should enable the new secretariat to make a considerable impact if one bears in mind the minuscule financing for current environmental operations by members of the UN system. On what will it be spent? This question raises the whole issue of functional responsibilities which has been more discussed than illuminated in the past months of preparation for the Stockholm conference. The approach of the secretariat has been that as regards institutional responsibilities, "form must follow function" or, in other words, that any new institutional arrangements must depend on what functions

[22] The budget of the UN Fund for Population Activities, which in the year of its establishment (1969) stood at only $1.5 million, rose to $15 million in 1970 and to $25 million in 1971; in 1972 the fund is expected to receive $35 million to $40 million in voluntary contributions.

should be performed internationally. Logical though this may appear as an approach, it has suffered from the fact that even when the conference secretariat's action proposals are all agreed to by the Preparatory Committee as being suitable for presentation to governments at the conference, it will still not be possible simply to reallocate functions among the various agencies and organizations concerned. If this task of allocation of responsibilities can be achieved at all, it can only be achieved in an evolutionary fashion, and it is precisely this process of evolution which calls for central funding and a "leadership" role in controlling this money to be placed in a central secretariat. So far, therefore, the conference secretariat has handled this problem of functions by suggesting that the agencies continue their current functions but that the possibility be reserved that future additional functions might be allocated by a central environmental secretariat.

VII. NEW FUNCTIONS

The new functions to be performed are grouped by the conference secretariat into three categories: the environmental knowledge, acquisition, and assessment function; the environmental quality management function; and the environmental technical assistance function. Under the first of these are grouped four subsidiary networks of functions, namely, research, monitoring,[23] information exchange, and evaluation of environmental knowledge. In each case the secretariat points out that new work will be required of existing parts of the United Nations system but at the same time environmental risks cannot be fully assessed or established without intersectoral and interdisciplinary review, definition, administration, classification, information transfer, and evaluation requiring a necessarily central function which is totally lacking in the United Nations system at present. Should there also be a central research facility for scientific study of global environmental problems? Various proposals have been put forward in the course of discussion of post-Stockholm institutional arrangements for a central scientific institute for the environment. They have not, however, found a clear consensus of support from the scientific community and, at least partly for this reason, have not been regarded with favor by governments which, together with the Stockholm secretariat, prefer the concept of close contact between

---

[23] "Monitoring" has become a key word in Stockholm conference jargon. When used in the context of the conference, it does *not* connote the policing or surveillance of compliance with regulations or standards "Monitoring" is here taken to mean the collection of "base-line" environmental data and information on changes in the quality of media which, directly or indirectly, may significantly affect the health or well-being of man.

the central secretariat and the international scientific community which should be convened in expert groups to give attention to problems on an ad hoc basis.

The environmental quality management function is subdivided by the Stockholm secretariat into "goal setting" or the establishment of standards of environmental quality (referring to the level of pollutant in a specified environmental medium or a minimum health or safety standard); discharge standards (rate of emission of pollutants from source); operational standards (relating to activities which cause pollution); and complete prohibitions, effluent charges, and price adjustments. Other standards, for example, for energy consumption, housing, water supply, quantitative and selective use of natural resources, and use and protection of endangered species of flora and fauna are also referred to as other goals that may in the future be advanced for intergovernmental agreement either in the form of nonmandatory recommendations and guidelines, uniform national codes of conduct, or international agreement through treaties, conventions, etc. In the case of almost all such standards setting the main international institutional function would be simply to provide a forum — with those proverbial corridors attached — in which international negotiation could take place. There is also, clearly, an important leadership and initiative function which should attach to the office of the executive head of the central secretariat.

However, according to the conference secretariat "goal setting" is not the only international environmental quality management function requiring new institutional arrangements. Others include the institutional means for consultation over proposed actions by international actors which may affect the global environment, the provision of a forum in which such questions as environmental education priorities or international scarcities of environmental manpower resources can be discussed and identified. Again, such functions would seem to be best performed by the proposed intergovernmental body or its committees.

Finally, in support of both the knowledge acquisition and assessment function and the environmental quality management function there is clearly a need for some central public information facilities. Only the most limited resources are likely to be made available by governments for such public information purposes. Yet it is vitally important to the success of all national and international environmental efforts that the need for a global environmental consciousness is recognized and provided for in international institutional arrangements. It therefore seems essential that a small specialized publications and publicity staff be established within the central environmental secretariat to publicize the results of central intergovernmental discussions and of symposia and other meetings organized under the intergovernmental body for the environment.

As regards the international environmental aid function — the task of providing help to countries in acquiring and assessing environmental knowledge and improving their environmental management — the Stockholm conference secretariat has spelled out three broad functional roles to be performed by the UN system as a whole: 1) formulation of appropriate environmental guidelines for international and national developmental programs; 2) provision of support for education and training of environmental professionals, including environmental education in schools and universities; and 3) provision of the resources — both men and money — necessary to integrate environmental considerations into development programs. This provision should include technical assistance in assessing and offsetting the economic and social impact of other countries' trade and investment controls to protect their environments.

The Stockholm secretariat has made it clear that both technical and capital assistance that falls under these three categories should be organized, financed, and executed by the existing machinery of the UN's development system. The secretariat has thus attempted to resolve the much-discussed issue of to what extent an environmental fund could or should be devoted to "topping up" existing aid resources to encourage or ensure an environmental protection dimension in developmental assistance activities, by suggesting that new environmental funds should be devoted solely to the accumulation and assessment of environmental knowledge and the application of its use for developing international agreement on common measures for protecting environmental quality. Politically, this was a necessary decision as donor governments from the start responded negatively to any suggestion that implied the possibility of "the environment" becoming a conduit for additional aid funds.

Much of the discussion on functional responsibilities inevitably sounds hazy and even evasive of the hard issues of jurisdiction that are unquestionably at stake. Yet from all the discussion of the new functions that need to be performed in any attempt to institutionalize international cooperation to protect the environment a picture of a central functional requirement does emerge. A central intergovernmental body and supporting secretariat appears to be essential. Inevitably and unavoidably the question of new functions to be performed is inseparable from that of the nature and role of the environmental secretariat.

VIII. AN INTERNATIONAL ENVIRONMENTAL SECRETARIAT

The approach to functional responsibilities outlined above implies a small environmental secretariat entrusted with the responsibility, under the supervision of the intergovernmental body, to lead and coordinate the ongoing environmental activities of the United Nations system. This secretariat would be responsible for the central functions of evaluation, assessment, transfer, and exchange of the knowledge acquired through ongoing research and monitoring activities which it would coordinate and other necessary research and monitoring work which it would, at the request of governments, initiate, finance, and supervise, though not conduct.

It is generally agreed that what is needed to carry out these responsibilities is a small secretariat of high quality working in intimate relationship both with the scientific community and the top-level decisionmakers in governments. It would have to have access to the best of the world's scientific and professional resources. Its own skills would be those required to relate the advice of scientists and technologists to the political decisionmaking process. It would have to produce the kind of information and recommendations that governments would find useful in making decisions concerning both national programs having international implications and international activities in which they are participating. It would complement and support the efforts of national governments to exercise effective coordination of their own policies, particularly with respect to the activities of international organizations.

The principal formal method by which information and recommendations from the secretariat would reach governments might be by means of an annual report to the United Nations General Assembly — in the nature of an annual "Report on the State of the World Environment." It might also hold meetings in particular countries and regions which would provide a basis both for receiving information and views on the particular environmental concerns of these countries and regions and of focusing public attention in such areas on these concerns and on important global issues.

To perform these functions the secretariat would need to undertake an active recruitment policy both from within and outside the UN system. Here the Stockholm secretariat has inclined to the cautious and, some observers will believe, disappointingly conformist view that the secretariat's establishment should conform closely to current interpretations of article 101 of the charter and that administrative costs at least of the environmental secretariat should come from the regular budget of the United Nations. This is certainly the line that will have the greatest initial appeal to governments and to the United Nations establishment. But it may be doubted whether, in the light, for example, of the recent revelations of glaring ineptitude in the UN Office of Personnel made in a report of the United Nations Joint Inspection Unit[24] the link which this solution implies with the central administration of the United Nations is likely to provide the type of scientifically and technically authoritative secretariat that will be needed if the central functions described above are to be adequately fulfilled.

There are, in fact, precedents for three alternative approaches to this problem of secretariat financing for subsidiary organs of the General Assembly (which is, inevitably, closely linked with other administrative arrangements). In the case of UNCTAD all the expenses of the secretariat are borne by the regular budget of the United Nations; in the case of UNIDO and the United Nations High Commissioner for Refugees (UNHCR) the administrative expenses of the organ are borne by the regular budget of the UN and other expenses are financed by voluntary contributions; finally, in the case of UNITAR, UNICEF, and the UNDP all expenses, both administrative and operational, are financed from voluntary contributions. The argument for a UNIDO- or UNHCR-type of solution is essentially that such a formula may give member governments, and the international civil servants involved, the proper degree of confidence in the continuing concern for multilateral action in the field of environment. The issue may not be particularly important if supplementary funds from voluntary contributions are in fact freely available for "special administrative purposes" such as the hiring of consultants. Yet it does seem that from the experience of recent times, and especially of recent months, the notion that the regular budget represents a surer basis for future operations than voluntarily contributed funds may need some reexamination. United States plans to reduce its overall contribution to the United Nations refer to the regular budget. Indeed in political terms it would seem that voluntary contributions for United Nations activities in such electorally popular fields as environment or population are likely to prove at least as secure and possibly a great deal more plentiful than the theoretically mandatory contributions which are at best liable to remain frozen in the foreseeable future. If the environmental concern is indeed just a passing electoral whim or fancy, then the most cautious and sagacious plans for international cooperation for environmental action will be of no avail. If it is not a whim but represents a commitment at least as solid and sure as that toward the developmental aid activities of the United Nations, then surely it is sensible and fitting for the financing and administration of the environmental secretariat to be so

[24] UN Document A/8545.

established that its head has flexibility in recruitment and other administrative and especially personnel matters equal to that accorded to the administrator of the UNDP.

IX. REGIONAL INSTITUTIONAL ARRANGEMENTS FOR THE ENVIRONMENT

On no aspect of the debate on future international institutional arrangements for the environment has there been such widespread agreement as that the great bulk of intergovernmental cooperation to deal with environmental problems must occur at the regional level. Three general principles regarding the establishment of new regional bodies for environmental action seem to have emerged from discussions concerning institutional arrangements. The first is that whenever possible, new regional organizations should be centered around specific common environmental problems. Another is that the geographical area of a region should, whenever possible, be ecologically defined, i.e., it should include not merely an international lake but also the lake's catchment area; not simply an international river but also its basin and preferably its whole catchment area; for some purposes, perhaps, a whole climatic region. The third principle is that such organizations must be defined by the states concerned.

It seems clear, too, that eventually a large number of regional organizations of many varieties and sizes will be necessary. Patterns of intergovernmental organization differ markedly in the major regions of the world as do their relations with the scientific communities of the respective areas. No standard format for regional environmental organizations can be suggested that is uniformly relevant. The organizational pattern must inevitably differ greatly from one area to another and from one subject-focus to another. Whether to build on existing organizations or to start afresh is a matter for governments of the regions to decide.

In many instances special financial and technical assistance will be required to launch such organizations and support them in their initial phases. This raises the question of the relationship between such regional institutions and the central United Nations mechanism for environmental matters. This relationship would be likely, because of the great variety of regional arrangements envisaged, to vary greatly from case to case. There will, however, be a major leadership role for the central United Nations environmental body to play in helping to establish such institutions. On occasion this role may call for some technical assistance "seed money" to enable negotiations between the countries concerned to go forward.

Apart from the need for regional groupings of countries organized around a specific common environmental problem or resource many commentators have seen the need for more general regional environmental centers. Such centers could serve the same areas as the regional economic commissions of the United Nations and might, for convenience, be located at their headquarters. Some observers, however, feel that, on the analogy of avoiding placing the central environmental secretariat within the UNDP, the environmental centers should operate under separate auspices, their central linkage being to the environmental body in the United Nations. There is also, however, a considerable body of opinion to the effect that no regional environmental center, whether of the specific-focus type or the general variety, should be in any sense a branch body of a global institution. Instead, it is felt that a close nonhierarchical working relationship should be sought. The regional organizations should both service and be serviced by the global facility in a co-operative world network of environmental organizations.

It is vital that regional organizations, whether general or problem-focused, avoid duplication of either existing or potential research knowledge transfer or training facilities that may be provided by other international organizations, either within the United Nations system or outside it. Some of these functions may, on occasion, and by mutual agreement with the other organizations concerned, be carried out under regional center auspicies, but they would not be the primary role of regional centers. The main task of such centers would be to provide a range of "stimulation" and "management-aid" services for governments, which in many parts of the world no existing agency is equipped to provide. Stimulation functions would include: 1) promotion of an integrated approach and interdisciplinary methods essential for effective ecological and environmental study; 2) ensurance that the views of scientists from the countries of the region are taken fully into account in the planning and conduct of cooperative international research programs in environmental affairs; and 3) provision of better scientific information about environmental conditions to decisionmakers of the region in question. Management aid functions would vary greatly from region to region. In the case of the more developed areas many are already being provided. The objective of new regional organizations in the less developed areas of the world would be to perform a parallel set of services.

As regards the more developed regions of the world, there already exist a number of well-established institutional arrangements. Their evolution should not, obviously, be impinged upon by any new United Nations regional machinery. In the case of the developing countries the preparatory process for the Stockholm conference has evoked considerable discussion of problems and the basis for continued intergovernmental negotiation within the context of the UN's four geographic regions.

As far as the regional activities of international organizations outside the United Nations system are concerned, one possible approach might be to establish, initially, ad hoc regional advisory groups which would include representatives of all the regional bodies involved or interested in environmental protection activities, whether they are within or outside the United Nations system. These could be formed at the initiative of the central environmental secretariat. In addition the central environmental secretariat of the United Nations should be in a position to encourage the activities of such nongovernmental regional bodies in relation to regional environmental problems and to help their establishment, perhaps with "seed-money" but certainly with arrangements for technical back-up facilities.

Having stressed the regional nature of almost all international environmental problems, I must conclude with the one aspect of the institutional issue which is unavoidably global in its scope and its institutional requirements and has emerged from the Stockholm process of "rolling debate" as the greatest single focus of institutional attention.

X. ORGANIZATION TO DEAL WITH MARINE POLLUTION: A SPECIAL PROBLEM

The concern of UN members with marine pollution has been manifested in recent General Assembly resolutions and in the Intergovernmental Working Group on Marine Pollution established by the Preparatory Committee. Although valuable measures of cooperation have already been undertaken to deal with marine pollution, it is clear that the organizational structure is not adequate to cope effectively with all the relevant aspects of this problem.

Marine pollution is an environmental problem in which international cooperation can be particularly valuable at the regional level. This is not only because common interests may be more readily perceived at the regional level but also because of the different characteristics of different bodies of water. Arrangements have already been embarked on to deal with the pollution of certain enclosed or semi-enclosed seas — the Caspian, the Baltic, the North, and the Mediterranean seas. At Stockholm governments may wish to encourage these efforts and call for additional measures to deal with other threatened bodies of water for which adequate arrangements do not yet exist. Institutions are also needed on the global level in view of the fundamental interrelation of the entire marine environment and in view of the fact that the most serious source of oceanic pollution is the outfall of wastes, sewage, agricultural chemicals, carbon dioxide, etc., from land-based human activities. Adequate measures to preserve the health of the oceans obviously require a global approach. A number of global institutions are presently concerned with the marine environment. A broad range of monitoring, evaluation, research, education, and training functions is performed by the Intergovernmental Oceanographic Commission (IOC) in collaboration with UNESCO, which provides its secretariat, and other specialized agencies. To avoid duplication of effort and to provide a common source of advice in this field the UN, together with the FAO, UNESCO, the WHO, IMCO, and the International Atomic Energy Agency (IAEA), have established the Joint Group of Experts on the Scientific Aspects of Marine Pollution (GESAMP). The administrative secretariat of GESAMP is provided by IMCO.

The responsibility for regulating different sources of marine pollution is presently divided as follows:

Marine pollution from maritime commerce. This is the responsibility of IMCO. At its 1973 conference IMCO will not only consider revisions of its 1954 convention to eliminate all intentional pollution by oil but will also consider agreements for the elimination of intentional pollution by substances other than oil, for the minimization of accidental pollution by oil and other substances, for the safe carriage of dangerous goods, and for the disposal or treatment of ship-generated sewage waste.

Marine pollution from offshore oil installations. This is within the purview of the UN Committee on the Peaceful Uses of the Seabed and the Ocean Floor beyond the Limits of National Jurisdiction and is to be considered at the law of the sea conference which it is hoped will be held in 1973. One proposal would entrust this responsibility to an international seabed authority.

Marine pollution from ocean dumping. Proposals for an international convention to regulate ocean dumping — the transportation by ship of waste materials to the oceans from land — are currently before the Intergovernmental Working Group on Marine Pollution established by the Preparatory Committee for the Stockholm conference. Under one proposal presented to the group responsibility for administering a convention on this subject would be entrusted to the international organization created as a result of the law of the sea conference and, pending the creation of such an organization, to a general conference of contracting parties.

Marine Pollution from land. Pollutants reaching the oceans from rivers, from outfalls, from land runoffs, and from the atmosphere are by far the most important sources of marine pollution. Yet they are totally unregulated except for IAEA standards on the disposal of radioactive wastes. These sources will have to be dealt with through international cooperation if the health of the oceans is to be protected. International action could take the form of monitoring pollution from these sources, setting standards of water quality for different parts of the marine environment, and eventually setting limits on the discharge of pollutants.

A general obligation to protect the health of the marine environment is contained in article 25 of the 1958 Convention on the High Seas which obliges states "to cooperate with competent international organisations in taking measures for the prevention of pollution of the seas or air space above, resulting from any activities with radioactive materials or other harmful agents." In the absence of an organization of general competence in this area, however, this obligation has not yet had much significance.

The institutional choices facing the international community would seem to be four. First, IMCO could take responsibility not only for marine pollution from maritime commerce but also for all the sources of marine pollution described above. This has the advantage of using the one existing UN agency with regulatory experience in the marine pollution area. It would build upon and incorporate the work going on in GESAMP, for which IMCO already provides the secretariat. On the other hand, the addition of these other responsibilities, particularly for land-based sources of pollution, would add heavily to IMCO's responsibilities and involve a major reshaping of that organization.

Second, IMCO could confine itself to pollution from maritime commerce; the international organization resulting from the law of the sea conference could be responsible for pollution from offshore oil facilities, ocean dumping, and perhaps land-based pollution as well. The problem with this solution is that it would have to await a satisfactory conclusion of the law of the sea conference, which is problematical and may, if indeed it is achieved at all, be a number of years away.

Third, the IOC could be strengthened and given the responsibilities assigned in the second choice above to the international organization emerging from the law of the sea conference. This solution would, of course, suffer from the same objection as choice one. Indeed perhaps more so, as the IOC, unlike IMCO, has no regulatory functions at present. If both scientific and regulatory functions were given to the IOC, its current institutional location as well as its nature as a part of UNESCO would, almost certainly, have to change. Inevitably, it would have to grow considerably from its present minimal establishment in staff and budgetary terms and would also have to develop close relations with other agencies of the UN system, in particular the WMO with whose global atmospheric monitoring activities the IOC's future oceanic monitoring will have to be very closely integrated. This now has led to a proposal, currently under consideration, for the relocation of the IOC in Geneva, a move which would probably be essential if the IOC is to play a central part in global oceanic monitoring in the future.

A fourth alternative would be to allocate the task of administering and conducting research and monitoring to the IOC and to make IMCO responsible for the operation and surveillance of intergovernmental maritime agreements on pollution, including the technical assistance support that will be vital to ensure the capacity of many countries to comply with agreed international regulations. The overall coordination of the two functions could be handled by the central intergovernmental environmental committee and its secretariat. This coordinating responsibility could be much more effectively undertaken if the funds supporting such activities were channeled through the central environmental machinery.

At some point in the future it seems inevitable that consideration will be given to establishing a world oceans authority with responsibility for all the scientific and regulatory functions discussed above, together with functions relating to fishery resources and other law of the sea issues. However, opting for this solution would clearly be premature at the Stockholm conference in view of the major political issues still unresolved and the work proceeding in other forums. It should perhaps, however, be made clear at Stockholm that present institutional arrangements were being made on a pro tempora basis.

If current considerations in various bodies do point to a new body with responsibilities for the marine environment, governments should retain the flexibility necessary to reallocate tasks at a later date. Here again the central mechanism for the environment may be the most effective place to mediate the eventual settlement. Indeed, the problem of maritime oceanic institutions and the marine environment serves to illustrate the general point that all the organizational arrangements for international environmental cooperation must be flexible and responsive enough to shape and support this ongoing process as it unfolds in technical, political, and economic circumstances that are now only dimly foreseeable, if at all. In fact, the requirement for Stockholm is not so much to establish an organizational *structure* as to set up a parallel *process* of institutional development capable of growth and renewal and of promoting and accommodating the specific organizational modes needed to deal with the infinite variety of new and unforeseen problems of environmental planning, management, and protection as they arise.

In an important sense such a process has already been set in motion by the preparations for the Stockholm conference. It is this — together with the technical work and intellectual ferment it has generated — that must be sustained and sharpened by the organizational arrangements adopted at the conference.

XI. CONCLUSIONS

To protect the planet and ourselves from the side effects of our drive to make it a more hospitable home is the largest opportunity and challenge ever offered to international cooperative efforts. It is daunting. But it is also unavoidable. So is the problem of designing institutions through which a divided mankind can cooperate effectively in this work.

In a world of sovereign states realism dictates the principle that we must rely, whenever possible, upon the capacity of states for action. The institutional design discussed in this article remits the execution of international policy primarily to national governments. At the international level the only sensible approach to institution building is one of flexibility, pragmatism, and caution. The hardest blows of heaven fall in history upon those who imagine that they can control events in a sovereign manner, playing providence not only for themselves but for the far future and gambling on calculations in which there must never be a single mistake. New international institutional arrangements there clearly must be. But they must grow gradually out of the perceived realities of need and of capacity.

APPENDIX 1. DISTRIBUTION OF ENVIRONMENTAL ACTIVITIES
AMONG INTERNATIONAL ORGANIZATIONS[1]

ATMOSPHERIC POLLUTION

Standardization of data collection	A1
Monitoring air pollutants of global significance	A2
Adoption of agreed air quality criteria	A3
Emission inventories, by specific source	A4
Standards for permissible amounts of selected pollutants	A5
Studies of air pollution effects, especially on health	A6
Analysis of the economic impact of air pollution	A7
Monitoring the upper atmosphere	A8
Expanding the existing solar monitoring network	A9

MARINE ENVIRONMENT

Oil spillage from ships	M1
Studies of oceanic pollution effects	M2
Monitoring pollutants affecting ocean quality	M3
Inventory of ocean pollution sources	M4
Economic impact of adopting ocean pollution standards	M5
Development of pollution control technology	M6
Sustaining yields of marine living resources	M7
Air-sea interactions affecting weather forecasting	M8
Man-made ecological upset of the sea	M9

WATER POLLUTION AND WATER RESOURCES DEVELOPMENT

Effects of air pollution on water quality	W1
Monitoring methods and water quality standards	W2
Controlling eutrophication of estuaries	W3
Controlling eutrophication of lakes	W4
Studies of regional water availability	W5

LAND USE AND CONSERVATION OF NATURAL RESOURCES

Surveys of land types and uses	L1
Analytical studies of land requirements	L2
Comprehensive land use planning	L3
Research on reduction of waste of natural resources	L4
Land utilization in regions with extreme climate	L5
Baselines for natural ecosystems	L6
Coordinated network of natural parks and preserves	L7

---

[1] This tabular description is based on an appendix to a working document
entitled "U.S. Priority Interests in the Environmental Activities of International Organizations" (December 1970), kindly made available to the author
by the Committee on International Environmental Affairs, Department of State.

URBAN ENVIRONMENTAL PROBLEMS
Urban growth and national settlement patterns   U1
Environmental management for large urbanized areas   U2
Improvement of squatter settlements   U3
Urban land reform   U4
Urban management   U5
Disposal of solid wastes   U6

CONTROL OF SELECTED POLLUTANTS
Development of pest control technology   P1
Control of pesticide residues in foods and feeds   P2
Control of pesticide residues in the environment   P3
Economic analysis of pesticide substitutes   P4
Studies of toxic metals in the environment   P5
Radioactive effluents from nuclear power stations   P6
Disposal of radioactive wastes   P7
Control of aircraft noise, especially the sonic boom   P8
Noise standards for appliances and equipment   P9

Column groups: Atmospheric Pollution (A1–A9), Marine Environment (M1–M9), Water (W1–W5).

Organization	A1	A2	A3	A4	A5	A6	A7	A8	A9	M1	M2	M3	M4	M5	M6	M7	M8	M9	W1	W2	W3	W4	W5
WHO	X[a]	O									O								O				
WMO	X	X						X	X							O	X						
FAO						O					O	X	X	O		X				O			O
IMCO										X	O	O	O	O									
ICAO				O	O																		
IAEA			O	O	O	O	O				O	O	O	O									
UNESCO[b]						X		O	O		X		X	O	X		X	X			O	O	
UN/REC[c]				X	X		X							X					X	X	X	X	X
Other UN[d]							O								O	O							
CCMS		O	X	X	X					X										O			
OECD		O	X	X	O	X	X							O					X			O	X
NGOs[e]		O					O	O	O						O	O	O	O			O	O	

[a] X = principal organization(s) involved in the project.
O = organization(s) performing an advisory or supporting role.
[b] Includes the IOC.
[c] UN regional economic commissions, chiefly the ECE.
[d] Includes the Department of Economic and Social Affairs, the United Nations Scientific Committee on the Effects of Atomic Radiation, etc., as well as UN Secretariat (for the 1972 conference).
[e] Nongovernmental organizations, chiefly the ICSU and IUCN.

Organization	Land and Conservation							Urban Environment						Selected Pollutants								
	L1	L2	L3	L4	L5	L6	L7	U1	U2	U3	U4	U5	U6	P1	P2	P3	P4	P5	P6	P7	P8	P9
WHO									O	O				O			O	O				
WMO	O[a]															X						
FAO	X	X	O	X	X	O		O						X	X	O	X					
IMCO																						
ICAO																					X	X
IAEA													O	O					X	X		
UNESCO[b]			O	O	X	X		O					X	O		X		O				
UN/REC[c]		X	X			O	O	O	O								O	O	O	O		
Other UN[d]	O	O	O	O				X	X	X	X	X	X				O		O	O		
CCMS										O	O	O									O	
OECD				O							O	O			X	X	X	X	X		O	X
NGOs[e]			O	O	O	O	X	O						O					O			

X = principal organization(s) involved in the project.
O = organization(s) performing an advisory or supporting role.
[a] Includes the IOC.
[b] UN regional economic commissions, chiefly the ECE.
[c] Includes the Department of Economic and Social Affairs, the United Nations Scientific Committee on the Effects of Atomic Radiation, etc., as well as UN Secretariat (for the 1972 conference).
[d] Nongovernmental organizations, chiefly the ICSU and the IUCN.

APPENDIX 2. ENVIRONMENTAL ACTIVITIES OF INTERNATIONAL
ORGANIZATIONS: DESCRIPTION OF ACTIVITIES[1]

1. INTERDISCIPLINARY OR COMPREHENSIVE APPROACH

Organization	Type and Nature of Work
United Nations	UN Conference on the Human Enviroment, Stockholm, 1972. Comprehensive consideration of international environmental problems, both physical and social.
Economic Commission for Europe	Governmental conference on the environment and its influence on society, Prague, 1971. (See also below.)
United Nations Educational, Scientific and Cultural Organization	Follow-up to 1968 UNESCO Conference on the Rational Use and Conservation of the Resources of the Biosphere. Establishment of operational program based on conference resolutions.
	1970 Helsinki Interdisciplinary Symposium on Man's Role in Changing his Environment. (See also below.)
Organisation for Economic Co-operation and Development	On the recommendation of the Ad Hoc Preparatory Committee on the Environment the OECD has established an Environment Committee which will direct the activities of the Sector Groups on Air Management, Unintended Occurrence of Chemicals in the Environment, Water Management, and Urban Environment.
Council of Europe	European Committee for the Conservation of Nature and Natural Resources has produced recommendations and declarations in many fields (see below). Its future work program following the European Conservation Conference of February 1970 is now under consideration.

[1] Based on material included in a working paper kindly made available by the United Kingdom Foreign and Commonwealth Office.

Organization	Type and Nature of Work
World Meteorological Organization	Weather and climate analysis, including hydrometeorology. Interpretation of meteorological effects on man's activities, such as transport, agriculture, industry, living conditions, etc. Prediction of future weather.
Science and Technological Research Committee of the European Community (Aigrain Group)	Nuisances constitute one of seven selected areas for multilateral research projects.
North Atlantic Treaty Organization	The Committee on the Challenges of Modern Society has commissioned national pilot projects on the physical and social environment with a view to stimulating national or international action in the appropriate body. They are at present: disaster relief, road safety, air pollution, open waters pollution, inland waters pollution, job satisfaction and productivity (United Kingdom pilot), transmission of scientific knowledge into the decisionmaking process, environment, and the strategy of regional development (United Kingdom co-pilot).
International Council of Scientific Unions	In 1969 the Special Committee on Problems of the Environment (SCOPE) was established with a view to identifying and indicating the research effort necessary for solving environmental problems of an international nature.
International Union for the Conservation of Nature and Natural Resources	Conservation of rare species and natural habitats.
Commonwealth Human Ecology Council	Promotion of integrated national case studies of environmental problems.

2. AIR POLLUTION

Organisation for Economic	Study groups on harmonization of

Organization	Type and Nature of Work
Co-operation and Development (Committee for Research Co-operation: Air Management Research Group)	national research policies and programs on monitoring, measuring, and control of air pollution from industrial or domestic sources, biological and physical effects, etc.
Council of Europe (Committee of Experts on Air Pollution)	Drafting of principles, recommendations, etc. for governments, comparison and harmonization of national legislation on air pollution from industrial and domestic sources.
Economic Commission for Europe (Working Party on Air Pollution Problems, Coal, Gas, Steel, and Inland Transport committees)	Studies of air pollution and control: economic effects and policy, motor vehicle pollution, drawing up of standards and regulations for vehicle construction.
North Atlantic Treaty Organization (Committee on the Challenges of Modern Society)	Pilot study by United States and Turkey on air pollution with view to joint discussion and recommendations to governments.
World Meteorological Organization (Commission for Atmospheric Sciences, Climatology, and Agricultural Meteorology; Executive Committee Panel on Meteorological Aspects of Air Pollution)	Studies on atmospheric pollution, its transfer, dispersion, and deposition: effects of air pollution on vegetation and climate, incidence and intensity of airborne pests and diseases. Prediction of pollution levels and the effect of control measures.
World Health Organization (Expert Committee on Urban Air Control)	Study of health and welfare aspects of air pollution including vehicle pollution, methods of measurement. Reference and training centers, publications.
International Labor Organization	Study of control of atmospheric pollution of working environment.

3. FRESHWATER POLLUTION

Organisation for Economic Co-operation and Development (Committee for Research Co-operation: Water Management Research Group)	Exchange of information on national policies for water management and research. Identification of research deficiencies in water management problems to stimulate national or international action. International

Organization	Type and Nature of Work
	collaborative investigation into a standard test for detergent biodegradability.
Organisation for Economic Co-operation and Development (Committee for Research Co-operation: Water Management Research Group)	Regional studies of the occurrence and distribution of pesticide residues in freshwater animals.
Council of Europe (European Committee for the Conservation of Nature and Natural Resources: Ad Hoc Study Group on Water Conservation)	Comparison of international legislation on water management, conservation, and pollution. Technical studies of forms of pollution. Preparation of draft conventions.
Council of Europe (Consultative Assembly Working Party on Freshwater Pollution Problems)	Preparation of draft conventions.
Economic Commission for Europe (Committee on Water Problems)	Activities and studies designed to promote cooperation in the rational utilization of water resources and in water pollution control, concentrating on water policy problems. Exchange of information and experience on water policies and exchange of experts on water problems.
	A seminar on river basin management was held in London in June 1970.
Economic Commission for Europe (Steel Committee Working Party on Chemical Industry)	An expert group has been considering problems of water pollution in the iron and steel industries.
North Atlantic Treaty Organization (Committee on the Challenges of Modern Society)	Pilot study on inland water pollution by Canada.
World Health Organization	Health aspects of water pollution: water pollution surveys. The European office has devised a long-term program on water pollution control

Organization	Type and Nature of Work
	in Europe. It held a conference in 1971 on Accidental Pollution of Inland Waters which will report to the UN Conference on the Human Environment in 1972.
World Meteorological Organization (Commission for Hydrometeorology)	Meteorological factors in water pollution.
Food and Agriculture Organization (European Inland Fisheries Administration Commission)	The EIFAC Subcommittee on Water Quality criteria lays down standards relating to water pollutants. The FAO undertakes field projects and technical assistance on water quality management and fisheries. Seminars and training centers on water use. Comparative studies of national legislation and practice.
United Nations Educational, Scientific and Cultural Organization (Committee for the International Hydrological Decade)	Ten-year program (1965-1975) of international efforts to promote the study of water resources, including scientific aspects of water pollution.

4. MARINE POLLUTION

Organization	Type and Nature of Work
Intergovernmental Maritime Consultative Organization (Subcommittee on Marine Pollution, Legal Committee, Maritime Safety Committee, Subcommittees on Marine Pollution, Carriage of Dangerous Goods, Ships Design and Equipment, and Safety of Navigation)	Negotiation of international agreements on measures to prevent pollution by ships and other equipment operating in the marine environment and to reduce the risk of marine casualties involving pollution. Legal rights of states in seeking redress. Exchange of information about methods of dealing with oil and other pollutants. (See Joint Group of Experts below.)
Food and Agriculture Organization	Studies of fishery aspects of marine pollution (See Joint Group of Experts below.) FAO Technical Conference on Marine Pollution and its Effects on Living Resources and Fishing (Rome, December 1970).
United Nations Educational, Scientific and Cultural	Study of the oceanographic aspects of marine pollution problems.

Organization	Type and Nature of Work
Organization (Intergovernmental Oceanographic Commission)	
Joint Group of Experts of FAO, UNESCO, WMO, IMCO, IAEA, WHO (GESAMP)	Studies on scientific aspects of marine pollution. Advisory body on information systems, research priorities, investigation of pollution accidents.
North Atlantic Treaty Organization (Committee on the Challenges of Modern Society)	Pilot study by Belgium and Portugal on open water pollution.
North Atlantic Treaty Organization (Science Committee: Oceanographic Subcommittee).	Study of the oceanographic aspects of marine pollution.
International Council for the Exploration of the Sea	Investigation of pollution problems in the North Atlantic, North Sea, and Baltic Sea.
Organisation for Economic Co-operation and Development ("Holden" Group)	Regional studies of the occurrence and distribution of pesticide residues in marine animals.

5. POLLUTION OF THE SOIL: PESTICIDES

Council of Europe European Committee for the Conservation of Nature and Natural Resources	
ad hoc Study Group on Pesticides Working Party on Fauna, Flora, and Landscapes	Studies and exchanges of information on the safe use of pesticides and methods of residual analysis.
Partial Agreement Committee Subcommittee on Industrial Safety and Health: Chemical Questions	Studies and recommendations.
Subcommittee on Poisonous Substances in Agriculture	Comparison of national legislation with a view to establishing a European convention.

Organization	Type and Nature of Work
European Conservation Year	General.
Organization for Economic Co-operation and Development (Study Group on Unintended Occurrence of Pesticides in the Environment)	Study of pesticide levels; movement, transformation, and accumulation of pesticides; analysis of pesticide residues and biological effects.
Food and Agriculture Organization (Committee on Pesticides in Agriculture)	Review of registration, use, and marketing of agricultural pesticides. Referee methods for residue analysis.
Joint Meeting of the Food and Agriculture Organization Working Party on Pesticide Residues and World Health Organization Expert Committee on Pesticide Residues	Studies and recommendations for acceptable daily intakes, tolerances, and methods of analysis.
Food and Agriculture Organization Working Party on the Official Control of Pesticides	Preparation of a model law for the official control of pesticides (section A) and preparation of internationally acceptable specifications (section B).
Food and Agriculture Organization Working Party on Pest Resistance to Pesticides	Collection of data on the occurrence of resistance and consideration of standard tests for determining incidence of resistance.
Codex Committee on Pesticide Residues	Proposing international tolerances for pesticide residue in specific foods. Preparation of list of priorities of those pesticide residues found in food commodities.
World Health Organization	Studies on the ill effects of pesticides on man; preventive measures. See also joint activities with the Food and Agriculture Organization.
World Meteorological Organization (Commissions for Agricultural Meteorology and Hydrometeorology)	Weather and fertilizer practice, soil moisture balance, and leaching.

Organization	Type and Nature of Work

6. RADIOACTIVE POLLUTION

Organization	Type and Nature of Work
International Atomic Energy Agency	Studies on radioactive contamination of atmosphere, soil, freshwater, and seas. Advice on waste disposal.
United Nations (FAO, WHO, UNSCEAR)	Monitoring of levels of radioactive contamination.
Organisation for Economic Co-operation and Development (European Nuclear Energy Agency)	Development of scientific and technical cooperation on questions of health and safety, including the publication of guides for handling radioactive products. Organization of joint disposal operations. Elaboration and harmonization of legislation for the protection of public health.
International Commission on Radiological Protection	Estimation of potential risks from radiation sources. Advice on maximum permissible levels of radiation exposure and dose.
World Meteorological Organization	Studies on transfer, dispersion, and deposition of airborne radioactive particles.

7. NOISE

Organization	Type and Nature of Work
Organisation for Economic Co-operation and Development (Committee for Research Co-operation: Transportation Group)	Studies of noise from urban transportation and sonic boom.
European Public Health Committee	Effect of noise on health.
Economic Commission for Europe	1971 Prague conference: urban man, including noise.
International Civil Aviation Organization	The development of international standards and recommended practices for aircraft noise abatement and the study and measurement of sonic boom.
World Health Organization	Studies of the effect of noise on health.

Organization	Type and Nature of Work
8. MISCELLANEOUS	
United Nations	1972 Conference on the Human Environment.
United Nations Educational, Scientific and Cultural Organization	Some existing work. 1970 Helsinki Interdisciplinary Symposium on Man's Role in Changing his Environment.
North Atlantic Treaty Organization	United Kingdom pilot study on job satisfaction and productivity.

THE ROLE OF SPECIAL PURPOSE AND NONGOVERNMENTAL ORGANIZATIONS IN THE ENVIRONMENTAL CRISIS

J. Eric Smith

J. ERIC SMITH is currently president, International Council of Scientific Unions, and of its Special Committee on Problems of the Environment.

The purpose of this article is to examine some aspects of the institutional structure which has been or is being developed within the United Nations to achieve, through international agreement and action and for the benefit of mankind as a whole, the most effective utilization of the earth's resources consistent with the minimum of disturbance of the environment in directions harmful to man and other living organisms.

Consumable materials, labor, and capital, from which are generated the means of life and standards of living, are ill distributed among the states and peoples of the world. The circumstances of geography and the events of history have given to some the occupation and use of land and waters rich in productivity, mineral reserves, and energy sources; for others the endowments of nature are meager and of little benefit. Rich and developed states well furnished with natural and capital resources can without much difficulty achieve through their labor a production comfortably in excess of chosen patterns of consumption; impoverished and less developed communities, often burdened with an exponentially increasing population, may be unable to maintain more than a marginal subsistence with frequent and widespread lapses into famine. In the more favored states capital, the accumulated product of private and national saving, is available for investment in services, machinery, education, and technological innovation; yet, with the expansion of productivity through industrial development, new dimensions and patterns of production develop which are unattainable by lesser developed societies.

The fundamental causes of the present environmental crisis lie in the failure of man to create for himself the conditions of social and economic development which he needs or desires without in the process destroying or gravely impairing the natural qualities of the environment necessary for life and acceptable standards of living. This failure stems from the fact that man has not as yet attained the power to adequately manage and control any one of the three elements of potential progress. Labor expands on a global scale in the unwanted numbers of a population increase which if sustained at existing levels will, in the 30 years remaining to the end of the present century, double the present population. The finite resources of the earth are, by virtue of the population increase and a greater per capita demand, being exploited and consumed at an ever increasing rate. Finally, as an additional strain on the environment technological advances incorporated into industrial processes frequently produce materials toxic or in other ways deleterious to man in quantities which are rarely known with accuracy. Many of these materials are persistent and cumulative in the environment, and their distribution and circulation in air, land, water, and living organisms are either unknown or ill defined. Moreover, the effects of these man-made materials on individual species and on the interspecies dependencies of ecosystems are largely a matter for speculation.

These and many other contributory causes and manifestations of the environmental crisis are markedly different in their regional character and presentation over the surface of the globe. More than three-quarters of the earth's surface has a cover of oceans and deserts which bears, as yet, only small and transient imprints of man's activities. But even virtually unpopulated areas are not wholly free from locally generated, man-made environmental disturbances. The continental margins of the seas, long exploited for their food resources, are increasingly invaded by industry in search of hydrocarbons and other minerals and are often used as dumping grounds for unwanted health-hazarding chemicals while deserts and other unpopulated regions are favored sites for the testing of nuclear devices.

It is, however, within the habitable parts of the globe that environmental stresses are mainly generated and most directly experienced. The nature and causes of environmental alteration and the reasons for concern about it are not, however, common to all regions and peoples. A sophisticated, highly industrialized society, relieved of the fears of staying alive and drawing its wealth from the trading of manufactured goods, sees industrial and domestic pollution as the main threat to the environment in its progressive spoliation of places of natural beauty, rest, and recreation. Less developed communities, with few industries and with difficulty wresting from the land sufficient food to satisfy hunger, will employ all means available to increase production even if these involve the use of methods and materials which depreciate or pollute the environment. In these circumstances the pressure of present need overrides all other considerations.

The problems of the scientific management and control of the environment, while presented in differing character and degree of complexity in different parts of the world, are nevertheless the concern of all. Population growth, the progressive concentration of peoples within rapidly enlarging cities, the expansion of industry, the improvement of agriculture, and the increasing exploitation of water and mineral resources are but a few of the issues which in varying measure engage the attention of all societies. Such issues, therefore, require the full benefit of international scientific discussion and collaboration for their better understanding, management, and control. Moreover, since the biosphere is the common heritage of all mankind, disseminating and conserving through the circulation of air and water all elements of persistent and cumulative change, problems of the environment are by their very nature capable of solution only through international cooperation and action.

I. PROCESSES OF INQUIRY

Before presenting a personal interpretation of the role of special purpose and nongovernmental organizations in promoting internationally collaborative inquiry into the state of the environment, the quality and quantity of man-made environmental changes, and the effects of these changes on man and living ecosystems it may be well to note briefly the nature, content, and purposes of some processes which must necessarily be contributory to and integrative of international cooperation and action. The first such process of the inquiry involves a review and evaluation of the present state of knowledge of all the many and varied phenomena implicit in the interactions of man and the biosphere. This task, immense though not impossible, can in a limited time be done only imperfectly. Two essential requirements for the optimization of this process are 1) the involvement of scientists of every kind of discipline concerned in any way with environmental phenomena and 2) the careful selection of the component parts of each area of study within the several disciplines that appear to be most relevant to the problems under review.

The range of scientific disciplines which must be brought to bear on the interactions of man and the biosphere cannot be, or ought not to be, categorized formally under conventional headings for environmental studies in their broadest sense admit of no well-defined boundaries of interaction between individual disciplines. Table 1 lists a few major fields of scientific inquiry without subdivision of their subject content and represents (by their placement in columns) the primary but not delimited engagement of these fields with different aspects of the biosphere. It is apparent from the great number of vertical and horizontal linkages that must be made between individual disciplines, and from the transpositions which must be allowed between one column and another, how each discipline is dependent on others for the full development of its capability and application and how each applies to almost every aspect of environmental study.

TABLE 1.   MAJOR FIELDS OF SCIENTIFIC INQUIRY

Physical Environment	Natural Ecosystems	Man
Physics	Biology	Medicine
Chemistry		Sociology
Geology		Economics
Geography		Geography
Mathematics		

The second process of inquiry entails the identification of areas in which further research is needed and the means by which it can be promoted. As in the assessment of present states of knowledge, this is an activity which can best be undertaken by scientists themselves through regional (usually national) collaboration or by consultation within appropriately constituted international forums. Insofar as these forums have a continuing function and some permanence of organization and purpose, they acquire an institutional status. The institutions with which we are concerned here, namely, the scientific forums within which the problems of the environment are defined, existing knowledge of environmental phenomena collated and assessed, and new fields of investigation proposed, are, at the present time, rarely represented by fully multidisciplinary associations. Though uniquely capable within the limits of their expertise, they are, in themselves, too numerous and large and above all too restricted in their viewpoints to achieve effective corporate integration of effort in the attack on environmental problems.

The third level of inquiry into environmental problems moves from the levels of problem assessment and action planning to the promotion of the research needed for the advancement of knowledge and to the formulation of the principles of environmental management. This is not the place to review the work that must be done at this stage but rather to emphasize the vastly increased extension of the institutional matrix which inevitably accompanies the process of the funding of research and the planning of patterns of integration necessary to ensure that investigations which require interdisciplinary participation make the most effective use of the organizations and agencies best able to contribute to them. With the involvement of a broad spectrum of operational bodies the need to review the programs which had seemed to be scientifically desirable from the point of view of their feasibility and cost becomes evident.

There remains for brief mention the final stage in the chain of processes of inquiry: its consummation in internationally agreed actions or measures designed to check and control the circumstances of environmental change of proven or potential hazard to man and other biota. The forthcoming UN Conference on the Human Environment, making full use in its judgments of a large-scale intellectual conceptual input of scientific information, will for the first time in history provide an international forum that is not only adequately equipped by a long period of carefully prepared planning to make an informed comprehensive review of environmental problems but is required to make recommendations to the UN with a view to their implementation through international agreement. Having briefly indicated the general nature of the processes and organizational relationships that have been marshaled for the present scientific, sociological, economic, and political confrontation with the environmental crisis, we may now turn more specifically to the role of special purpose and nongovernmental organizations as contributors to these processes and as integral parts of the total system.

II. SPECIAL PURPOSE AND NONGOVERNMENTAL ORGANIZATIONS

Shortly before the end of World War I, when it became clear that communication between scientists of different states would again be possible, an international conference called on the initiative of scientists themselves, acting through their academies and research councils, was held in the rooms of the Royal Society in London to consider the ways and means by which communication and collaboration could best be achieved. After further conferences in Paris and Brussels the International Research Council was formed in 1919 for the purpose of facilitating international cooperation in scientific work and promoting the formation of international unions in different branches of science. Simultaneously, four unions were created and admitted to the International Research Council; by 1923 the number had grown to seven. The council, which had excluded Germany from its membership, was reconstituted in 1931 as the International Council of Scientific Unions (ICSU) which now incorporates sixteen such unions. The ICSU in its rejection of political discrimination as an unacceptable impediment to the free communication of scientists thus maintained, both in character and intent, a strictly nongovernmental status.

The formation of the United Nations in 1945 brought with it the desire and opportunity for more effective international collaboration. The vital role of science in society and the need to apply the benefits of science to constructive rather than destructive ends were given practical expression in the creation by the UN of a series of largely autonomous agencies, funded through member states of the UN and charged with specific and largely complementary tasks. It is notable that three of the agencies, the Food and Agriculture Organization (FAO), the World Health Organization (WHO), and the World Meteorological Organization (WMO), founded respectively in 1945, 1948, and 1950, have a direct involvement with problems of the environment. They emphasize physical phenomena (WMO), man and his environment (WHO), or man and the exploitation and management of food-yielding ecosystems (FAO). Each, moreover, has conceived its operation as requiring the cooperation of many scientific disciplines and has directed its activities not only to the alleviation of problems that are of world concern but to the needs of particular states and regional communities. It must, however, be conceded that this system of independent agencies, each concerned with largely separate facets of environmental studies, has not, as yet, proved to be readily amenable to the integration required for a synoptic evaluation of the interrelated states of flux within the biosphere as a whole and of the nature, quantity, and flow of man-made disturbances of the environment. The opportunity to bring to this problem the full benefit of scientific advice and thinking came with the establishment in 1946 of the United Nations Educational, Scientific and Cultural Organization (UNESCO) to promote and develop international and national efforts in the fields of education, natural sciences, and social sciences and to these ends to foster international cooperation between specialists and nongovernmental organizations.

At the conference which drafted the UNESCO constitution a resolution was passed instructing its Executive Board to consult with the ICSU on methods of collaboration to strengthen the programs of both bodies in the area of their common concern. The plans thus formulated, including recommendations for a suitable working arrangement with the ICSU, were to be reported to the first General Conference of UNESCO. By the terms of the agreement subsequently approved by the two bodies UNESCO, in promising financial and secretarial assistance to the ICSU and its unions, recognized the scientific unions of the ICSU as the natural and appropriate forms of nongovernmental institutions for the international organization of science and the ICSU as their coordinating and representative body. The ICSU in turn recognized UNESCO as the principal agency of the UN in the field of international relationships. The creation of a close working relationship between the ICSU, the principal nongovernmental association of scientists of a wide but as yet not fully comprehensive range of disciplines, and UNESCO, a support-enabling and powerfully operative intergovernmental agency, has provided the structural basis on which it is becoming possible to develop, through appropriate collaborative linkages, the full potential of scientific involvement with the environmental crisis.

Hugo Rudolph Kruyt in his presidential address to the ICSU General Assembly in 1946, while emphasizing the high standing of the ICSU as the international organization representing the national academies of science of countries all over the world, drew attention to the weaknesses inherent in the fragmentation of international science if the component unions were to operate solely within the restrictive limits of their subject disciplines. He therefore called on the ICSU to organize scientific activities in domains intermediately between those of two or more unions by means of joint commissions. Interunion commissions have proven to be a useful device for uniting the efforts of related scientific disciplines in addressing themselves to specific and well-defined tasks of limited duration. They do not, however, provide for the broader interdisciplinary attack needed for studies involving phenomena of many different kinds and manifestations present on a global scale. For this purpose the scientific (or special) committees of the ICSU have provided a more effective answer.

THE INITIATION OF INTERNATIONAL RESEARCH

The first essay by the ICSU of planning and research operations by a scientific committee was initiated in 1952 with the formation of the Special Committee for the International Geophysical Year to study the feasibility of launching a simultaneous worldwide cooperative effort of states in the description and elucidation of geophysical events encompassing all, or a great part, of the earth. During the International Geophysical Year (IGY), which in fact extended from July 1, 1957, to December 31, 1958, continuous and detailed observations were made of sunspot activity and of the auroral, magnetic, and ionospheric disturbances of the upper atmosphere. Rockets and satellites were developed to explore the upper atmosphere, to identify and measure the properties of the earth's outer magnetic field, and to register changes in them. Weather observations were made on a comprehensive scale guided by the WMO which also undertook the task of data collecting. The scale of the international effort and of national participation, and the extended use of vastly improved scanning devices, made it possible to construct considerably more accurate models of the thermodynamic and hydrodynamic events which activate the general circulation of the atmosphere by the transfer of heat, momentum, and water vapor between different latitudes. Important studies were made on glaciology and, in particular, on the snow and ice cover of Antarctica. In the field of oceanography large-scale measurements were made of surface and subsurface currents.

The organization of the IGY embodies elements of design which ensured the effective interaction of national and international endeavor. First, the initial planning was undertaken by a nongovernmental and internationally constituted scientific committee financed from international funds channeled (mainly) through UNESCO and the ICSU. Second, the organization of contributory research projects was undertaken by individual states through the machinery of national committees by which means governments were encouraged to respond favorably to requests for support knowing that the proposals had been planned and endorsed on the basis of the most informed scientific advice available to them. Third, research was stimulated that might otherwise not have been done, for example, the scientific exploration of Antarctica. Fourth, the scale of the activities of the IGY captured the imagination of the scientific world and engendered cooperation in and enthusiasm for projects and goals which had previously seemed to be unrealizable.

Above all, as the first internationally mounted exploration of the world environment the outstanding success of the IGY directly stimulated ongoing and extended investigations depending, in large measure, for their initial planning and continual review on the work of ICSU scientific committees. The organization of these committees and their institutional relationships within the UN system were of a similar pattern to those of the Special Committee of the IGY.

Of the nine scientific committees that have been set up within the ICSU during or subsequent to the IGY all have, in greater or lesser degree, been concerned with environmental studies. The Committee on Space Research (COSPAR), set up by the eighth General Assembly of the ICSU in 1958, was designed to further studies in space research to which the IGY program had given initial impetus by aiding the progress on an international scale of all kinds of scientific investigations which are carried out with the use of rocket or rocket-propelled vehicles. As a nonpolitical organization COSPAR, in line with the function of all the nongovernmental special committees of the ICSU, does not initiate programs of mutual assistance between one state and another but, keeping itself informed of UN or other international activities in the field of space research, endeavors to promote international programs to the maximum advantage of these activities. Thirty-five countries adhering to the ICSU are represented in COSPAR. The committee has seven working groups in operation: Five are primarily concerned with extraterrestrial phenomena, but the working group on the application of space techniques to meteorology and earth surveys is of particular interest as it is engaged in a field which, perhaps more than any other, will provide information about the states of atmospheric flux and about the distribution and changing patterns of the biomes on the earth's surface. The working group on space biology promotes, moreover, a complementary function of the extraterrestrial inspection of biosphere phenomena and environmental changes.

The Scientific Committee on Antarctic Research (SCAR), constituted in 1958 as a direct outcome of the IGY development of Antarctic-based programs and of the successful collaboration achieved during those eighteen months of international activity, is by its constitution charged with furthering the coordination of scientific activity in Antarctica with a view to framing a scientific program of circumpolar scope and significance. The purposes of SCAR uniquely illustrate the importance of bringing to bear the full force of international and national advice in the study of a regionally defined area of the globe, a region where environmental processes are generated that are not only particular to the region but of global significance and where, in an area which is relatively undeveloped by man, the problem of the interaction of organisms within ecosystems of comparatively simple composition and of man's capacity and adaptation to live and work with a harsh environment present special opportunities. The working groups of SCAR, assembled under the general headings of biology, geodesy and cartography, geology, glaciology, logistics, meteorology, oceanography, solid earth geophysics, and upper atmosphere physics, sufficiently indicate the comprehensive coverage and environmental significance of the phenomena which require investigation.

SCAR has, in addition to its officers, representatives of six scientific unions and of the WMO together with twelve nationally appointed delegates and representatives of scientific committees whose programs have a direct involvement with Antarctica. This follows the established custom of the ICSU in providing for a membership representative of scientific unions contributing to the disciplines contained within the general studies and of the academies of states having, in this instance, through the terms of the Antarctic Treaty (which entered into force June 23, 1961), a long-sustained regional interest. The scientific programs of SCAR have so far been developed mainly at the national level, but the international aspects of its work have been kept constantly under review by the international committee and by symposia reporting on the progress of Antarctic studies and the lines along which they can be developed.

Investigation of Water Resources

The Scientific Committee on Oceanic Research (SCOR) is the

most senior of the existing ICSU special committees. It was founded in 1957 to further international scientific activity in all branches of scientific research. The domestic functions of SCOR as outlined in its constitution follow closely the lines of the first and second processes of scientific inquiry referred to above, namely, the review of the present state of research on the oceans and the identification of areas in which further research is needed. As befits an organization which must draw on the expertise of scientists of all disciplines in the promotion of physical and biological oceanography, SCOR places great emphasis on the value of collaborative discussion and action not only with other organizations within the ICSU family but with all national and international organizations concerned with scientific aspects of ocean affairs. It comprises in its membership the nominated members of national committees, nominees of the ICSU and of such ICSU scientific unions and scientific and special committees as may wish to participate in SCOR and, in order to ensure the best possible advice and counsel, SCOR invites to its membership individual marine scientists from countries that do not have the benefit of a national committee. Further, in order to create an organization that is comprehensive and flexible in seeking working relationships with other bodies SCOR invites to its meetings such additional representatives of nongovernmental and of intergovernmental organizations as are appropriate to the matters under discussion. Of special value to the institutes and laboratories from which much of the present-day research in oceanography is carried out is the expressed intent of SCOR to foster the recognition of their work, to advise on specific problems which would benefit from their consideration, and to encourage an adequate level of support for their activities.

Shortly after its inception SCOR, having reviewed the areas of fundamental oceanographic research to which it could contribute, made clear its awareness of the growing environmental crisis in identifying three long-range problems critical to the future welfare of mankind. The first of these concerns the sea as a receptacle for the waste products of our industrial civilization and the danger of the accumulation of persistent toxic materials to levels which would endanger the food resources of the sea. The second refers to the finite resources of the oceans and the need, in order to exploit these resources rationally and to the optimal level, to understand more fully the processes of nutrient enrichment and of the causation and distribution of fertile areas of the sea. The third concerns the role of the oceans in climatic change and the need for a vastly increased program of research on the thermal, gaseous, and water exchanges at the air-sea interface and between the deep and surface waters of the oceans.

The part played by SCOR in initiating scientific research in oceanography, in planning cooperative exercises, and in integrating the activities of the many organizations and bodies concerned in oceanographic studies may be briefly indicated by some examples of its participation. In its early years SCOR was mainly occupied with the planning of the International Indian Ocean Expedition of which it was cosponsor with UNESCO and in which process it drew on advice from intergovernmental agencies, notably the FAO and the WMO. Mainly through the medium of national committees the interest of twenty governments was solicited. Thirteen of these were ship-operating countries, and some 40 of their vessels participated in the investigation which began in 1962. The scientific program of the expedition, covering a wide variety of projects within the general fields of physical and biological oceanography, geology and geophysics, and meteorology, extended from 1961 through 1965. Through these investigations knowledge of the physical and biological processes which prevail within large parts of the 28 million square miles of this previously little-known ocean was greatly extended. The many thousands of plankton samples taken during the biological surveys have been maintained and sorted at the Indian Ocean Biological Center. The facilities and staff of the center are provided largely by the Indian government while UNESCO furnishes a curator and provides funds for research fellowships and training.

SCOR has similarly acted as the principal nongovernmental scientific advisory body in the development of the Cooperative Study of the Kuroshio (CSK), of the International Cooperative Investigation of the Tropical Atlantic (ICITA), and of the Cooperative Investigation of the Caribbean (CICAR). (The principal intergovernmental organization concerned with these studies, the Intergovernmental Oceanographic Commission [IOC], is the forum for generating national participation and the coordination of programs.) The web of institutional relationships within which SCOR effects its linkages is very extensive as the following selected examples show. It contributes, with the IOC, to the Group of Experts on Scientific Aspects of Marine Pollution (GESAMP); to the Integrated Global Oceans Stations System (IGOSS); with the Advisory Committee on Marine Resources Research (ACMRR) to the FAO; with the WMO to a working group on scientific aspects of international oceanographic research; and to the International Council for the Exploration of the Sea (ICES). (The ICES, a scientific and research operating consortium of European countries, is the oldest [1902] and one of the most active oceanographic bodies; its area of interest is the Atlantic, the North Sea, the Baltic, and the Mediterranean.) SCOR is also conjoined with SCAR as an international coordination group on the Southern Ocean and directly advises UNESCO.

The Scientific Committee on Water Research (COWAR) was set up by the ICSU in 1964 to study the problem of international water resources in all its aspects, to formulate and promote programs of research, to establish contacts with international governmental and nongovernmental organizations concerned with water resources, and to act on behalf of the ICSU as scientific adviser to UNESCO and the environmental agencies of the UN (the FAO, the International Atomic Energy Agency [IAEA], the WHO, and the WMO) on the programs of the International Hydrological Decade (IHD). COWAR serves in some measure as the freshwater counterpart of SCOR in the surveillance of world water cover. The division of interest is not, however, absolute nor are the activities of the two bodies strictly comparable for COWAR lays particular emphasis on the physical and chemical qualities of water, the importance of these qualities in defining programs of improved management of resources, global water distribution and balance, and the means of optimizing available resources. There is as yet rather little biological content in the COWAR program itself though within the context of the projects planned as part of the IHD the hydrological aspects of water pollution bear fundamentally on more general environmental studies and of course on marine pollution. Apart from the close association developed between COWAR and the International Union of Geodesy and Geophysics (IUGG) in its division of the International Association of Scientific Hydrology (IASH), COWAR has established important working relationships with the WMO and the FAO. Moreover, a symposium on man-made lakes organized by COWAR in 1971 has formed the starting point of an extended study to be undertaken by the Scientific Committee on Problems of the Environment (SCOPE). The scientific expertise developed within COWAR and the crucial importance of freshwater studies to knowledge about and understanding of biosphere processes makes COWAR an essential scientific component in the institutional relations that must be developed in the evaluation of the environmental crisis.

The environmental studies developed by the ICSU through the activities of the IGY, the International Year of the Quiet Sun (IQSY), COSPAR, SCOR, SCAR, and COWAR had been prompted by the special timeliness of international investigations (IGY, IQSY), by the need to further research involving highly sophisticated equipment and apparatus with a unique capacity for synoptic environmental surveillance (COSPAR), by the desire for knowledge of the extensive bodies of salt and fresh water which cover the greatest part of the earth's surface (SCOR, COWAR), and by the opportunities offered by man's increasing interest in and occupation of one of the least known regions of the world, Antarctica (SCAR). Of these endeavors only those of SCOR and SCAR had a substantial biological content, and no provision had been made for a comprehensive review by world scientists of the nature, biological relationships, and environmental interactions of the many kinds of plants and animals which populate the seas, fresh waters, and land.

Biological Investigations

In order to facilitate international collaboration and the planning of biological investigations having these purposes in mind the tenth General Assembly of the ICSU set up in 1963 the Special Committee for the International Biological Program (SCIBP) charged with planning and ensuring the execution of a program on the biological basis of productivity and human welfare to be elaborated as a worldwide study of 1) organic production on the land, in fresh waters, and in the sea and of the potentialities and uses of new as well as of existing resources, and 2) human adaptability to the environment and to its changing conditions. The SCIBP has organized its activities under the seven sections of production processes (PP) concerned with photosynthesis and the utilization of solar energy, terrestrial production (PT), freshwater production (PF), marine production (PM), terrestrial conservation (CT), use and management of resources (UM), and human adaptability (HA).

Countries wishing to participate in the International Biological Program (IBP) are required to adhere to the SCIBP, to designate a national committee for the IBP, and to contribute toward the operational expenses of the central planning, coordination, and organization of the IBP. Moreover, it has been made clear that, while the general character of the scientific program is defined by the international committee, the review and arrangements for funding of individual research programs are the responsibility of national committees in consultation with the appropriate sectional committees of the SCIBP. The membership of the SCIBP includes, in addition to its officers, representatives of the ICSU, of five unions of SCOR and SCAR, and of three international nongovernmental unions (the International Union of Nutritional Sciences [IUNS], the International Union for Conservation of Nature and Natural Resources [IUCN], and the International Union of Anthropological and Ethnological Sciences [UISAE]) none of which is in the ICSU family but each of which provides a necessary liaison with sciences which are essential in their contribution to the programs. By 1970, 58 countries had made formal contributions to the IBP, 33 countries had made less formal linkages, and more than 2,000 research projects covering 83 separate themes had been entered into the program.

Space does not permit a review of the immense range of research projects which have been undertaken under the umbrella of the IBP. Some of its more important organizational and procedural achievements must, however, be mentioned. It has sometimes been remarked, and more often in the earlier than in the later stages of the program, that much of the work within the IBP would have been done if there had been no IBP. There is some truth in this criticism which, however, fails to give credit to the enormous benefits which derived from the international support of the program, from the frequent meetings of scientists to discuss the methodology, purposes, and progress of their investigations, and from the publication of the excellent series of handbooks reviewing the progress made in the work of the several sections and the validity and accuracy of recommended procedures, the acceptance and use of which enables work done by individual workers and teams of investigators to be more readily compared and evaluated. Nor does the criticism take into account the interest and support generated in developing countries participating as equal partners in a common enterprise. Perhaps most of all the program has been beneficial in promoting the education and training of scientists and technicians, particularly of the developing countries.

The IBP was initially planned to have two phases. The first phase, 1964-1967, was devoted to the preparation, submission, and consideration of the national programs and to central planning, the second phase, 1967-1972, to operational research. A third phase of two years ending on June 30, 1974, has been added for the continuation of uncompleted projects and for the preparation of the final documentation of the program. In the initial stages of the IBP the need for cooperation with other nongovernmental organizations both within and outside the UNESCO complex of unions and committees was clearly foreseen, and, in addition, close working relationships were established with many UN agencies and other intergovernmental institutions, either through the creation of intersecretarial committees, collaborative working groups, or the organization of conferences and symposia. As an example of the progressively widening extension of the interdisciplinary connections necessary for the study of environmental problems, mention may be made of the discussion of the human adaptability aspects of the IBP program by the UISAE in Toyko in 1968 and of the cooperation of the International Union of Psychological Science (IUPS) with the human adaptability section in the discussion of psychological performance tests. The value of these associations may encourage UNESCO to give greater recognition and support than it has in the past to the social, psychological, demographic, economic, and engineering sciences all of which must play an important part in a united scientific confrontation with the environmental crisis.

As the IBP draws to a close, the importance of continuing its programs and of preserving the many invaluable interdisciplinary relationships evolved during its lifetime has become increasingly evident. The SCIBP, therefore, has reviewed the ongoing activities of its several sections in light of surveys and projects which it must necessarily leave uncompleted and of its experience of the relationships developed during its ten years of operation, and it has come to the point of making recommendations for the future designation of its sectional programs. It seems clear that marine production is a field well provided for in SCOR, and that terrestrial conservation lies within the special scientific expertise of the IUCN. The productivity of fresh water falls within the purview of the limnological section of the division of environmental biology of the International Union of Biological Sciences (IUBS) but will need an organizational backing of broader interest in order to maintain, in association with COWAR, an adequate level of national and international research. The three major activities which the SCIBP wishes to see developed further are production processes, biome studies, and investigations of human adaptability. A joint commission of the SCIBP and SCOPE is presently inquiring into the possibility of including some or all of these activities within the programs of SCOPE.

Investigations of the Relationship Between Man and His Environment

SCOPE, the most recently established special committee of the ICSU, originated at the twelfth General Assembly of the ICSU held in Paris in 1968. The assembly resolved that the IUBS and the IUGG, in consultation with the SCIBP, should set up an ad hoc Committee on Problems of the Environment to report on environmental characteristics which man was altering and to emphasize problems of international concern whose solution the scientific competence of the ICSU could further. The resolution recognized that the mounting progression of man-made changes of the world environment and the effects of these changes on man called for an urgent and continuing appraisal by the scientific community. While its existing unions, scientific committees, and organizations in collaboration with existing agencies and other intergovernmental bodies were well able to advise on and to promote investigations of particular aspects of environmental change, the ICSU resolution indicated a need for an organization providing a scientific forum for a more comprehensive and world-ranging review of the phenomena contributing to the changing states of the biosphere and their effects on man.

In reporting to the ICSU the ad hoc committee created by the resolution drew attention to some ways in which a comprehensive organization could usefully contribute to the ICSU's engagement with the environmental crisis. In particular the committee noted the potentiality of such an organization for promoting and coordinating research relevant to environmental quality control and the rational use of natural resources by setting up commissions and working groups to assess present knowledge and the direction of future research and its potential value as a source of scientific advice to the ICSU and (when requested) to UN agencies and other program-operating organizations. The committee also stressed the importance of promoting a responsible public awareness of environmental problems through education, publications, and other media and further recommended the setting up of an international center for the environment for the secretariat of the new organization and its center of operations.

The Executive Committee of the ICSU, having received the report of the ad hoc committee and noting its recommendations, decided at its meeting in October 1969 formally to establish the Special Committee (later renamed Scientific Committee) on Problems of the Environment. In its charge to SCOPE the ICSU outlined its reasons for constituting the committee. It mentioned particularly the primary causes of environmental stress, the general nature of depreciatory environmental changes and of their present and potential effects on man under differing social conditions, the need to quantify environmental changes and to measure this impact on man and the world biota generally, the need to provide decisionmakers in local and national governments and intergovernmental bodies with sound and unbiased information concerning the environmental consequences of alternative courses of action and remedial steps, and the need to involve a broad spectrum of talents such as engineering, social, and medical sciences, as well as the natural sciences in providing this advice.

SCOPE at its first meeting (in Madrid in September 1970) considered how it might most effectively respond, in its initial stages of operation, to the directives given to it by the ICSU in formulating its first scientific programs and in defining its attitudes, purposes, and mode of development. An evident danger was seen in attempting too much too soon, straining the resources of the organization beyond its capacity through uncontrolled and unrestricted growth. As a general statement of its philosophy the committee thought that SCOPE should present itself as a body whose primary purpose would be to assemble, review, and assess the information now available on man-made environmental changes and the effects of these changes on man; to assess and evaluate the methodologies of environmental measurements; and, by assembling the best available scientific information and constructive thinking, to establish itself as a source of informed advice for the benefit of centers of fundamental research and of the organizations and agencies operationally engaged in field studies of the environment. To this end SCOPE would need, in the first instance, to be rigorously selective of the problems to be investigated and would then probe them in depth. In making its choice it would include among the criteria of selection the urgency of the problem, the feasibility of studying it, and the importance of the problem to developing countries. In entering into the investigation of problems of the environment SCOPE would not intrude on the activities being undertaken by the already very large number of existing committees, organizations, and agencies but should evolve as a body complementary in function to and cooperative with existing organizations.

Working groups have been established for the following projects: 1) methods of determining materials which may significantly alter the biosphere; 2) the scientific basis of the construction and management of man-made lakes; 3) a pilot study on the feasibility of an international registry of chemical compounds; 4) a planned system of global environmental monitoring; and 5) environmental problems in developing countries.

The projects, four of which have been supported by generous grants from the Ford Foundation, have drawn freely on the advice and expertise of a variety of other nongovernmental bodies and of intergovernmental organizations, and three of them have now been completed for publication and transmission, at the request, by letter, of the secretary-general of the conference, as contributions to the 1972 UN Conference on the Human Environment. The feasibility of further working groups is now being studied, namely groups to consider toxic substances and their toxicity levels in a selected range of plants and animals including man, the acoustic environment, tropical savannas, and model building in ecological predictions.

The planning of the two major enterprises now being developed within the UN system, the UN Conference on the Human Environment and the Man and the Biosphere program (MAB) to be undertaken by UNESCO, has presented early opportunities for SCOPE to contribute scientific advice and recommendations. In December 1970 Maurice Strong, secretary-general of the Stockholm conference, specifically requested that the SCOPE Commission on Environmental Monitoring should prepare for the conference a report recommending the design, parameters, and technical organization needed for a coherent global environmental monitoring system making maximum use of available capabilities of existing and planned national, regional, and international networks together with such data collection and processing centers as may be required. While recognizing that other SCOPE studies are in an earlier stage of development, Strong urged that a prompt review should be made within these areas in order to determine whether proposals might emerge as potential items for inclusion in the active plan on which agreement of governments might be achieved at the Stockholm conference. The proposals of the working groups 2, 3, and 5 referred to above have been forwarded with recommendations in response to this request.

The MAB program which is undergoing refinement by the International Coordinating Council of the MAB will, at the invitation of UNESCO, be developed in collaboration with SCOPE along with many other cooperating organizations. In developing close relationships with the MAB, SCOPE would of necessity have to be selective of fields on which it had the competence to advise and, complementing MAB activities, would continue to initiate its own programs in conformity with its natural development.

In addition to the development of its scientific programs SCOPE, in its second year of operation, is giving careful consideration to the means of creating internal working arrangements and external relationships by which to ensure the least complicated and most effective use of its opportunities. A major internal concern is the generation of the full potential of national committee/central committee interactions. Environmental problems by their nature require both national and international attention, and, while it will be essential for the international committee regularly to inform and seek advice from individual national committees on the operation of internationally mounted exercises, it will be equally important for national committees to make known the extent of their expertise and their engagement with national problems of special interest to them. Moreover, though this is not yet determined, SCOPE may well be disposed to benefit from the admirable arrangements made by the SCIBP in promoting, through the financial support of individual states, individual and team investigations that contribute to planned programs. Another problem which SCOPE must face is how best to incorporate within its councils the full range of scientific disciplines which must be brought to bear in gaining a full appreciation of the multifaceted character of each of the many aspects of the interactions of man and the biosphere. Large and long-lasting bodies of fixed constitution are often too ponderous and unwieldy for easy and productive discourse, and considerable flexibility of structure is desirable and can be obtained through delegation to working groups having a representation of individuals and organizations appropriately chosen for the particular problem under review.

In concluding the brief survey of the nature, role, and interrelationships of the nongovernmental organizations within the ICSU family of scientific advisory bodies a word should be said about the special committees of the ICSU which, though not primarily concerned with environmental studies, nevertheless provide an essential service to them. The Committee on Science and Technology in Developing Countries (COSTED) has shown a strong awareness of the peculiar environmental impact of technological advances in developing countries. In this and other respects it plays a complementary role to the Advisory Committee on the Application of Science and Technology to Development (ACAST) under the aegis of the UN Economic and Social Council (ECOSOC). The creation of SCOPE as the central ICSU advisory body on problems of the environment will entail increasingly close relationships between UNESCO and ECOSOC on environmental questions, and it is notable that, in conjunction with the first General Assembly of SCOPE (held in Canberra in 1971), a SCOPE-ACAST working group jointly prepared for the Stockholm conference a report on the impact of the environmental crisis in developing countries.

In the development and rationalization of international storage and retrieval information services, on which environmental studies are greatly dependent, the ICSU in collaboration with UNESCO has been active in initiating an ICSU-UNESCO Joint Project to Study the Feasibility of a World Information System (UNISIST) the results of which have now been reported. Through its Committee on Data for Science and Technology (CODATA) the ICSU is seeking to promote and encourage on a worldwide basis the production and distribution of compendia of critically selected numerical and other quantitatively expressed values of properties of substances of importance in science and technology, while the Panel on World Data Centers is the coordinating link between the scientific advisory bodies of the ICSU and the centers and acts as an advisory body to the centers as required.

III. CONCLUSION

The main intent of this article has been to review the purpose and achievements of presently constituted nongovernmental organizations as a source of scientific advice and constructive thinking on environmental problems and to give some impression of the manner in which collaboration between the different organizations has been and is being effected for the better scientific understanding of the changes which are being progressively imposed on the biosphere as the result of man's activities and of the effects of these changes on man and other biota. Almost inevitably this article may have failed to expose sufficiently the imperfections of the present institutional arrangements for the marshaling of evidence, the identification of urgently needed lines of inquiry, the facilitation of research and of its funding, and the presentation of an adequate and well-substantiated body of evidence as a basis for policy framing and decisionmaking. The character of the component organizations and of the institutional matrix which may best serve the interests of a fully informed and politically effective system for international environmental policy and administration is an issue which will assume a considerable importance on the agenda of the Stockholm conference in preparation for which numerous bodies have already contributed suggestions and recommendations. In reviewing the capabilities of the present system I will do no more than express a personal view of some ways in which the present institutional arrangements may perhaps be better utilized and of some areas in which, for better coordination, communication, and implementation, institutional innovations may be necessary.

First, let us restate the sequences of inquiry and of action which must be brought into play between the initial assessment of the changing states of the biosphere and the implementation of internationally agreed-on decisions and measures of enforcement designed to ensure the control of biosphere modifications in the best interests of man and the world biota. These may for convenience be categorized under the headings listed below. However, they ought not to be regarded as constituting strictly compartmentalized divisions of the total institutional matrix. Rather, an important feature of the matrix should be that it shall provide both for unrestricted collaboration of all interests relevant to each stage and for the passage of personally interpreted information from one stage to another. Much time can be saved and misunderstanding avoided if the contributions, purposes, and attitudes of people trained in different disciplines and with different types of responsibilities are made evident through free communication and counsel between scientists, representatives of industry, and administrators at every stage of environmental inquiry and action.

The sequences of inquiry are: 1) the evaluation of the changing states of the biosphere and of the problems of environmental control and management; 2) research promotion and funding; 3) environmental policy formulation and review, decision preparation, and decisionmaking and decision implementation.

1) Since the first of these processes of inquiry involves a strictly objective assessment of the physical and biological phenomena associated with naturally occurring and man-made changes within the biosphere, the inquiry is essentially scientific. The main purpose of the institutional organization that services it is to ensure that while

studies in depth of particular aspects of the environment are fully and continuously developed, changes which affect the biosphere as a whole are not neglected. In their contributions as a nongovernmental scientific advisory service the ICSU complex of unions, commissions, and scientific committees draws on a body of scientific advice which, if fully utilized by flexible arrangements for collaborative discussion, is potentially capable, within the range of expertise deployed, of developing a soundly based evaluation of the physical and chemical states of the environment and of the effects of environmental modifications on living ecosystems. It must be admitted, however, that the institutional arrangements operating within the ICSU have not as yet been utilized to their full capacity. With few exceptions sufficient opportunity has not been taken to draw into the system the knowledge and expertise of the medical, social, economic, and engineering sciences. Studies on the ecology of man, to which these sciences are essentially contributory, are now seen as among the most urgently needed fields of investigation. Within the ICSU system of advisory bodies SCOPE, as the organization most directly charged with the synoptic review of environmental problems, has a major responsibility to remedy this deficiency.

2) The direct promotion of programs of environmental research by internationally constituted nongovernmental advisory bodies such as those contained within the ICSU organization of unions and committees is strictly limited by budgetary considerations. The financial support given to unions and special committees by national dues, grants from the ICSU, and allocations of UNESCO's subvention to the ICSU meets the working expenses of administration and meetings and, when supplemented by grants from private foundations, trusts, and industry, enables working groups to carry out their evaluation of specific environmental problems. However, the funding and operational resources needed for the promotion of environmental research on an adequate scale require support on a level which can only be given by governments. The ICSU advisory committees have explored and used a variety of channels to mount, fund, and operate research programs designed within international advisory forums. To mention a few examples: The SCIBP developed its programs through national committees and research councils; the IGY, SCOR, and SCAR enlisted through intergovernmental organizations the participation of governments and agencies in large-scale and long-term international endeavors bearing on various aspects of environmental analysis; and, somewhat less directly, the scientific expertise of the nongovernmental organization has been fully deployed in the UNESCO-WMO interagency programs of the Global Atmospheric Research Program (GARP).

In recognizing the immense value of these programs in the furtherance of environmental studies it must be acknowledged that neither in their concept nor in the sum of their results can they be regarded as part of an integrated global study of the environment. The work requirements of such a study demand not only that the naturally occurring states of flux of the biosphere and the superimposed man-made modifications of the world environment be viewed as changes which are transmitted throughout all parts of the biosphere through the media of air, land, and water but that they be watched continuously. Moreover, a continuing review is essential for the planned evolution of a program of environmental research requiring at each stage of its development an appraisal and selection of problems having a particular timeliness or urgency.

Considerations of this kind have led many environmentalists to question whether the institutional matrix which now services environmental studies is adequate, in its present form, to meet the requirements of a time-extended and spatially integrated global program of investigations which must be generated at a pace that matches the urgency of the growing environmental crisis. Considerable thought has been given to this question within the councils of governments, by the secretariat of the Stockholm conference, by bodies such as the International Institute for Environmental Affairs (in the Aspen report), and by nongovernmental scientific advisory committees such as SCOPE to name but a few examples. While, however, there is almost general agreement that planned programs of global environmental studies involving wide international and interdisciplinary participation will require for their formulation and progressive development a central international service of considerable creative and organizational capability, it is more difficult to define in detail the kind of organization that it should be. Various opinions have been expressed concerning the purposes it should serve; the size, scale, and variety of its initial and eventual operations; the level within the processes of inquiry and action on environmental questions at which it should concentrate its activities; its nature—whether it should be an intergovernmental or nongovernmental service or a combination of the two; and, according to the nature of its constitution, its funding.

Perhaps the first question to be resolved is whether the kind of central institute for the environment that is needed is one that should be concerned primarily with the scientific evaluation of environmental problems and research planning together with the necessary advisory, educational, publicity, and administration functions or whether the institute should have the additional capability of funding and operating research. There are compelling reasons for the creation of an institute capable of servicing the first series of functions if for no other reason than that this kind of central organization is necessary for the implementation of the purposes for which SCOPE was founded. The charge given to SCOPE by the ICSU in constituting the committee required the committee to examine the primary causes of environmental stress and of depreciatory environmental changes and their effects on man under differing social conditions, to consider means of quantifying environmental changes and of measuring their impact on man and living organisms, and, by the scientific evaluation of the interactions of man and the biosphere, to provide decisionmakers in local and national governments and intergovernmental bodies with sound and unbiased information concerning the environmental consequences of alternative sources of action and remedial steps. These are not activities and responsibilities which can be effectively discharged solely through the medium of committees and working groups but require for their continuing surveillance and promotion a center within which to gather environmental data and to process it. Such a center would provide a permanent meeting place for the broad spectrum of scientific talents which must be brought to bear on environmental problems and, apart from the servicing of the necessary processes of administration, could be used as the office for the preparation and publication of scientific, advisory, and educational reports and papers.

Whether or not an international center for the environment equipped for these functions should have the further capacity to fund and operate international research programs is a matter which requires cautious and careful appraisal. A center having these capabilities could only be justified if the present system of international organizations engaged in environmental research, notably the UN agencies, were unable to redesign and expand their programs to include fully collaborative interagency investigations of the nature, fluctuations, and interactions of environmental phenomena as manifested throughout the biosphere as a whole. The MAB program to be launched by UNESCO may succeed in bringing into operation integrated studies of this kind. It would therefore seem premature and unnecessarily replicative of functional machinery already complicated enough to suggest the addition at this stage of another further research operating institution unless subsequent experience shows the present institutional arrangements cannot be successfully deployed for research of broader vision and engagement.

In summary, this discussion of the second stage in the sequence of inquiry has emphasized several points concerning the promotion and funding of environmental research and the role of nongovernmental scientific bodies in facilitating these processes. First, the international forum for the scientific evaluation of problems of the biosphere should be nongovernmental in character and designed for the collaborative assembly of scientists of all relevant disciplines speaking as scientists and not as representatives of governments. Second, the international scientific forum should be equipped with the services of a permanently constituted center for environmental studies in order to give it continuity of function, the opportunity to make broad and flexible arrangements for interdisciplinary collaboration, and the promotional capability to develop its scientific advisory, educational, and administrative services. Third, the scientific advisory body should seek to promote research by involving the interest and participation of existing research operating organizations both at the national and international levels and should not, at least at the present time, operate its own field research programs. It is further suggested that SCOPE, both by its terms of reference and its declared intention to serve as a scientific advisory forum complementary in function to existing organizations and nonintrusive on activities already adequately serviced, is the body best equipped to develop and to administer an international center for the environment.

3) In the formulation of environmental policy and in the review of the issues involved in achieving international agreements to implement this policy the corpus of objectively prepared scientific advice on the nature of man-made modifications of the world environment and the effects of these changes on man must be subjected to value judgments of the gains and losses attendant on alternative courses of action. The benefits to be gained from industrial development must be weighed against the environmental hazards that will surely follow from unrestrained industrial expansion. The need to extract from land, sea, and fresh waters a sufficiency of food and other natural resources to maintain hungry populations or to improve their standards of living may create conditions that are in other ways socially and economically unacceptable; the preservation of amenities for enjoyment and recreation can rarely be accomplished without loss of alternative benefits.

Full opportunity must be given prior to the framing of environmental policy and decisions for all sections of the world community to articulate their interests as users of the environment. The logistics of such a debate are almost impossible to conceive, but if they are to be achieved they must clearly be processed through institutional arrangements which channel and summarize widely drawn information and advice for transmission and interpretation by representatives at a conference table. The 1971 annual conference of nongovernmental organizations at UN headquarters, which took as its theme "The United Nations and the Human Environment," included representatives of 169 organizations in addition to independent delegates and observers. It is clear from the conference report to the secretariat of the Stockholm conference that this process of assembling value-judgment advice to aid in framing environmental policy is not only necessary but is practicable if organized in the right way and on a scale which requires the initiative and capability of a high-level directive force. The secretariat of the Stockholm conference provides at the present time the initiative and drive for the utilization and full deployment of the expertise of existing nongovernmental institutions through which advice on value judgments and environmental management can be recruited. It would seem important that, following the conference, the secretariat should have the continuing function of promoting through UNESCO, ECOSOC, and other agencies of the UN the recruitment and evaluation of this advice for the appraisal and formulation of future environmental policy.

The final, consummatory stages of environmental inquiry and action—the preparation of recommendations on which to propose international agreements and on which to base their implementation —extend beyond the levels of nongovernmental inquiry to intergovernmental action. They are therefore complementary additions to the first three stages. However, these processes engage a political and legal expertise to which scientists and other members of the world community concerned with the preservation of the environment cannot directly contribute. It is important therefore that those to whom the ultimate decisions are entrusted not rely solely on the documentation prepared for them but be enabled through the advice of national academies and other informed bodies to gain a full appreciation of the content, arguments, and attitudes embodied in the presentations on which their decisions are made.

THE ROLE OF THE WMO IN ENVIRONMENTAL ISSUES

David Arthur Davies

DAVID ARTHUR DAVIES is secretary-general of the World Meteorological Organization.

I. INTRODUCTION

The World Meteorological Organization (WMO) is a specialized agency of the United Nations. By definition it is concerned with the atmosphere and atmospheric processes and, hence, with the human environment, for whatever definition of the human environment may be adopted, the atmosphere is clearly one of its essential elements. Many atmospheric processes are intimately, indeed inextricably, related to processes and phenomena the study of which falls within the compass of other geophysical disciplines — notably hydrology and oceanography. The WMO has therefore certain responsibilities in these fields also, and as a result its interest in the human environment is somewhat wider than its title may suggest.

Man's concern with his environment stems mainly from two factors. First, he needs to understand natural environmental processes and to utilize his acquired knowledge for useful and positive purposes. From a practical point of view such activities may be described as the efficient use of natural resources. Second, he needs to ensure that his own activities do not interfere unduly with natural environmental processes, and, hopefully, he will be able to rectify some of the damage already done in this respect. In both cases meteorology is directly involved. As regards the first aspect, the acquisition of knowledge of atmospheric phenomena, particularly those phenomena we call weather and climate, and the application of such knowledge for practical purposes has been the raison d'etre of national meteorological services and of the WMO (and its predecessor, the International Meteorological Organization [IMO]) for about a century. This aspect of environmental studies by meteorologists and others working in various geophysical disciplines has tended to be taken for granted although in recent years there has been a growing realization of the importance of such studies, especially in relation to the problems of economic development. Indeed, until relatively recent times man's interest in, or even awareness of, his environment seems to have been confined mainly to times of disasters occasioned by such natural phenomena as floods, droughts, tropical cyclones, gales, etc., and the need for more effective systems for giving operational warnings of such disasters is in fact still one of the most urgent of modern-day environmental issues.

It is, however, toward the second aspect, i.e., the need to protect the natural environment, that great attention is now being directed and rightly so. This is because man is learning that if he allows his own activities to interfere unduly with natural environmental processes he does so at his peril. Fortunately, the awareness of the world has been aroused to the dangerous situation which has developed from excessive pollution of the air, land, and water.

The convening by the United Nations of the Conference on the Human Environment in Stockholm in 1972 is a clear and most welcome indication of the intention of the states of the world to take remedial action. Indeed this conference has become the focus of world interest and of hope for the solution of environmental problems.

The WMO has formally pledged its support for the conference and to this end is taking part in the collective assistance being given to it by the Administrative Committee on Coordination (ACC) as a whole. In this way the WMO has, with other specialized agencies concerned, provided technical material for the use of the conference secretariat in the preparation of certain conference documents. It has also contributed to the preparation of an important conference document put together by the ACC entitled "The United Nations System and the Human Environment" which reviews the current activities of the UN system and describes the functions and perspectives of the system from the environmental point of view.[1] The document shows that the WMO is concerned in varying degrees with most present-day environmental issues. To describe in all its aspects the role of the WMO in such issues would be, to a large extent, a repetition of relevant sections of this ACC document, and, as the document will in due course become generally available, such repetition seems unnecessary. In this article attention is accordingly confined to those areas in which WMO activities are particularly relevant to the problems arising from environmental pollution.

Before leaving the subject of the ACC document it may be mentioned that while it provides a valuable review of the role which each part of the UN system plays in this field, it also provides a reassuring confirmation that a coordinated approach is being taken by all the bodies represented on the ACC. The need for a high degree of co-

[1] UN Document A/CONF. 48/12.

ordination in dealing with a subject so complex and so vast as the human environment may be taken as axiomatic, and the Stockholm conference will doubtless give much attention to the question of future coordinating machinery.

II. MONITORING THE ATMOSPHERE

Long before atmospheric pollution became a problem an atmospheric monitoring system had been developed for purely meteorological purposes. The need for such a system arose from the fact that neither the prediction of the weather nor its long-term study (climatology) could be seriously attempted without a knowledge of the state of the atmosphere at frequent intervals and over large areas. Thus, initially under the aegis of the IMO and later its successor, the WMO, an international system of meteorological reporting was established. In recent years the whole system has been reviewed and modernized to take into account such important developments as the introduction of meteorological satellites and the increasing use of high-speed electronic computers for meteorological purposes. The result of this exercise, which was incidentally undertaken at the instigation of the General Assembly of the United Nations,[2] was a plan for a comprehensive and fully coordinated system to which the name World Weather Watch (WWW) was given. Implementation began in 1968, and since then remarkable progress has been made. By means of the WWW the atmosphere is now kept under constant surveillance, and all countries of the world receive, on a routine daily basis, the meteorological data necessary for them to meet national requirements. At the same time each country makes its own contribution to the system by establishing and operating specified facilities and services within its own territory; arrangements for assisting the developing countries of the world in this task have, however, been introduced.

Because of its direct relevance to any future plans for monitoring the atmosphere for purposes related to the solution of present-day environmental problems a brief description of the WWW seems appropriate. Such a description is also necessary since the references in recent literature to the WWW as one of a number of basically similar atmospheric monitoring systems suggest that there is still a lack of understanding as to its full scope, complexity, and basic importance to environmental issues. Comparisons of the World Weather Watch with most if not all other atmospheric monitoring systems may be of so little significance as to be seriously misleading.

[2] See General Assembly Resolution 1721 C (XVI), of December 20, 1961.

At present the WWW includes about 8500 observer stations on land at which a comprehensive range of meteorological elements are observed at standard international hours (generally every six hours) and coded into standard international figure codes (to overcome language problems and to maintain brevity). The observations are then collected at national centers and exchanged on a worldwide basis by means of an intricate world meteorological telecommunications network linking all countries of the world. After processing by electronic computers or other means the raw data is then distributed for use at the national level for many practical purposes, including weather forecasting.

In order to cover the oceans of the world some 5500 merchant ships of many states take part in a scheme whereby, at the same fixed hours, meteorological observations are taken on board these ships while at sea. The observations are also coded in a special code for transmission to designated coastal radio stations and are then fed into the general international exchange of meteorological information already described. In a few ocean areas the need for data is so important that special ocean weather ships are maintained. In many uninhabited regions, such as Antarctica, meteorological stations are maintained which also send in their reports on a routine basis. In addition, commercial aircraft take part in the reporting system, and, in a few places, special aircraft reconnaissance flights are made.

For climatological purposes a much denser network of stations is maintained by the states of the world; there are well over 100,000 stations in the global network at present. Here the observations are of a simpler kind and, in some cases, may only include daily readings of rainfall; but, in all cases, the methods of observation are standardized internationally. In general, each country publishes its own climatological statistics, but limited information is published on an international basis.

As already mentioned, meteorological satellites have recently been introduced into the system and may be said to have marked a turning point in meteorology. For the first time in human history man has the means to observe the atmosphere on a truly global scale and at frequent intervals. It would take too long to describe the full effects of the introduction of satellites for meteorological purposes. Suffice it to repeat that it was largely as a result of this development that the World Weather Watch was conceived, planned, and introduced by the WMO.

From this rather sketchy description it will readily be appreciated that the WWW is a highly organized operation involving a very high degree of international cooperation both in planning and execution. It is, moreover, a system in which the main responsibility for the establishment and manning of the associated world, regional, and national centers lies with the countries themselves.

How then does all this affect the modern need for atmospheric monitoring? The answer to this depends, of course, on the purposes which the monitoring is to serve, but, whatever the purposes, it is clearly necessary to utilize existing facilities and experience to the maximum extent possible. Indeed, it is difficult to see how any new monitoring system even remotely approaching the WMO system could be introduced within any acceptable period of time. But let us look at the reasons which make it necessary to monitor pollution in the atmosphere.

Directly or indirectly atmospheric pollution affects almost all human activities. In the first place it may have a direct effect on the health of all persons in the polluted regions. It may also have a bearing on the overall planning and management of human settlements; it may affect plant growth and agricultural crops; it may affect proper management of natural resources in many ways; and so on. Much is known about such effects by the specialists in these fields, but much remains to be learned; without appropriate monitoring techniques a full knowledge of the effects of atmospheric pollution cannot be attained. The nature and scope of the atmospheric monitoring system which the specialists in these fields will need must be decided on by the specialists themselves. Some aspects may be essentially of purely national concern but, as the atmosphere is in constant motion, many aspects will be of international concern. Apart from repeating that the organizations represented on the ACC are well aware of these problems in their respective fields and have taken appropriate action I shall not pursue these subjects further but will return to the meteorological aspects of atmospheric pollution.

In the present context these aspects are twofold. First, it is important to know whether the pollutants interfere to a significant extent with natural atmospheric processes and, if so, whether such interference is having long-term effects on the earth's climate. Second, the atmosphere serves as a means of transporting airborne pollution from its original source and depositing it in distant places — sometimes in other countries. Both of these questions are dealt with in later sections of this article. The significant thing to note at the moment is that they both give rise to a need to monitor atmospheric pollutants in a systematic manner.

To meet this need the WMO approved, in 1969, a plan for measuring on a global basis a wide range of atmospheric pollutants, and already good progress has been made in its implementation. The plan provides for the establishment of pollution-measuring stations of two kinds. Stations of the first type are named *baseline stations*.

Located in isolated areas, they are designed to provide data about long-term changes in atmospheric environmental parameters of particular significance to weather and climate, such as carbon dioxide, particulate matter, and the chemical composition of precipitation. In addition to these compulsory parameters these stations may, on an optional basis, measure a number of other gaseous and metallic parameters which could have repercussions on the world climate or the atmospheric environment in general. It is estimated that it will be sufficient to establish ten to twenty such stations at suitable locations around the globe with a minimum interference from local and regional factors. Already national governments have selected sites for seven such stations, according to specific criteria laid down by the WMO, and the stations are expected to come into operation shortly.

Stations of the second type are named *regional stations*. Situated in rural areas, they are also designed to provide data on the chemical content of precipitation and on particulate matter. In addition they are intended to reveal long-term changes in atmospheric composition due to changes in regional land-use such as urbanization, industrialization, new agricultural land management, etc. In this network, which was inaugurated in July 1970, nineteen countries have notified the WMO of their selection of sites for a total of 46 regional stations, again according to specific WMO criteria. The network is gradually expanding, and it is hoped that the number of regional stations making measurements of atmospheric composition will rise to between 100 and 200 in the course of the next few years. When that stage is reached, this network will provide, as an additional benefit, the data necessary for studies on the transformation and long-distance transport of pollutants in the atmosphere from one region to another.

It is, of course, essential that measurements at the above stations be carefully standardized both as regards methods of measurement and of analysis. An operations manual has been published by the WMO to facilitate such standardization of observations at regional stations, and a similar one for the more sophisticated observations to be taken at baseline stations is in preparation.

III. CLIMATIC CHANGES

The significance of the earth's climate as an all-pervading environmental factor is too evident to need emphasis. Thus, in the present context the question of whether atmospheric pollution is causing significant climatic changes is posed. The simple answer is that we do not know for certain; but clearly we should find out. As already explained, it is the need to answer this question which is one reason why the WMO has introduced a system to monitor the pollutants in the atmosphere in an internationally standardized and coordinated manner.

There are several processes by which a change in air composition might modify the climate. For example, an increase in the amount of particulate material or of carbon dioxide in the atmosphere would result in interference with the natural radiation budget, that is, the balance between incoming solar radiant energy through the atmosphere and the outward directed terrestrial radiation returning to space. The combustion of fossil fuels by industry — principally for power generation — is the largest source of man-made pollutants, and a close relationship has been found between the increase in use of coal and petroleum products over the past century and the measured changes in the concentration of carbon dioxide and particulate matter in the atmosphere. If the current trends continue, it is possible that the concentration of carbon dioxide, which has risen by 10 percent in the past 100 years, may increase by another 20 percent by the year 2000. Although a fully satisfactory model to forecast the climatic consequences of greater levels of carbon dioxide is not available, the best current predictions indicate that by the year 2000 the effect of added carbon dioxide will be about a one-half degree Celsius warming of the average global temperature which, in some sections of the world, could have significant effects on weather patterns and agricultural and industrial productivity.

On the other hand, recent studies indicate that the amount of particulate matter in the atmosphere has increased over large populated regions during the last decades. Such an increase might reduce the incoming radiation reaching the earth's surface which may in turn cause cooling and a lowering of the temperature of the earth. It has been argued that even a comparatively small lowering of the temperature could act as a trigger mechanism which could result in a considerable expansion of the ice packs over the earth.

Atmospheric pollution is not the only possible cause of climatic change. Nature itself has in the past produced major changes in the earth's climate but the time scale of such changes is very great. Changes in local climate may occur following changes in the natural state of the earth's surface such as those due to agricultural and water management procedures. For reasons already explained, however, these questions are not pursued further at this time. Suffice it to say that the meteorologist has to take all factors into account in considering climatic changes.

IV. TRANSPORT OF POLLUTANTS BY THE ATMOSPHERE

As already mentioned, one of the reasons the WMO is concerned with atmospheric pollution in the context of environmental problems is that the atmosphere acts as a channel for airborne pollution to pass from its source to other places on the earth's surface. The horizontal currents in the atmosphere carry with them the pollutants they contain and may then deposit them on land, rivers, or oceans far removed from their sources. The process of "wash-out" by rainfall is a particularly important means of transferring pollution from the atmosphere to the surface. It is indeed fortunate that nature provides such atmospheric cleansing mechanisms. One has only to think of the smog which results when nature temporarily halts such mechanisms to realize what would happen if atmospheric pollutants were retained in the atmosphere.

It is now well recognized that pollution conveyed to the surface by atmospheric processes constitutes a very significant source of surface pollution. The increased acidity of land and water resulting in this way from the presence of sulphur dioxide in the atmosphere is for example a particularly serious problem in some regions. Much of such pollution thus finds its way into the rivers, lakes, and oceans. For this reason and also because of the intimate relationship between meteorology, hydrology, and oceanography referred to above the WMO has an important role to play in the two environmental fields of water resources and the oceans.

V. WATER RESOURCES

The WMO's role in water resource development arises mainly from its responsibility for that branch of hydrology known as operational hydrology. Its work in this field, although not yet as highly developed as in meteorology itself, is nevertheless of great and increasing importance. Operational hydrology includes such questions as hydrological network design, standardization of hydrological instruments and methods of observation, collection, transmission, and processing of hydrological data, and supply of meteorological and hydrological data for design purposes and hydrological forecasting. Particular emphasis is laid on surface water, and it is in this field that the WMO finds itself increasingly involved in environmental problems, especially the monitoring and prevention of inland water pollution. Thus, in hydrology the WMO is involved in the operational aspects including such items as flood forecasting and the mitigation of natural disasters which may so often result. The organization is, however, no less concerned with the long-term monitoring aspects of inland waters with particular reference to water pollution.

These latter activities are in some respects analogous to those which, insofar as the atmosphere is concerned, are covered by the

World Weather Watch. In much the same way as the WWW has been extended to include measurements of the composition of the atmosphere with particular reference to pollutants the appropriate bodies of the WMO are currently studying what action the WMO needs to take in the detection and measurement of water pollutants as part of its overall work in the field of operational hydrology in general and water quality in particular.

VI. THE OCEANS

As regards oceanography, the WMO is playing an important role in developing, with other agencies, the Integrated Global Oceans Stations System (IGOSS) which is also, in many respects, analogous in this field to the World Weather Watch in the atmosphere. In addition, the WMO is cooperating with other agencies in many other oceanographic problems including that of direct marine pollution, particularly oil pollution from ships. This is in fact one of the most pressing of all environmental issues at this time. The relevance of the WMO's activities in this connection arises from the relationship between movement and dispersion of oil "slicks" and current weather conditions. However, as already explained, there is in addition a transfer of certain pollutants from the air to the sea, and, moreover, in some cases there is the reverse process, as with carbon dioxide which is taken from the ocean in some regions and is returned to the ocean in other regions.

VII. CONCLUSION

As mentioned at the outset, this article is not intended to be a comprehensive review of the role of the WMO in environmental issues. It deals only with those WMO activities related to pollution problems. The consolidated document on the "United Nations System and the Human Environment" gives a more complete indication of the wide range of the WMO's activities in this field and moreover places these activities within the overall pattern of the activities of the whole UN system.

As regards possible climatic changes due to pollution, the WMO has already taken appropriate steps for the necessary data to be obtained and studied. The transport of airborne pollution and its deposition on the earth's surface is another field which evidently falls within the field of responsibility of the WMO and for which appropriate action is being taken. As regards water resources, the WMO is taking action within the field of operational hydrology, particularly with respect to the monitoring of water pollution and water quality in general. The WMO is involved in the study of marine pollution because of the interchange of pollution between the ocean and the atmosphere and because the movement of floating pollutants (particularly oil slicks) depends upon weather conditions.

In all these activities the WMO is cooperating as necessary with other agencies in the UN system and recognizes that a coordinated approach to the solution of environmental problems will be even more necessary in the future than it has been in the past. In particular the WMO, with other agencies of the UN system, is cooperating in every appropriate way in support of the Stockholm conference. Whatever may be the outcome of the conference, it is clear that a detailed and farsighted reappraisal of world environmental problems will have been made and that the issues to be faced will have been more clearly identified. Recommendations for facing these issues will doubtless be formulated.

The ACC's "The United Nations System and the Human Environment" shows the wide range of environmental activities in which the UN system (including the WMO) is already engaged, and the conference will doubtless wish to ensure that the fullest use is made of the agencies in the future. For its part the WMO is pledged "to participate fully in the implementation of any decisions taken by the Conference in so far as they relate to the activities of the Organization."[3]

[3] WMO Resolution 16 (VI), paragraph 9, of April 1971.

ENVIRONMENTAL CONSIDERATIONS IN DEVELOPMENT FINANCE

James A. Lee

JAMES A. LEE is environmental adviser in the Office of the Director, Projects, of the International Bank for Reconstruction and Development (IBRD).

The current concern with the human environment, which has given rise, in part, to the United Nations Conference on the Human Environment in 1972, comes at a time when the energies, efforts, and resources of the developing countries are being harnessed as never before to achieve their respective development objectives. The compelling urgency of the third world's development efforts found endorsement in the proposals for the Second United Nations Development Decade (DD II). While to a large extent the concern with environmental issues has arisen out of the problems experienced by the industrially advanced countries, the developing countries are not unconcerned with or even immune from these problems. It was with this general thinking in mind that the Preparatory Committee for the Second United Nations Development Decade unanimously decided to include in the strategy for the decade the following statement which was accepted by the General Assembly: "Governments will intensify national and international efforts to arrest the deterioration of the human environment and to take measures towards its improvement and to promote activities that will help to maintain the ecological balance on which human survival depends."[1] The General Assembly in a recent resolution on the matter of the human environment further affirmed that environmental policies should be considered in the context of economic and social development, with account taken of the special needs of development in developing countries.[2]

It may be recalled that the General Assembly in its earlier resolutions on the human environment,[3] which were unanimously adopted, underlined the importance of taking environmental factors into account

---

[1] See General Assembly Resolution 2626 (XXV) of October 24, 1970.
[2] See General Assembly Resolution 2657 (XXV) of December 7, 1970.
[3] See General Assembly Resolutions 2398 (XXIII) of December 3, 1968, and 2581 (XXIV) of December 15, 1969.

in planning for economic and social development. General Assembly Resolution 2398 (XXIII) emphasized the collective views of its members that increased attention to environmental problems is essential for sound economic and social development. It further expressed the hope that the developing countries would, through appropriate international cooperation, derive particular benefit from the mobilization of knowledge and experience about the problems of the human environment so that those very problems might be avoided. In resolution 2581 (XXIV) the assembly reaffirmed this latter point by endorsing the main purpose of the Conference on the Human Environment as a practical means to encourage, and to provide guidelines for, action by governments and international organizations to protect and improve the human environment and to remedy and prevent its impairment by means of international cooperation.

Developing countries have an obvious and vital stake in environmental problems which affect the biosphere, themselves, and their economic relations with the developed countries. They would clearly wish to avoid, insofar as it is possible and feasible, the development patterns of the industrialized countries which have been responsible for the great concern over environmental matters in the richer states. The environmental problems of the developing countries are essentially of two kinds. First, there are the problems of rural and urban poverty characterized by poor housing, nutrition, water supplies, sanitation, and disease. Under these conditions in which the biophysical environment exhibits the ravages of long years of mismanagement not merely the "quality" of life but life itself is endangered for the environment often exhibits an inability to renew its life-supporting capabilities. Second, there are the environmental problems that tend to accompany the very processes of development itself. Rural and urban poverty affect the greater mass of mankind and clamor for attention; they are seen as problems that can only be overcome through development. However, as the development process moves ahead at an accelerated pace under the pressure of easing urgent social problems, the hazards and threats to the environment and health associated with the development process become greater.

The process of agricultural growth and change, for example, can involve construction of irrigation and drainage systems, clearing of forests, adoption of monoculture practices involving use of fertilizers and pesticides, creation of new disease-transmission routes, and establishment of human settlement patterns. All these processes and others associated with them have environmental and health implications. Industrialization results in the release of pollutants to the environment and in other environmental problems attendant on the extraction and processing of raw materials and the growth of related urban trade centers. Indeed, the growth of the entire economic infrastructure of transport and communications has implications for the environment and for human health and well-being.

Urbanization, while a global phenomenon, is a serious and growing problem for many developing countries. Population growth, when not accompanied by adequate economic development, gives rise to unemployment of formidable dimensions which further impoverishes the rural environment and swells the drift to the cities, thereby intensifying human problems of the gravest nature. In the absence of adequate land use planning, industrial pollution control, provision for water supplies and sewage disposal, and adequate housing the population pressures that have produced unfavorable rural land use patterns impinging increasingly on the cities have become intolerable to the psyche and soma of the inhabitants.

Exploitation of both natural and human resources is a necessary ingredient of economic development. It can and does have profound and lasting effects on the naturally occurring environment, on its biota, and on people. Increasingly we read of "ecological boomerangs" occurring in connection with development schemes in which unwelcomed and, sometimes, unexpected consequences have arisen. Yet, economic development cannot proceed without disruptions for man and nature. The developing countries and their peoples have made it clear that they *must* expand their economies and modernize their social institutions; they *must* provide themselves with an opportunity to build more productive and rewarding lives. Clearly, economic development calls for the continued export of technology from the developed to the developing countries. This export is already of significant proportions. At the same time, however, the environmental record of the developed countries in reaping quick economic benefits only to comprehend later the greater and more lasting social costs attributable to premature application of new technology should be noted. But the question cannot be viewed as one of economic and social development versus the environment. Rather, we must ask how this development can proceed in ways minimally disruptive to the environment and in ways promising of individual self-fulfillment and social progress.

Both the developed and developing countries, in their respective ways, are beginning to realize they stand face to face with the finiteness of the biosphere, their only habitat. They are also realizing that there is no choice other than to husband and manage by some means the biophysical resources that sustain them. This realization comes as states begin to comprehend, albeit too slowly perhaps, the implications of the interrelatedness of their life-supporting ecological systems, the man-made environment, human societies, and individual welfare. The linkages and interdependences of ecological systems comprising the global biosphere that are now coming to light suggest that *all* states must take an interest in protecting the integrity of these life-supporting systems. Practices which give rise to regional and global environmental problems clearly call for corrective action in the best interests of *all* the states concerned.

Yet, having this in mind, one must also be cognizant of the very real dichotomy that discussions of environmental problems and issues provoke throughout the world. One must ever be conscious of the fact that while ecological concerns are emerging as issues of high priority in developed countries, particularly in the United States, they do not command nearly the same amount of attention in the third world — and understandably so. Dwelling on the "quality" of life and environment may seem an almost luxurious preoccupation indeed for societies afflicted with widespread malnutrition and disease, high infant mortality, low life expectancy, high illiteracy levels, endemic unemployment, and severely skewed distributions of per capita income. If one adds to this litany of travail the widening gap, both absolutely and relatively, in material advances between developed and developing countries, it is easy to appreciate the dichotomy.

On every count the contrast in values, in interests, in priorities, and in capacities between developed and developing countries is marked. In matters affecting the environment, its use and protection, the contrast is, if anything, even more marked. The new-found concern of the developed countries for the environment strikes no resonant chord in much of the still developing world. If the dialogue between the worlds of the "haves" and the "have nots" about such matters is to be at all productive, it must be based on a frank and honest recognition that the viewpoints on both sides are different and that solutions to the world's environmental problems must be complementary to and not at the expense of efforts to advance the economic and social development of third-world countries.

In the preparations currently under way for the 1972 United Nations Conference on the Human Environment regional environment–development seminars have recently been concluded in Bangkok, Addis Ababa, Mexico City, and Beirut. Those seminars had the benefit of a report of an earlier meeting of development planning experts at Founex, Switzerland.[4] This report makes clear that the issue of the human environment is and ought to be of great importance to developing countries and that it must be regarded as an integral aspect of their own development process. The seminars, in fact, addressed themselves

[4] *Development and Environment,* Report submitted by a panel of experts convened by the secretary-general of the United Nations Conference on the Human Environment, Founex, Switz., June 4-12, 1971. (Mimeographed.) This report was described as a "historic turning point in the development-environment dialogue" by Maurice Strong, secretary-general of the conference, in a statement to the Preparatory Committee for the Conference on the Human Environment at its third session, September 13, 1971.

to three basic elements in the report which are of interest to developing countries. These are, in brief:

1) Developing countries share with the entire community of states a common interest in preserving and utilizing for the benefit of all mankind that portion of the earth's environment — the oceans and the atmosphere above them — which lies outside the jurisdiction of any state, and they must join in common action to protect it;

2) developing countries will be greatly affected by the actions taken by the more industrialized countries in dealing with their environmental problems, and such actions present both new opportunities and new risks to which developing countries must be prepared to respond;

3) developing countries themselves have serious environmental problems, many of them related to poverty and underdevelopment, and international cooperation is needed to enable them to deal with these problems and to build into their own development processes measures which will tend to prevent unnecessary abuse and degradation of their environment.

Thus, a major challenge faces developing countries: They are attempting to find ways to achieve their own social and economic goals at an accelerated rate and to avoid, as far as possible, the social costs of environmental degradation. Concern for the environment is coming to be viewed, therefore, as an integral part of the development process. This is especially so because, under the conditions prevailing in developing countries, any additional costs involved in improving the quality of the environment can only be envisaged in the context of accelerated growth. Only with great difficulty can resources be diverted from the urgent needs of development. The problems should not be viewed, however, exclusively in terms of a tradeoff between the rate of growth and environment-oriented actions. The situation prevailing in most developing countries is such that preventive action may be taken now at only a part of the cost which would be incurred later on. This type of tradeoff — between short-term economic effects and long-term development — is one that is constantly faced by development planners.

The regional UN seminars on the human environment have also made it clear that the formulation of environmental goals, as indeed the formulation of economic and social policies in general, is seen by the developing countries as coming within their sovereign competence. Each country indicated that it must find its own solutions in the light of its own problems and within the framework of its own political, social, and cultural values.

While it is important that environmental policies are integrated with development planning and are regarded as a part of the overall framework of economic and social planning, it should be stressed that concern about the environment is only another dimension of the problem of development in developing countries. It is not viewed by them as something separate and apart from their development efforts. The objective is, rather, to regard the safeguarding and improvement of the environment as a part of the multiple goals in a development plan. Developing countries have certain inherent advantages in intgrating environmental and developmental policies. Most of them are already so committed to planning that the imposition or acceptance of social controls is nothing new for them. They are also making a fresh start in many fields and can thus anticipate environmental effects and provide for them in their current planning. The overriding constraint in developing countries is, of course, money, the lack of which necessitates fairly sharp choices between various objectives of planning. Since environmental improvement can be regarded as only one of the multiple objectives of planning, its priority in relation to other objectives will be determined by each society in the light of its own urgent economic and social problems and its own stage of development. Basically, this is a question of alternative uses of resources within the framework of comprehensive economic and social planning.

Parallel to the integration of environmental goals with developmental policies at the macro level developing countries must also turn to the micro level to devise appropriate techniques and guides for including environmental factors in the appraisal of their development projects. Application of adequate criteria and procedures to project design and appraisal presupposes a better knowledge of the environmental, health, and sociocultural impacts of development projects. While environmental experts would be the first to recognize and admit the inadequacies and shortcomings of predicting accurately the full range of consequences attendant on development schemes, sufficient information, data, experience, and expertise do presently exist so that "reasonable" predictions can be made about the consequences of environmental alteration and manipulation. Knowledge of the structure and function of ecosystems, while still at a relatively rudimentary level, is being developed due, in part, to the efforts of the International Biological Program (IBP). Disease problems attributable to development are becoming both better known and understood, and measures for their prevention or mitigation are being developed. Sociocultural impacts are perhaps less well understood, but the increasing participation of social scientists in the planning, appraisal, conduct, and auditing of development activities is an encouraging sign.

It would seem, however, that it is not within the present state of the art to make available definitive guidelines which would provide firm directives to development planners on how to plan, design, construct, operate, and evaluate projects in such a way as to ensure that all potential environmental, health, and sociocultural consequences and remedial measures are identified and costed out and proper values assigned to benefits in cost-benefit analyses. Guides to environmental considerations presently being used and under development would seem to represent, in part, a way to reach the stated goals of developing countries, namely, the pursuit of economic development in a manner that is minimally disruptive to life-supporting ecological systems, with minimal adverse effects on the physical and mental health of affected peoples and with minimal dysfunctional effects on the sociocultural processes by which peoples conduct their interpersonal and intergroup affairs. Whatever form they may take, environmental considerations should, to the extent possible, ensure that environmental quality, human health, and social well-being need not be sacrificed or unduly injured, let alone irreversibly altered, as a result of economic development. Further, these considerations should, by their very existence and application, point the way toward bringing about increased awareness of development-associated environmental problems in developing countries, the marshaling of the necessary resources and expertise to study such problems, the stimulation of the need for appropriate research and training, and the encouragement of exchanges of information and experience between countries.

Purposeful and systematic evaluation of the impact of development activities on the environment and on public health and social well-being is a rather recent innovation in direct response to the growing concern over threats to the very survival of man. This is not to imply that all economic development activities in the past proceeded in the absence of any such evaluations. However, it has only been within the past several years that development planners and their institutions have been alerted to the necessity of carrying out "preproject" evaluations in something of a systematic manner. Most of these activities have been centered in the developed countries in which new legislation has imposed restrictions on activities potentially damaging to the environment and health. In the United States, for example, the Environmental Quality Act of 1969 provides for an accounting of probable environmental impacts of federally financed projects in advance of and as a prerequisite to their implementation. Environmental impact statements are prepared by the project sponsor and subjected to review by interested agencies at the federal, state, and local governmental levels. More recently economic development institutions such as the IBRD, the Swedish International Development Authority, the United States Agency for International Development (AID), and the United Nations Development Program (UNDP), among others, have indicated their intention to include environmental considerations in the planning and appraisal of projects prepared by or submitted to them for financing.

In its own distinct way the IBRD, by way of example, has striven to serve the basic goal of economic development without undue adverse consequences to the environment. It has greatly increased its activities in recent years. One measure of this increase is the financial commitments of the World Bank Group for high-priority projects in developing countries, which have risen from $1 billion in 1968 to $2.3 billion in 1970.[5] In the five years from 1968 to 1973 commitments are expected to total $12 billion, or more than double the figure for the previous five years. But the World Bank Group's goals are not merely financial or quantitative; they are also qualitative. For it is the improvement of the human condition, not of statistical abstractions, that is the object of its endeavors.

In expanding its activities the IBRD attaches particular importance to the promotion of agriculture, education, and family planning. This ordering of priorities is dictated by the facts that one-third to one-half of mankind suffers from hunger or malnutrition, that 800 million illiterates have been bypassed by educational systems that remain both inadequate and out of tune with manpower needs, and that the population explosion has become one of the greatest threats to the economic and social progress of the human race. The experience of the IBRD — not only in these sectors but also over the entire range of its activities — has underlined for it the need for an improved understanding of the social and environmental implications of economic change. That need will increase as the bank grapples in the years ahead with the growing problems of urbanization, unemployment, industrialization, land reform, health, income distribution, and threats to the environment.

Speaking to the UN Economic and Social Council (ECOSOC) in 1970, IBRD President Robert McNamara stated:

> The problem facing development finance institutions, including the World Bank, is whether and how we can help the developing countries to avoid or mitigate some of the damage economic development can do to the environment, without at the same time slowing down the pace of economic progress. It is clear that the costs resulting from adverse environmental change can be tremendous . . . witness, for example, the harm to human life that some water-storage projects in Africa and Asia already have done by encouraging water-borne diseases — to say nothing of the implications of the rising use of pesticides throughout the develop-

[5] International Bank for Reconstruction and Development and International Development Association, *Annual Report 1970* (Washington, 1970), p. 5.

ing world. . . . It is equally clear that, in many cases, a small
investment in prevention could be worth many times over what
would have to be expended to repair the damage.[6]

To this end the World Bank Group is taking steps to assure that
projects financed by it do not have seriously adverse environmental
and health consequences or, if they are likely to have such consequences, that measures are taken to avoid or to mitigate them. Indeed, the president and the World Bank Group's top management
have already initiated changes that will ensure to every extent possible a consideration of the environmental, health, and related social
consequences of development projects proposed for financing.

The policy of the World Bank Group regarding the environmental
consequences of the activities for which it makes loans, simply stated,
is to pursue its economic development objectives with a careful and
studied regard for the consequences to the environment and to the
health and well-being of affected peoples. This policy statement is
intended to leave no doubt that the bank fully intends to press forward with its primary job of assisting developing countries to achieve
a higher standard of living and economic growth. At the same time
the statement is also designed to leave no doubt that the bank does
not intend that its activities should knowingly contribute to short-
term economic gains at the price of long-term human ecological misery.

Bank-financed projects that might have adverse consequences for
the environment or health are reviewed and studied (including appropriate field investigations) with a view to identifying the nature
and dimensions of problems and providing for their solution. Similarly,
opportunities for environmental enhancement are sought out for often
such benefits can be incorporated without significant alteration of the
project's intended purpose. Environmental safeguards deemed necessary are considered by the borrower, the member government, and
the bank in the preparations for negotiating the loan and, finally,
by the bank's Loan Committee and Board of Directors which must
authorize the loan. When environmental provisions are incorporated
into the project, their costs are included in the terms of the loan.

The World Bank Group is of the opinion that environmental
quality, human health, and social well-being need not be sacrificed
or unduly injured, let alone irreversibly altered, as a result of economic
development activities. It seeks to convince its developing member
countries that ecologically oriented planning, appropriately combined
with sociocultural awareness and sensitivity, is a necessary prerequisite
of project identification, design, and implementation. Not surprisingly, it is finding much sympathy for this approach on the part of

[6] See UN Document E/SR. 1730.

many of the developing countries which it serves. While these countries rightfully and predictably seek to share in the fruits of technology and industrialization, in expanded agriculture and improved yields, they are becoming more aware of the unwanted consequences that can attend these efforts. Increasingly, they are seeking advice and assistance on ways to avoid or mitigate these adverse consequences while at the same time moving forward toward their respective economic and social goals.

It would seem that looking ahead into the 1970s financial institutions, public and private, will ignore at their peril the consequences of their operations for the human environment. More and more they will be held accountable for the environment-affecting activities whose financing they provide and in whose preparation and execution they increasingly play a major role. Further, it is not unreasonable to expect that development finance institutions will find themselves called upon to fund new types of projects designed to rehabilitate and clean up urban chaos and associated environmental pollution: pollution of lakes, rivers, estuaries, and fjords; pollution of the air over densely populated urban and industrial areas where disturbing clinical signs are beginning to reveal themselves; pollution of valuable urban lands from growing mountains of solid wastes; pollution from toxic substances that slowly and insidiously take their toll of wild animals and birds; and pollution of the human organism, the effects of which can be expected to be reflected in changing morbidity and mortality statistics.

Further, no country and no people are exempt from the current effects and ultimate consequences of threats to the biospheric integrity of the planet, from dangers such as global pollution of the oceans, large-scale atmospheric and climatic changes, or the worldwide effects of persistent and pervasive biocides. Some encouraging signs are apparent, however. The forthcoming UN Conference on the Human Environment could prove to be a turning point for international cooperation in averting what in some quarters is viewed as an approaching "crisis." The International Biological Program is offering new hope for an early understanding of the structure and functions of ecosystems and, hence, the development of a capability for predicting the consequences of alterations and disturbances to them. The proposal for a global network for environmental monitoring could provide the tools for measuring changes and allow for surveillance over critical elements and factors. Though ecological research is, itself, on the upswing, it is still deserving of greater support for, as Marston Bates so correctly prophesized a decade ago, "ecology may well be the most important of the sciences from the viewpoint of long-term human survival."[7]

Ecologically speaking, 1980 is the day after tomorrow . . . the year 2000 is next week . . . and if we truly intend to become responsible trustees of the biosphere, we must better understand how it functions and what the effects of our tampering might be. Development finance institutions are becoming aware that the global challenge — the survival of mankind — must be met by resolving the basic conflict between man's creativity and his destructiveness. The issue of the environment provides a new imperative, a new opportunity, a new mandate to measure development assistance in terms other than growth of output — for man himself is the ultimate measure.

[7] Marston Bates, "Man and Other Pests," *Nation*, October 6, 1962 (Vol. 195, No. 10), p. 202.

THE UN REGIONAL ECONOMIC COMMISSIONS AND ENVIRONMENTAL PROBLEMS

Amasa S. Bishop and Robert D. Munro

AMASA S. BISHOP is the director of the Environment and Housing Division, Economic Commission for Europe (ECE). ROBERT D. MUNRO is an associate of the division. The authors, while assuming sole responsibility for the text, wish to acknowledge the constructive comments and suggestions of M. Fagen, B. F. Reiner, and S. Kalnins. The views expressed are not necessarily those of the United Nations.

I. INTRODUCTION

A cursory glance at a map, a university curriculum, or a government organization chart will confirm that man has a remarkable capacity for establishing arbitrary boundaries. Moreover, he has usually claimed a degree of sovereignty within those boundaries which he would energetically defend and, if possible, extend. We would continue to believe that we could reasonably afford our independent behavior except for the recent "discovery" that the human environment is not only a complex but also a finite system. Environmental problems, or, more particularly, the harmful effects of man's activities on his environment, challenge our exclusiveness and affect our existing territorial, disciplinary, and institutional boundaries simply because they transcend them. Of the many factors to be taken into account in dealing with environmental problems two have particular importance: the identification of the geographical level at which action can effectively be taken and the choice of the appropriate legal and institutional instruments to be employed.

The majority of environmental problems occur within national boundaries and can appropriately be dealt with at that level. However, environmental problems extending or occurring beyond the boundaries of a single state have increasingly become a major concern of governments. These international environmental problems have two major dimensions, global and regional; of these, the greater number occur at the regional level. In the case of the latter the need to develop comprehensive regional approaches is clear. But even in the case of the former there are many practical reasons and advantages for including regional approaches as an integral part of global strategies and programs, as has already been illustrated by the extensive regional activities of the United Nations specialized agencies and by the preparatory process for the United Nations Conference on the Human Environment.[1] As the immediate causes and effects of international environmental problems can be more readily identified and analyzed in the various regions, the development of global strategies has depended and will continue to depend extensively on the assessments undertaken and the views expressed at the regional level. Environmental guidelines and programs that may be developed at the global level will require some adaptation to specific regional conditions and needs, and, because of the relatively greater interdependence and more extensive contacts between governments at the regional level, they are likely to be applied regionally with a higher degree of effectiveness. But in order to be applied at all, at either level, they will require agreement within and between governments on the appropriate intergovernmental organizations to be employed.

The need to contend with existing international environmental problems and to avoid future ones will increasingly limit the national policy choices available to governments. When in the past international problems have arisen, governments have usually had the choice whether to cooperate or not; intergovernmental organizations became and remained important "precisely to the extent that such multilateral co-ordination is the real and continuous aim of the national governments."[2] But as the failure to deal effectively with international environmental problems will eventually affect all countries equally, international cooperation will increasingly become for governments not an alternative but an imperative of national policy. The choice remaining to governments will be which intergovernmental organizations to use, adapt, or create for dealing with international environmental problems.

A review of the functions and work of existing intergovernmental organizations relating to problems of the human environment is consequently both necessary and timely. As one contribution, this article

[1] Five major regional meetings on environmental problems were held during 1971. In three regions — Asia and the Far East, Latin America, and Africa — seminars were jointly sponsored by the respective regional economic commissions and the secretariat for the United Nations Conference on the Human Environment. In the Near East the regional seminar was held under the joint auspices of the UN Economic and Social Office at Beirut and the UN conference secretariat. In the fifth region, Europe, a symposium was held under the auspices of the ECE. The reports of the five meetings were designated as basic papers for the UN conference and used in developing the major position papers.

[2] Gunnar Myrdal, "The Intergovernmental Organizations and the Role of their Secretariats" (The W. Clifford Clark Memorial Lectures, 1969), reprinted from *Canadian Public Administration,* Fall 1969 (Vol. 12, No. 3), p. 12.

will deal with four similar intergovernmental organizations, the regional economic commissions of the United Nations.[3] In section II the common characteristics and formal functions of the regional commissions are briefly reviewed. The activities and views regarding intergovernmental cooperation on environmental problems of ECAFE, the ECA, and ECLA are reviewed in section III, and those of the ECE in section IV. Section V includes several concluding remarks and observations on the potentialities of the regional commissions, especially their role in the development of comprehensive regional approaches to environmental problems.

II. THE UN REGIONAL ECONOMIC COMMISSIONS

The intention to extend the work of the proposed world security organization into social, economic, and other fields was originally expressed in the Dumbarton Oaks proposals and was later confirmed at San Francisco in 1945.[4] As a consequence intergovernmental organizations and administrative units were established at both the global and the regional levels within the UN system, but the relationship between them at the regional level was not precisely defined. Yet, when considering regional structures within the UN system, it remains important to distinguish between the different character and role of those, such as the regional economic commissions, which have a regional focus and a general mandate, and those, such as regional units of specialized agencies, which are part of a larger structure with a specific sectoral mandate. While at the regional level both types of organization are clearly interrelated, with programs that should be complementary, their respective roles and responsibilities are not the same and were not intended to be.

The four regional economic commissions have these general purposes in common: 1) to initiate and participate in measures for facilitating concerted action on economic problems in the respective regions; 2) to maintain and strengthen economic relations between members and with other countries of the world; 3) to conduct or sponsor studies of economic and technological problems arising within the region;

[3] The four commissions and the year in which each was established are: the Economic Commission for Europe (ECE), 1947; the Economic Commission for Asia and the Far East (ECAFE), 1947; the Economic Commission for Latin America (ECLA), 1948; and the Economic Commission for Africa (ECA), 1958. Near East countries are served by a bureau of the Department of Economic and Social Affairs at Beirut.

[4] For a skeptical review of the Dumbarton Oaks proposals on this question see Gunnar Myrdal, "Relation to the Specialized Agencies in the Economic and Social Field," in *Peace and Security after the Second World War* (Stockholm: Almquist and Wiksell, 1945), pp. 173-190.

and 4) to conduct or sponsor projects for the collection, evaluation, and dissemination of economic, technological, and statistical information. In addition, three regional commissions — ECAFE, ECLA, and the ECA — are also formally charged 5) to devote special attention to problems of economic development, including an obligation to assist in the formulation of coordinated policies and in the implementation of technical assistance programs in the region, and 6) to concentrate as well on the social aspects of economic development and the interrelationship of economic and social factors.[5]

The regional economic commissions are, for purposes of decision-making, exclusively intergovernmental organizations. Their principal membership consists of all countries in the region belonging to the United Nations.[6] The membership of three commissions also includes some member countries of the UN which are not located in the region.[7] Under the terms of reference of ECAFE, the ECA, and ECLA territories in the region may participate as associate members but without the right to vote. In principle, any member of the UN may participate in a consultative capacity on matters of particular concern to that country. The terms of reference for the ECE include a special provision allowing the commission to admit in a consultative capacity countries in the region which are not members of the United Nations and to determine the conditions of their participation.

The development of comprehensive and effective programs for dealing with regional problems requires both agreement between the governments and cooperation with other organizations in the region. The terms of reference of each regional commission contain provisions concerning liaison with other organizations working either in the region or a related general field. The commissions must ensure that necessary liaison is maintained with other UN bodies and, formally for all but the ECE, with the other regional economic commissions in particular. Representatives of the UN specialized agencies must be invited, and

[5] The terms of reference for each commission are contained in the following documents: ECE (UN Document E/ECE/788); ECAFE (UN Document E/CN.11/539, Rev. 1); ECLA (UN Document E/CN.12/544); and ECA (UN Document E/CN.14/111/Rev. 4).
[6] There are significant exceptions. For example, the Federal Republic of Germany, while not a member of the United Nations, is a member of the ECE. The Republic of South Africa, while both a member of the United Nations and located within the ECA region, was precluded from participation in the work of the ECA by ECOSOC Resolution 974 D IV(XXXVI), July 22, 1963.
[7] Countries which are full members of the regional commissions although not located in the region include: ECE — the United States; ECLA — France, the Netherlands, and the United Kingdom; ECAFE — France, the Netherlands, the Union of Soviet Socialist Republics, the United Kingdom, and the United States. (The Soviet Union, though geographically part of both Europe and Asia, is a member of the ECE.)

those of other intergovernmental organizations may be invited, to participate in a consultative capacity on matters of particular concern to them. Unlike many international or subregional intergovernmental organizations outside the UN system the four commissions must also make appropriate arrangements for consultations with nongovernmental organizations which have been granted consultative status by the Economic and Social Council (ECOSOC).

The regional commissions have a common, worldwide institutional context and similar powers. Each acts within the framework of UN policies and is subject to the general supervision of ECOSOC, to which each reports annually. The commissions are specifically empowered to make recommendations on any matter within their competence directly to their member governments, to governments admitted in a consultative capacity, and to the UN specialized agencies concerned. The commissions may not take any action concerning a country without the agreement of that country and, for proposed activities which would have an important effect on the economy of the world, prior consideration by ECOSOC is required. This last provision may become increasingly important as the effects on trade of regional agreements and actions regarding environmental problems become more apparent.

Finally, the terms of reference permit each regional commission, after discussions with specialized agencies at work in the same general field and with the approval of ECOSOC, to establish principal subsidiary bodies to carry out its responsibilities. As a reflection of their extensive responsibilities and the willingness of governments to cooperate at the regional level, the regional commissions have subsidiary bodies and task forces at work in a wide variety of economic sectors and problem areas. These sectoral bodies are a particular asset of the commissions in attempting to deal with environmental problems. Separately, and often in cooperation with other sectoral committees in the commissions or other international organizations, these committees have been particularly effective in identifying and assessing specific environmental problems in the various sectors and, more important, in supporting preventative and remedial actions. The combination of these groups within one structure, the regional economic commissions, already provides a comprehensive and flexible economic, social, and political framework for effective action in resolving environmental problems on a region-wide basis.

Despite these fundamental and common characteristics shared by the regional economic commissions there are important differences between them. Each commission serves a large continent with a great diversity in geography and problems, and each includes among its members countries of widely differing economic and social systems, conditions, and prospects. As a consequence there has been a gradual but different evolution for each commission in response to the distinctive needs and concerns of the governments which compose that commission. The differences are nowhere more apparent than in the commissions' views and activities regarding problems of the human environment.

III. ECAFE, THE ECA, ECLA, AND THE HUMAN ENVIRONMENT

The extensive consultations that have been so constructive a part of the preparatory process for the conference in Stockholm have reinforced the recognition of the wide range in the nature of problems of the human environment. An eminent panel of economic experts, convened at Founex, Switzerland, in June 1971 by the secretary-general of the Stockholm conference, described some of the differences as follows:

> The major environmental problems of developing countries . . . are predominantly problems that reflect the poverty and very lack of development of their societies. They are problems, in other words, of both rural and urban poverty. In both the towns and in the countryside, not merely "the quality of life," but life itself is endangered by poor water, housing, sanitation and nutrition, by sickness and by natural disasters. These are problems, no less than those of industrial pollution, that clamour for attention in the context of the concern with human environment. They are problems which affect the greater mass of mankind.[8]

The greater mass of mankind lives in the regions served by three regional economic commissions: ECAFE, the ECA, and ECLA. A brief review of their major concerns and activities related to environmental problems follows.

The Economic Commission for Asia and the Far East

ECAFE includes among its major concerns the problems of population growth, particularly their effect on the environment, and problems of water resource development.[9] Through an extensive pro-

---

[8] See *Development and Environment,* Report submitted by a panel of experts convened by the secretary-general of the United Nations Conference on the Human Environment, Founex, Switz., June 4-12, 1971 (UN Document GE.71-13738), p. 1.

[9] For a complete list and review of the environmental problems most commonly experienced by the countries in the region see *Report on the Seminar on Development and Environment,* Bangkok, August 17-23, 1971 (UN Document E/CN.11/999), p. 11 ff.; see also the *Report of the Regional Seminar on the Ecological Implications of Rural and Urban Population Growth,* Bangkok, August 25-September 3, 1971 (UN Document E/CN.11/L.312).

gram of research, regional seminars, and multilateral assistance ECAFE has made a substantial contribution to the understanding of population problems and to the formulation and implementation of policies and improved programs of population and family planning in the region. In seeking to anticipate and develop today the programs required for tomorrow ECAFE is attempting to strengthen and extend data collection systems for population and other demographic information in order to assess the patterns of population growth and distribution and their relation to environmental conditions.

It is already anticipated that within 30 years the ECAFE region, representing 17 percent of the world's land area, will contain a population equal to that of the world in 1970. About 75 percent of the existing population inhabits rural areas. With 80 percent of the available arable land in the region already being cultivated, sustained agricultural growth is imperative yet not always reconcilable with environmental considerations.[10] Apart from already apparent concerns about the extensive use of chemical fertilizers and pesticides, other more subtle and intractable problems emerge. For example, increased productivity in the agricultural sector will require, among other things, more extensive irrigation and, to provide both the necessary equipment and financing, greater growth in nonagricultural economic sectors. Yet in some cases the consumptive loss of water for irrigation could result in serious depletion of water supplies needed for industrial and domestic use and for diluting and transporting municipal wastes.[11]

Water resource development has always been a prominent concern of ECAFE members, and the commission has promoted long-range planning and integrated river basin development, such as the Mekong Development Project undertaken in cooperation with the United Nations Development Program (UNDP). ECAFE has also conducted extensive research and manpower training programs in the water resource field and will sponsor a Southeast Asian Regional Workshop on "Water Resources and National Development" to examine the critical role of water in the economic development and quality of life in the region.

In addition to this work ECAFE activities regarding environment also include a pilot survey on the extent and nature of pollution in the region; discussions on deforestation and on problems of erosion; studies of air pollution caused by fuel burning and thermal power stations; and, as a major concern, problems of rapid urban growth. It was proposed at the regional seminar on "Development and Environ-

[10] Report on the Ecological Implications of Rural and Urban Population Growth, p. 17.
[11] Ibid., pp. 12-13.

ment" to establish a separate unit in the ECAFE secretariat to deal exclusively with environmental problems,[12] with particular emphasis on serving as a regional clearinghouse for information on the human environment and on programs for the education and training of environmental engineers and scientists.[13]

The Economic Commission for Africa

The ECA, with its major emphasis on activities supporting economic development in the region, has undertaken a comprehensive program on the preparation of natural resource inventories, using air survey methods, as a necessary basis for future management and planning. Associated projects include the training of personnel in survey techniques and a cooperative program for standard mapping. Other major activities related to environment include programs on water resource development, agriculture, and problems of urban growth and housing.

In the field of water the ECA is engaged in the planning and establishing of networks for the collection of water resource data. At the national level the ECA promotes and, on request, assists in preparing coordinated water resource development plans and, between some members, the integrated development of international river basins. Problems of agriculture and rural water supplies in the region, a special concern, will be assessed by a working party established following a recent conference sponsored by the ECA in cooperation with the Food and Agriculture Organization (FAO), the UN Educational, Scientific and Cultural Organization (UNESCO), and the World Health Organization (WHO). The problems and particular importance of agriculture in the region led to the establishment of a joint ECA/FAO division. To promote integrated rural and urban development the ECA is actively engaged in the formulation and implementation of programs in housing, building, and physical planning. A study to examine the effect of pollution on living conditions in African cities has recently been undertaken and will eventually include the consideration of preventative measures.

Problems of the human environment were identified as a major priority for the region at the first All-African Seminar on the Human Environment. Held at Addis Ababa in August 1971 under the joint auspices of the ECA and the secretariat for the Stockholm conference, the seminar adopted a comprehensive set of recommendations on environment for submission to the governments.[14] The proposals in-

---

[12] *Report on the Seminar on Development and Environment,* Bangkok, p. 36.
[13] Ibid., p. 15.
[14] See *Report of the First All-African Seminar on the Human Environment,* Addis Ababa, August 23-28, 1971 (UN Document E/CN.14/532).

cluded a request for the ECA to establish for the region an all-African steering committee in preparation for the UN Conference on the Human Environment in Stockholm.[15]

The Economic Commission for Latin America

ECLA, in common with ECAFE and the ECA, had not previously emphasized problems of the human environment as a distinct and unified area of activity. Earlier studies and programs considered special problems such as the deterioration of the natural resource base of the region and specific environmental problems caused by industrialization and urbanization.[16] Concerning water development, ECLA has conducted for several years — with the support of the UNDP, the Pan American Health Organization (PAHO), and the WMO — a Natural Resources and Energy Program which involved a series of studies on the use of water resources in nearly all the countries of the region. The pollution of water, of estuaries, and beaches, problems of flood control and of erosion, and zoning policies based on the availability of water were included in the studies.[17] ECLA is currently conducting a study on the application of systems analysis to water resource planning and, with the UNDP and the PAHO, advises countries in the region on problems of municipal and industrial water supply and disposal, on water quality planning, and on legal and institutional aspects of water resource development. ECLA also prepares population projections for the region and has undertaken studies on population growth and problems of regional and urban development.

At a recent regional seminar on "Problems of the Human Environment and Development" convened by ECLA in cooperation with the secretariat for the Stockholm conference the following overall needs at the regional level were stressed: a greater exchange between the ECLA countries of scientific and technical information on environmental problems; more technical and research assistance from other countries; the conduct of joint studies of environmental problems in border and common maritime areas; greater coordination between the technical organizations working in the ECLA region; the standardization of criteria, concepts, and terminology for environmental problems; and the strengthening of a general or interregional system for controlling the quality of the atmosphere.[18] The seminar recom-

---

[15] Ibid., p. 12.
[16] See *Report of the Latin American Regional Seminar on Problems of the Human Environment and Development*, Mexico City, September 6-11, 1971 (UN Document ST/ECLA/CONF.40/L.5/Rev.1); see also *The Human Environment in Latin America* (UN Document E/CN.12/898).
[17] *The Human Environment in Latin America*, p. 18.
[18] *Problems of the Human Environment and Development*, Mexico City, pp. 21-22.

mended that the countries in the ECLA region convene a further intergovernmental meeting prior to the UN Conference on the Human Environment.

In spite of the many differences between the three regions ECAFE, the ECA, and ECLA consider their environmental problems fundamentally similar in kind and quite different from those occurring in the developed regions of the world. Common to the three regional seminars was an emphasis on the fact that environmental problems of many countries in each region often derived from their status as developing countries. On this point the Founex panel drew a distinction between environmental problems arising from the process of economic development and those created by lack of development.[19] As these problems are apparently inextricably linked, the Founex report stressed that development programs should serve both economic growth and environmental goals. When the latter support or reinforce economic growth, priorities can be clearly established. But, as the report emphasizes:

> Where conflicts are involved, particularly in the short or medium run, more difficult choices would have to be made regarding the "trade off" between these and narrower growth objectives. These choices can only be made by the countries themselves in the light of their own situations and development strategies and cannot be determined by any rules established *a priori*.[20]

While working to develop cooperative programs to deal with environmental problems at the regional level the members of ECAFE, the ECA, and ECLA share a common concern about actions to be proposed at the global level. They are particularly concerned about the possible effects on economic development within their countries and their economic relations with developed countries. These concerns, originally expressed at the three regional seminars and other international meetings,[21] are summarized in a resolution adopted by the UN General Assembly on December 20, 1971.[22] The resolution was passed by a vote of 85 to 2, but without the support of any developed countries. The voting pattern, foreshadowing the discussions to be held in 1972 at the third session of the UN Conference on Trade and Development (UNCTAD) at Santiago in April and at the UN Conference on the Human Environment at Stockholm in June, clearly illustrates the many differences that must be reconciled before agree-

---

[19] *Development and Environment,* Founex, p. 6.

[20] Ibid., pp. 2-3.

[21] See, for example, *The Declaration and Principles of the Action Programme of Lima,* adopted by the Group of 77 at the Second Ministerial Meeting, Lima, November 7, 1971 (UN Document TD/143), especially pp. 30-31.

[22] General Assembly Resolution 2849 (XXVI), December 20, 1971.

ments can be obtained at the global level while at the same time indicating the need for such international consultations on environmental problems. The voting pattern also suggests that intensified regional approaches may be a prerequisite. The Founex panel proposed that developing countries should discuss the formulation of specific guidelines concerning, inter alia, the favorable and unfavorable impact of projects on the environment, "at the level of the regional economic commissions, regional banks and other relevant international agencies."[23] As an integral part of future work, exchanges of views and information on environmental problems need to be extended on a continuing and systematic basis within and especially between the respective regions.

IV. THE ECE AND ENVIRONMENTAL PROBLEMS

The ECE includes among its members most of the highly industrialized countries of the world, and it is largely as a result of the industrial, diplomatic, and other activities of these countries that environmental problems have become a matter of international concern. It is consequently in these countries, and in the ECE among the various regional commissions, that the necessary remedial and preventative actions will be first required. J. Stanovnik, the executive secretary of the ECE, has repeatedly emphasized this in unequivocal terms.

> It is those who are polluting who should start first. Since the developed world today commands 80% of technology, uses 80% of the world's resources and produces 80% of the world's wastes and pollution, it is only normal that it should be the task of the developed world to suppress pollution and wastes at their origin. It is the developed world that is creating an environment which is unacceptable to human society, and it is therefore the task first of the developed world to do something about it. That is why in our Commission we consider that we cannot possibly make a better contribution to the global Stockholm Conference than by starting an action to suppress pollution and to improve the environment within our own area.[24]

A second distinction of the ECE is that it includes among its members countries from both Eastern and Western Europe. The

[23] *Development and Environment,* Founex, p. 32.
[24] J. Stanovnik, "The Human Environment — International Dimensions of the Problem," an address to the Annual Conference of Non-Governmental Organizations listed with the United Nations Office of Public Information, May 25-26, 1971, p. 32.

differences in economic, social, and political viewpoints have certainly complicated and have sometimes limited the work of the ECE, but it is precisely because the differences exist that the work of the ECE is unique and of special importance.[25] But, as has been suggested earlier in this article, environmental problems represent a new kind of international issue and are not amenable to solution within exclusive physical, economic, or political boundaries. An article in the Soviet journal *International Affairs* supports this view: The author argues for the development of a broad international approach because "the problem of protection of the environment cannot be solved within the framework of bloc policy, but only on the basis of broad cooperation between all countries concerned."[26] Similarly, it was suggested in an article in the American journal *Foreign Affairs* that the emergence of international environmental problems may be regrettable but timely, as the countries of both East and West "have need to replace the waning fixations of the cold war with interests which they can pursue in common and to everybody's benefit."[27]

Problems of the environment have been an international concern in the ECE for over fifteen years. To cite three prominent examples, water pollution problems first appeared on the agenda of the Inland Transport Committee in 1956, and studies on problems of air pollution were included in the work program of several ECE subsidiary bodies in the early 1960s. Separate groups were eventually established to deal with each of these problems on a continuing and regular basis. Concern for proper land use, the safeguarding of recreation areas, slum clearance, and other urban development problems have long been dealt with by the Committee on Housing, Building, and Planning. These examples illustrate a general point that the original concern and work for environmental problems began at the ECE within the various sectoral committees and have increased within them ever since. By 1969 the concern was sufficiently evident and wide-

[25] See Gunnar Myrdal, "Twenty Years of the United Nations Economic Commission for Europe," *International Organization,* Spring 1968 (Vol. 22, No. 3), pp. 617-628. Myrdal was the executive secretary of the ECE during the first decade of its work, 1947-1957.

[26] See B. Ganyushkin, "Pollution: An Important International Problem," *International Affairs,* January 1971 (Vol. 47, No. 1), p. 33.

[27] See George F. Kennan, "To Prevent a World Wasteland," *Foreign Affairs,* April 1970 (Vol. 48, No. 3), p. 413. Problems of security and environment have been directly linked. Premier Alexei Kosygin has been reported as suggesting that the Soviet Union and the United States negotiate an agreement to cooperate in a major fight against environmental pollution, using funds diverted from defense budgets following an arrangement at the SALT talks. See the *New York Times,* July 17, 1971, p. 36. Environmental problems are also a major item on the agenda developed by the Warsaw Treaty Organization for the proposed European security conference.

spread that work on environmental problems was established by
the commission as one of the four major priorities for all future programs.[28] At present nearly all ECE committees are in one way or
another engaged in major studies or cooperative programs on environmental problems resulting from industrial and other activities in their
respective fields. A chart illustrating the extent and nature of their
work is included as table 1.

The concern for environmental problems in Europe gradually
shifted in the mid-1960s from their sectoral characteristics to their interrelationships, and it became increasingly apparent that comprehensive and coordinated approaches would have to be developed within
both the countries and the region to deal with them effectively. At
the ECE Jubilee Session in April 1967 — more than a year before
the Stockholm conference was proposed — the member governments
unanimously decided to convene a meeting of senior officials from
each country to undertake a comprehensive examination of environmental problems in the region.[29] It was subsequently decided to
promote the meeting to the level of a formal international conference
and to hold it in May 1971 at Prague.

The 1967 commission decision inaugurated a fairly intensive period
of exchange of information and experience on environmental problems
between senior officials and experts in the European governments.
As an essential part of the preparations for the conference in Prague
each ECE country undertook to prepare a background study describing the major environmental problems in that country and the existing
legal, administrative, and institutional framework for dealing with
them.[30] Between the date the country reports were requested and
the time they were submitted a surprising number of changes occurred
in the legal and institutional approaches to environmental problems
in many ECE countries, some quite sweeping. Within a few months
of the circulation of these reports among the various governments
there were sufficient changes within many countries that their reports
as source documents were quickly out of date. Such changes occurring
during the preparatory period for the conference clearly reflected the
increasing importance that ECE governments attached to environmental problems and their desire to deal with them effectively. Their
concern led to the convening, six months prior to the conference,
of a special ad hoc meeting of senior governmental advisers for preliminary but in-depth discussions on several key topics including gov-

[28] ECE Resolution 5(XXIV), April 23, 1969.
[29] ECE Resolution 5(XXII), April 28, 1967.
[30] See "Review of Country Monographs on Problems relating to Environment,"
in *ECE Symposium on Problems relating to Environment,* Prague, May 2-15,
1971 (UN Document ST/ECE/ENV/I), pp. 31-38.

TABLE 1. SUMMARY OF THE MAIN ENVIRONMENTAL ACTIVITIES BEING CARRIED OUT BY ECE PRINCIPAL SUBSIDIARY BODIES

Bodies Primarily Responsible	Major Responsibilities and Activities Relating to Environmental Problems	Responsible Division within the ECE Secretariat
Senior Economic Advisers to ECE Governments	Long-term aspects of economic strategies, policies, and plans and their impact on current decisionmaking, including economic aspects of environmental problems.	Projections and Programming Division
Senior Advisers to ECE Governments on Environmental Problems	Survey and assessment of the state of the environment, national environmental policies, institutions, and legislation in ECE countries; study of environmental effects of various economic activities; organization of environmental information exchange; examination of tools and methods for decisionmaking; promotion of international arrangements between contiguous countries to solve environmental problems in areas of common interest. Through its Working Party on Air Pollution this body also deals with such topics as economic and technical problems concerned with air pollution control and prevention and air quality amelioration.	Environment and Housing Division
Senior Advisers to ECE Governments on Science and Technology	Methodological problems in studying the interrelationships between environmental problems, technological progress, and economic development.	Trade and Technology Division and Environment and Housing Division
Steel Committee	Examination of problems of air and water pollution arising in the iron and steel industry.	Industry Division
Timber Committee	Location of, and water and air pollution by, forest industries; damage to forests caused by smoke from thermal power stations; evaluation of social benefits of forests; study of long-term timber trends and prospects will include consideration of impact of demand for indirect benefits of forests on their traditional wood-supplying function.	ECE/FAO Timber Division
Committee on Water Problems	Surveys, reviews, analyses, and forecasts in the field of water resources utilization; (thirteen) selected problems of water pollution control; various projects on the formulation and administration of water management plans.	Environment and Housing Division

Committee	Description	Division
Committee on Agricultural Problems	Environmental problems connected with the application of fertilizers, weed and pest control, manure treatment, and technical means for reducing noise and exhaust fumes of agricultural machinery.	ECE/FAO Agriculture Division
Chemical Industry Committee	Study of air and water pollution caused by the chemical industry.	Industry Division
Conference of European Statisticians	Statistics relating to environmental questions, including statistics on housing, building, planning, health (in cooperation with the WHO); population; tourism; also regional statistics.	Statistical Division
Coal Committee	Selected environmental problems connected with coal mining, restoration of land, and utilization of wastes.	
Committee on Electric Power	Study of problems of air and water pollution, noise, etc., caused by power stations or resulting from transmission of power.	Energy Division
Committee on Gas	Environmental problems connected with gas pipelines and with the underground storage of gas in water-bearing soil.	
Committee on Housing, Building, and Planning	Selected environmental problems in the field of housing; environmental aspects of building materials and construction; selected environmental problems in the field of urban development and physical planning.	Environment and Housing Division
Inland Transport Committee	Specific agreements and recommendations, particularly in the field of road safety; air pollution by motor vehicles; vibration and noise from various vehicles; water pollution arising from transport of toxic or other dangerous substances, from inland water craft, from pipelines, etc.	Transport Division

ernmental objectives, policies, and priorities in the field of environment and governmental organizational methods for dealing with environmental problems.

The discussion papers and agenda for the Prague conference were designed to permit an examination of the major environmental problems from several distinctive perspectives. Two principal themes were emphasized: the socioeconomic aspects of environmental problems and the sources of environmental disfunctions. To avoid the usual media approach (air, water, soil, etc.) the problems were examined by both economic sector and geographic occurrence (problem area). A chart illustrating the preparatory process, with a detailed summary of the major studies and agenda topics, is included in table 2.[31]

Several weeks before the conference a political problem arose concerning the participation of the German Democratic Republic, which was not an ECE member and had not been admitted to the ECE in a consultative capacity. After extensive consultations during the commission session in April 1971 a successful compromise was obtained. The status of the meeting was changed from that of a formal conference to that of a symposium, and arrangements were made for experts from the German Democratic Republic to participate as the guests of the host government.[32]

The topics for discussion at the meeting remained largely unchanged. In attendance were senior officials and experts from most ECE countries and, in a consultative capacity, from Canada, Chile, India, Japan, and Tunisia. Representatives from the UN specialized agencies and 28 other intergovernmental and nongovernmental organizations also attended. The meeting successfully served the original purpose for which it was designed: a thorough exchange of information and views between senior officials and experts on the major environmental problems in the region. As indicated in table 2, a series of general and tentative conclusions were obtained which, in combination with the views expressed at preparatory meetings and in the discussion papers, provided an indication of the major concerns of governments and a basis for developing a comprehensive program for dealing with the environmental problems of the region.

At its 26th session in April 1971 the commission created a new principal subsidiary body: the Senior Advisers to ECE Governments

---

[31] The discussion papers and studies are included with the proceedings of the symposium in the document cited in the preceding footnote.

[32] For a summary of the commission discussions on the participation of the German Democratic Republic see UN Document E/5001, pp. 7-10. For the discussions on the conference see pp. 56-57.

TABLE 2. ECE SYMPOSIUM ON PROBLEMS RELATING TO ENVIRONMENT
MAY 3-10, 1971 (PRAGUE, CZECHOSLOVAKIA)

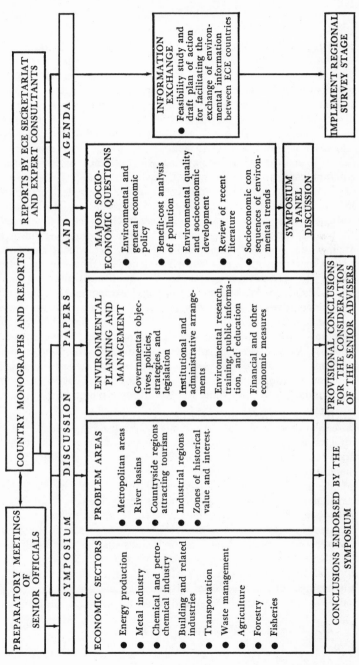

on Environmental Problems.[33] A work program for this body was developed to provide a comprehensive approach to environmental problems in the ECE region, combining broad and continuing policy considerations with specific problem-focused activities reflecting the expressed needs and priorities of the ECE governments. This proposed work program includes the following major items: 1) a survey and assessment of the state of the environment in the ECE region; 2) the examination of national policies, legislation, and institutions; 3) a continuing review of the work related to environment undertaken and proposed by other ECE committees and international organizations; 4) a program for improving the exchange of information on environmental problems between ECE governments; 5) the assessment of alternate fiscal policies and economic incentives designed to maintain or improve the quality of the environment; 6) a study of the existing and possible future effects on foreign trade of national environmental policies; 7) the development of indicators of environmental quality; 8) an intergovernmental seminar, in cooperation with the ECE Committee on Agricultural Problems, on the effect of activities within the agricultural sector on the quality of the environment; 9) assistance in developing international arrangements between contiguous countries to assess and resolve specific international environmental problems; and 10) an intergovernmental seminar on problems concerning the collection, disposal, treatment, and recycling of solid wastes. The program of work was not formally adopted in 1971 as the convening of the first session of the senior advisers was delayed because of unresolved difficulties concerning participation at the meeting, similar to the problems for the Prague symposium.

During 1971 considerable progress was made in the ongoing environmental programs of the various ECE subsidiary bodies and working groups. A limited but representative selection would include: the adoption by the Committee on Water Problems of a set of recommendations to ECE governments on river basin development; the adoption by the Working Party on Air Pollution Problems of a set of recommendations to ECE governments on the control of sulphur oxide emissions; the establishment of a working group by the Committee on Electric Power to study the interrelationship between environment and electric power and to initiate studies on the standardization of permissible values for air pollution, water pollution, and noise at thermal power stations; a successful seminar in Leningrad, held under the auspices of the Steel Committee, on air and water pollution problems associated with the iron and steel industry; the drafting by the

[33] ECE Decision J(XXVI), April 29, 1971.

Inland Transport Committee of a set of regulations on the control of noise and air pollution caused by motor vehicles; the completion of a seminar held in Krasnodar, the Union of Soviet Socialist Republics, under the auspices of the Timber Committee which included the consideration of methods for the protection of soil against erosion caused by logging; and, under the auspices of the Conference of European Statisticians, the launching of a major program to determine the objectives of international work on statistics for environmental studies and policies and, subsequently, to develop detailed proposals concerning the nature, scope, and content of a system of environmental statistics.[34]

Of the many activities planned for the immediate future two merit special mention because of the intersectoral cooperation involved. For the conduct of the first activity three subsidiary bodies — those for Timber, Water, and Agriculture — will combine their respective expertise to examine at a seminar the water pollution problems caused by agricultural and forestry activities. A second seminar, to be convened by the Committee on Housing, Building, and Planning with the support of the Inland Transport Committee, will examine "The Role of Transportation in Urban Planning, Development, and Environment."

What new environmental problems and issues are likely to arise in the ECE region? As one example among many, the executive secretary has suggested in a recent report to ECE governments that:

> The increasing concern of ECE Governments with the human environment also puts in the forefront of attention a number of new issues connected with the development of transport. International co-operation for the prevention of air pollution by noxious gases emitted by motor vehicles needs further intensification and development. Similarly the problem of safety of motor vehicles is of urgent region-wide concern. The prevention of river, lake and coastal pollution is important not only for environmental reasons but also must be taken into account when planning the further growth of transport systems. . . . Growing urbanization confronts ECE Governments with a number of environmental problems particularly in respect to intra-urban distributive transport.[35]

In addition to anticipating new problems there are several ways in which the existing work of the ECE could usefully be extended.

---

[34] For a review of all activities in 1971 related to environmental problems see the recent report to ECE governments by the executive secretary on *The Commission's Activities and Implementation of Priorities* (UN Document E/ECE/817), paragraphs 19-22.

[35] Ibid., paragraphs 81-83.

Certainly one of the most important relates to problems of environment and development, for the experience and knowledge acquired
by European countries concerning environmental problems created
by intensive urban and industrial development could usefully be shared
more extensively not only within Europe[36] but also with other countries
and regions in the world. The former secretary-general of the United
Nations has encouraged such efforts on several occasions.

> It is its integration within the global system that makes it possible
> for ECE to make its contribution to the Organization's efforts to
> extend to the less fortunate countries of the world the knowledge
> and the skills which have flourished, and continue to flourish so
> markedly, in your continent.[37]

As a general conclusion relating the problems of Europe to those
in the rest of the world, U Thant also made the following observation:

> Change is overtaking many quarters nowadays. Those countries
> which were first touched by the industrial revolution are now
> confronted with new problems. And this is happening before this
> revolution has even reached many of the less developed countries
> of the world. Economic growth is beginning to encounter ques-
> tioning and resistance in the affluent societies and will have to
> submit to new social and even ecological criteria. It was timely,
> therefore, that the concern of your Commission should have ex-
> tended to these new areas. The ECE may turn out to be one
> of the most sensitive barometers of new currents in economic and
> social thinking.[38]

V. CONCLUDING REMARKS

In an article assessing the effect of environmental and related
problems on the conduct of intergovernmental relations and, in
particular, their likely impact on international organizations, Eugene
Skolnikoff has observed that:

> In the technologically related societal issues with which we are
> concerned, nations today speak with a plurality of voices. This
> situation is likely to be intensified rather than moderated. Given
> the difficulty of harmonizing the views of more than 120 such
> governments, it may be that we must look to the international level

[36] At the commission session in May 1971 Resolution 1(XXVI) committed
the ECE to devoting greater attention in implementing priority tasks to those
programs of special interest to the least developed members.
[37] U Thant, *Address by the Secretary-General of the United Nations to the
Twenty-Sixth Session of the Economic Commission for Europe* (UN Document
E/5001, Annex 1), p. 4.
[38] Ibid., p. 4.

rather than primarily to the national level, to provide the necessary integration. If so, this would be another way in which the focus of decision making is likely to move toward the international scene.[39]

The existing organizational resources available to governments at the international level are already extensive, but nowhere is the overall pattern of international organizations more complex than at the regional level. A brief consideration of possible future roles and potentialities of the regional economic commissions follows.

A review of existing regional structures within the UN system and their activities relating to development was initiated in 1970.[40] Although the review is not yet complete, governments have indicated, in response to questionnaires which were circulated, that the regional economic commissions should become focal points for UN economic and social programs in the region and that a greater decentralization of these UN activities could be made to them.[41] But even within regions, as within a world system, centralization may not necessarily be an advantage,[42] especially for dealing with environmental problems. The complexity of existing patterns of regional and subregional groups both within and outside the UN system may represent a present difficulty but a long-term asset. For all intergovernmental organizations at the regional or subregional level, comprising a system to the extent that they have identical and overlapping membership, the competition for resources may lead to better planning and justification of the use of those resources. Despite the confrontation and occasional lack of harmony involved the organizational components may as a consequence become more complementary, the choices for action wider, and the organizational system within the region more flexible, viable, and responsive. For those kinds of problems now emerging at regional and global levels, such as environment, it is precisely those properties of an organizational system that are likely to be necessary.[43]

[39] Eugene B. Skolnikoff, "Technology and the Future Growth of International Organizations," *Technology Review,* June 1971 (Vol. 73, No. 8), p. 47.

[40] Following ECOSOC Resolution 1553(XLIX), July 30, 1970.

[41] The views of governments are expressed in the following documents: ECE (UN Document E/ECE/788); ECAFE (UN Document E/CN.11/L.285); ECLA (UN Document E/CN.12/895 and Add. 1 and 2); and the ECA (UN Document E/CN.14/513).

[42] See Walter Balk and James J. Heaphey, "Centralization of the International Civil Service: A Critique," *Public Administration Review,* May/June 1970 (No. 3), pp. 254-257.

[43] The articles by Anthony Judge in *International Associations* over the last several years explore some of these needs and possibilities for future international organizational arrangements. See, for example, "The World Network of Organizations: A Symbol for the 70s," *International Associations,* January 1972 (24th Year, No. 1), pp. 18-24.

In support of these attributes and the goals of the system the role and work of the regional economic commissions can be constructively extended in several ways in order to deal effectively with environmental problems within the respective regions. The commissions, for example, already combine in one structure a comprehensive set of intergovernmental committees of senior officials and experts for particular economic sectors and problem areas. This committee structure, particularly if complemented by the addition of an intergovernmental committee of senior officials responsible for dealing with environmental problems in their respective countries, can be effectively used for developing, in cooperation with the regional and sectoral units of other international organizations, a comprehensive program and priorities for environmental concerns to be assessed at the annual commission meetings for its overall priority relative to other social and economic problems in the region. A comprehensive plan for environmental problems in the various regions is certainly needed and would be helpful to committees and other international organizations in determining their own priorities within their respective economic, social, and other sectors. *The practical value and usefulness of such a plan would vary directly with the amount of intergovernmental and interagency cooperation involved in developing it.* The advice and assistance of the UN specialized agencies, in particular, with their established competence and experience in specific fields, would be essential.

The regional economic commissions may also make unique contributions with respect to subregional organizations and environmental problems. They could, for example, attempt to obtain agreement for applying on a region-wide basis some of the effective programs developed by subregional organizations for dealing with environmental problems. There are also environmental problems which occur at the subregional level between contiguous countries which do not belong to the same subregional organizations. In such cases the good offices and experience of the regional commissions could be used as a means of obtaining international agreements for solving them.

A further consideration is that the terms of reference and rules of procedure for regional economic commissions contain specific provisions for cooperation with the many nongovernmental organizations. Although no fundamental change would be required, there are for environmental problems many practical advantages in establishing close and more systematic relations with these organizations.[44]

[44] It has been suggested that "the time lag between detection of, and action on, a growing problem by a non-political body and recognition of a problem by political bodies may be precisely the difference between a minor problem requiring few resources and a major problem requiring much more resources." See Anthony Judge, "Planning for the 1960s in the 1970s," *International Associations,* 1970 (22nd Year, No. 3), p. 140.

In conclusion, it is apparent that for dealing with *specific* environmental problems at the regional and subregional levels there are many existing organizational alternatives available to governments. But for developing comprehensive regional approaches and programs for problems of the environment there is at present one alternative: the regional economic commissions of the United Nations.

INTERNATIONAL INSTITUTIONS FOR ENVIRONMENTAL MANAGEMENT

Gordon J. MacDonald

GORDON J. MACDONALD is a member of the Council on Environmental Quality in the Executive Office of the President, Washington.

The degradation of the human environment is a worldwide problem which has increasingly led to worldwide concern. All countries, whether rich or poor, young or old, irrespective of political and economic institutions, are finding that they must understand and improve the relationships between man's activities and the total environmental system. The recognition that the planet's resources and its capacities to absorb waste are definitely limited raises important questions as to how to approach solutions in a way that not only safeguards legitimate national interests but in the long run protects and enhances those resources essential to the future welfare of all states.

In examining possible international institutional mechanisms it is crucial from the beginning to recognize several characteristics of environmental problems. Typically, such problems are enormously complex, having their origins rooted in the political, economic, and social structures of individual countries. Solutions often will depend on major reform of national institutions. Such restructuring cannot be accomplished overnight. Environmental problems will be with us for many years, and any institutional approach must take into account the long time scales involved for problem definition and solution. Second, there are great gaps in our scientific and technical knowledge of problems and potential solutions. In the face of uncertainty temporary measures may have to be taken that later may be drastically altered. The constantly changing perception of cause and effect relations requires that while environmental questions may need a long time for solution, the institutional base must provide sufficient flexibility to adjust to new knowledge. Many environmental values, particularly those not associated with human health, depend on the peculiar cultural history of the society. A set of values appropriate to one country may be wholly irrelevant in a different setting. In addition to stability and flexibility any international mechanisms for environmental improvement should provide for different national views of what the quality of life really means. Finally, abstract discussion of institutional innovation is likely to be fruitless unless some analysis of the kinds of environmental problems is undertaken. Environmental quality cannot simply be equated to pollution control; any institutional framework should be responsive to actual environmental needs.

There exists today within the United Nations and in other contexts a rich variety of organizations, many of which have been involved in environmental problems of one sort or another for many years. Some of these organizations involve states on a global basis, others on a regional level, and some involve only two neighboring states. In recent times it has become fashionable to criticize certain of these organizations for their bureaucratic ways, their incapacity for arriving at decisions, their massive sluggishness, and their remoteness from the real problems as seen by governments. Because of these views there exists a great temptation to propose the establishment of new institutions designed to deal with newly perceived problems. I believe that for the environment this temptation must be resisted strongly. New organizations have been established in the past just because of alleged deficiencies in existing bodies, and these new groups have soon come under fire for failings attributed to previously existing organizations. Problems of environment are all-pervasive, and to remove environmental responsibility from existing bodies would not only weaken current efforts but deny the basic concept of the complex dependence of man's surroundings on all of his activities. The creation of new, independent institutions to deal with environmental problems would be justified only if it could be established that the existing, even if poorly functioning, mechanism did not have and was incapable of developing the capacity to deal with new responsibilities. Indeed, it is my view that awareness of the environment offers an opportunity to strengthen existing efforts directed not only toward those problems of immediate environmental concern but also toward the vast array of related issues. In such a strengthening one could achieve not only a greater effectiveness of international organizations but also an opportunity to restore public confidence in these bodies.

I. CATEGORIES OF ENVIRONMENTAL PROBLEMS

Environment encompasses such a wide variety of concerns that it is helpful to classify these in broad categories. The classification cannot be clear-cut because the basic premise of ecology is that everything is linked, however tenuously, with everything else. For present purposes four major categories appear sufficient: pollution, the economic consequences of environmental controls, the development of natural resources, both renewable and nonrenewable, and the broad question of land use with particular reference to problems of rapid urbanization.

By pollution I mean those problems created when the capacity of natural systems to dispose of waste produced by man's activities becomes overtaxed. The effects of pollution are usually thought of in terms of public health, but pollution can also endanger much more controversial values such as those associated with amenities and recreation. Pollution control costs money. Additional costs can put strains, even if temporary ones, on the internal economies of countries. Differing methods of assigning pollution control costs and setting product standards may give rise to dislocations between trading states. Environmental control measures can give rise to changing demands for natural resources, and these changes can have a major economic impact. The development of natural resources, whether these be water, mineral, or living resources such as fish and forests, can bring about major ecological changes, some of which may be irreversible. Great shifts in the use of land and in the distribution of population create difficulties by themselves and exacerbate problems of pollution, economic adjustments, and resource development. A recurring theme in this article is that the great diversity of environmental problems, having a myriad of international implications, makes it clear that there can be no single, one-shot answer to the question of how best to organize internationally. Rather, we should build on the strengths of existing institutions, recognizing that environmental considerations will play a larger role in decisionmaking in a wide variety of problem areas.

Pollution Control

Man releases directly, through intended discharges, or indirectly, for example, through fuel combustion, a vast variety of chemical elements and compounds. Some of these, in high enough concentration, may be directly injurious to human health or to other living species. Others may form new, potentially dangerous compounds or be concentrated in biological processes. Still others may react with natural constituents to bring about potentially undesirable changes in the overall system. Given these complexities, it is helpful to partially order the pollutants by considering their lifetime or resident time in air, water, or land, where they are introduced, and what the potential effects are. Once we do so, it becomes clearer which problems are best treated by bilateral, regional, or worldwide institutions.

If the resident time for a potentially harmful pollutant is long compared with the mixing times in the medium, either the atmosphere or a body or water, then the pollutant will have the chance to travel considerable distance and in so doing may cross national borders or enter into a clearly international area. If the resident time is long enough, the pollutant can become worldwide in its distribution. Table 1 illustrates this notion. The entries in the table are intended to be illustrative and certainly not all-inclusive. The list of potential pollutants is virtually endless, and in many cases the applicable resident time is not known.

Sulfur dioxide, once introduced into the atmosphere, has an average lifetime in the atmosphere, before being removed by some form of

TABLE 1. RESIDENT TIMES OF REPRESENTATIVE POLLUTANTS IN AIR AND WATER

Pollutant	Place of Introduction	Resident Time
Atmospheric		
Sulfur dioxide	Ground level	Four-eight days
Hydrocarbons	Ground level	———
Carbon dioxide	Ground level	About two years
Carbon monoxide	Ground level	About one year
Particulate matter	Ground level	Hours to days
	Stratosphere	One-two years
Water	Ground level	About one week
	Stratosphere	One-two years
Oxides of nitrogen	Ground level	Three-four days
	Stratosphere	One-two years
Bodies of water		
Oil	Nearshore	Days to weeks
	Open water	Can be long
Chlorinated hydrocarbons	Open water	Can be long due to biologic uptake
Heavy metals	Open water	Can be long due to biologic uptake

precipitation, of four to eight days. During such a time normal atmospheric movements will carry the sulfur dioxide distances of a few hundred to 1000 or 2000 miles. In areas where countries are in close proximity sulfur dioxide in high enough concentration can lead to transnational pollution. The resident time for sulfur dioxide is too short for the pollutant to be carried across oceanic distances, so this is not a pollutant requiring global action. However, in certain areas it can become of regional concern.

At present it would seem that sulfur dioxide presents a special problem to the North European countries. Concentrations have not reached such levels as to be of regional interest in other industrialized areas of the world. However, reports of increasing acidity of precipitation and soil as well as damage to forests in the Scandinavian countries indicate that this is a transnational pollution problem requiring regional attention. In Europe a number of international organizations could play a role in dealing with the possible transport of sulfur oxides from countries such as Belgium, the Federal Republic of Germany (West Germany), the German Democratic Republic (East Germany), the Netherlands, and the United Kingdom into the Nordic regions as well as from one highly industrialized country to another. The Organisation for Economic Co-operation and Development (OECD) has for many years provided a forum for the exchange of views on national research programs. The OECD, under its Environment Committee, has undertaken a study of transnational pollution by sulfur oxide. In this work the OECD will be drawing upon national competencies. However, the OECD's strengths in analysis, and particularly economic analysis, do not necessarily make it an appropriate forum for drawing up regional regulations with respect to air pollution. The Economic Commission for Europe (ECE) has the merit of including East European countries, presumably at some time including East Germany. It could serve as a basis for dealing with regional air pollution problems. Alternatively, a new regional grouping consisting only of directly affected countries might provide a faster moving and more effective method of dealing with regulatory procedures as contrasted with research efforts.

Hydrocarbons and oxides of nitrogen can react under the influence of solar radiation to form smog. In general this pollutant is confined locally and will not give rise to international concerns except in border cities. However, nitrogen oxides as well as water vapor and particulate matter, when discharged into the stratosphere by aircraft flying in this medium, remain there for at least a year. In this time these pollutants are dispersed at least through the hemisphere in which they were introduced and possibly globally. These pollutants may undergo reactions with the normal constituents of the stratosphere that result in potentially harmful effects, such as increased surface dosage of ultraviolet radiation resulting from a decreased ozone content in the stratosphere. Such a result, with its potential effects on man's health as well as on vegetation, would be of interest to all countries. Thus, stratospheric pollution would be a truly international concern even though only a few states actually fly supersonic aircraft in the stratosphere.

A number of existing United Nations organizations could play a role in the management of stratospheric pollution. The World Meteorological Organization (WMO) could bring together research results from various national programs as well as coordinate the monitoring of conditions in the high atmosphere. The International Civil Aviation Organization (ICAO), with current responsibilities in the development of standards and recommended practices, could assume the responsibility for negotiating whatever regulations would seem appropriate for governing civil aircraft operations in the stratosphere, drawing upon the research results brought together by the WMO.

Carbon dioxide has a long resident time in the lower atmosphere and is well mixed. Increasing the carbon dioxide content of the atmosphere can lead to a warming of the atmosphere. The potential climatic effects would affect all countries. Carbon monoxide also has a long lifetime, but as yet the long-term effects of carbon monoxide at low concentrations have not been identified. It would seem appropriate for the WMO to play a role in coordinating research and monitoring efforts on both gases on a worldwide basis.

In bodies of water oil, if spilled or dumped nearshore, can be carried by tides and currents onshore where it becomes a problem of beach, shore, and facility cleanup. In general this will be a national problem except when two countries border on or share a body of water, such as Iran and the Union of Soviet Socialist Republics on the Caspian Sea or Canada and the United States on the Great Lakes. In these cases regulatory policies for control and contingency plans for cleanup can be coordinated or developed jointly by the affected countries.

On the open ocean oil or its derivative hydrocarbons can have a long lifetime. The hydrocarbons can enter the food chain and affect an international resource, the world's fisheries. The oil can also be carried substantial distances by ocean currents to be deposited on the shores of countries that may or may not engage in the overseas transport of oil. Clearly, open-ocean oil pollution can affect many countries and is probably best dealt with by a truly international organization. In particular the Intergovernmental Maritime Consultative Organization (IMCO) of the UN family has taken the lead in negotiation of international agreements with respect to equipment specification and operating procedures for tankers. At the same time certain regions may find themselves particularly vulnerable to deliberate or accidental spills, and whatever international agreements are reached may need to be supplemented by regional agreements. For example, the Southeast Asian countries of Cambodia, Indonesia, Malaysia, the Philippines, the Republic of Vietnam (South Vietnam), and Thailand border on waters heavily traveled by tankers as well as continental shelf areas rapidly undergoing exploration and development. The Environmental Control Organization (ECO) proposed by Singapore and possibly involving at least some of these Southeast

Asian countries could provide the regional framework to reach whatever special regional agreements are needed under the umbrella of international agreement, negotiated through IMCO. Heavy metals and chlorinated hydrocarbons illustrate the problems of controlling potentially toxic materials that enter the open oceans in a variety of ways. Such compounds are disposed of in the high seas by actual dumping from ships and barges. However, the quantities entering international waters in this way are small compared with the amounts flowing into the oceans from the rivers draining continental areas. Atmospheric transport can also contribute significantly to the influx of certain compounds and elements. For example, some coal and oil contain appreciable concentrations of mercury which volatilize on combustion and can be transported to the oceans.

Both heavy metals and chlorinated hydrocarbons can enter the food chain and become widely distributed through the ocean by means of biologic action and ocean currents. In fact, ocean areas in the vicinity of heavily industrialized countries not requiring strict effluent limitations will receive heavier loads of heavy metals than open oceans far from industry. The control of toxic discharges into enclosed or semi-enclosed bodies of water presents special problems since the natural flushing times may be quite long. Control of river runoff into such regions as the North, the Baltic, the Mediterranean, and the Black Seas will certainly require regional cooperation. Similarly, ocean areas adjacent to countries where pesticides are heavily employed in support of agriculture and malaria control will bear heavier burdens of chlorinated hydrocarbons than, for example, the remoter regions in the Pacific Ocean. Thus, the fishing industry in the Indian Ocean will in the long run depend on actions taken by those countries bordering on the ocean.

The International Joint Commission (IJC), established by the Boundary Waters Treaty of 1909 between Canada and the United States, illustrates how a regional water problem, that of the Great Lakes, can be dealt with by the countries involved. The IJC consists of six commissioners, three appointed by each government, and a small secretariat. The treaty provides that the governments can refer matters to the IJC for study and report. Indeed, as early as 1920 both governments asked the IJC to prepare appropriate measures to regulate pollution of the boundary waters. Unfortunately, the proposals of the IJC were not negotiated successfully. In recent years the IJC has been far more active as both governments have become increasingly concerned about the conditions in the Great Lakes. In 1964 the United States and Canada asked the IJC to study the pollution of Lake Erie, Lake Ontario, and the international section of the St. Lawrence River and recommend appropriate measures for pollution control. Prior to the issuance in late 1970 of the final IJC report the United States and Canada met at the ministerial level to consider how the two governments could deal with the expected IJC recommendations. This meeting led to the establishment of ten joint working groups which examined in detail such problems as allowable phosphate loadings, joint contingency planning for oil spills, controls on the handling of hazardous material on the lakes and at lake ports, control of pollution from pesticides, joint research, etc. These reports and recommendations were accepted in principle by the two governments at a meeting in June 1971 between the Canadian minister of foreign affairs and the chairman of the Council on Environmental Quality. Detailed negotiations on the exact form of an agreement began in December 1971, and it is expected that these, unlike the previous negotiations, will be concluded successfully.

A special problem involving the oceans is the dumping of waste on the high seas. Control of such practices can probably best be achieved through national regulatory efforts at the ports of loading. Otherwise, problems of surveillance, to say nothing of enforcement in the international regime, become unmanageable. The control of the use of oceans for the deliberate disposal of matter at sea could best be negotiated through IMCO. This would appear to be particularly appropriate because of IMCO's role in developing agreements regarding the control of deliberate spills of oil. Alternatively, negotiations could be carried out under the auspices of the United Nations law of the sea conference presently scheduled for 1973. This conference will also have to deal with the technically difficult area of the control of pollution associated with resource development. The massive oil spill in the Persian Gulf in December 1971 illustrates some of the problems. An Iranian-based company with international participation was drilling from an Italian-owned rig when the blowout occurred. The oil slick threatened not only Iranian beaches but also the southern shores of the gulf, including several Arabian states.

Table 2 summarizes the situation with respect to several representative pollutants. In all cases responsibilities exist within agencies with respect to research, monitoring, exchange of information, and fostering of negotiations. The international organizations do not in general set standards though they encourage countries to arrive at agreed upon standards. For example, through the Codex Alimentarius, set up jointly by the Food and Agriculture Organization (FAO) and the World Health Organization (WHO), countries set maximum allowable residues for foodstuffs entering into international commerce. In general international organizations do not have responsibility for enforcement, nor do they have the means to enforce any agreed upon

TABLE 2.   REPRESENTATIVE PROBLEM AREAS AND INTERNATIONAL
ORGANIZATIONS

Problem Area	International Organization
Stratospheric pollution by civil aircraft	WMO - meteorological research, monitoring ICAO - regulations WHO - health effects research
Carbon dioxide	WMO - research, monitoring
Oil	IMCO - regulations and safety standards Regional organizations - special problems in such areas as North Sea, Mediterranean Sea, Persian Gulf, and Straits of Malacca
Heavy metals in oceans	IMCO - regulations WHO - health effects IOCᵃ - research FAO - fishery aspects Regional organizations

ᵃ The IOC is the Intergovernmental Oceanographic Commission.

regulation. The impotence of international regulatory efforts is well illustrated by the failure of the International Whaling Commission in regulating the taking of whales. In environment, as in other areas, enforcement of regulatory measures will have to remain the responsibility of states. In the present stage of development of international institutions it would be unrealistic to assume that these could take on and enforce internationally agreed upon standards or procedures. Rather, international organizations should encourage states to take the required legislative and enforcement actions.

One feature of the current and expected situation that may require institutional innovation is the fact that several of the UN specialized agencies will have some responsibility in the same problem area. The situation is not unlike that found in national governments. No matter how much environmental responsibility is centralized the pervasive nature of the problems implies the need for coordination at least at the policy level between departments or agencies. As environmental concern in the international arena matures, there may be a need for policy coordination between the specialized agencies. At present the heads of the specialized agencies form an Administrative Committee on Coordination (ACC). It is unlikely that such a group, with individuals representing the interests of their respective agencies, can succeed in developing coordinated programs. At least in other national context committees, equals tend to negotiate out compromise positions rather than to formulate policy that would guide agency activities. The coordination function could be carried out by a small secretariat lodged high in the UN structure, reporting directly to the secretary-general. Even at this level, however, coordination will be far from easy. The specialized agencies, with their massive bureaucracies and their independent budgets, are unlikely to be swayed by persuasion by a coordinating group unless that group has the strong backing of a secretary-general who takes a personal interest in its work. However small the chance of success of a coordinating group, the need is clear. For without close cooperation the research fostered by the WMO on the stratosphere may not meet the needs of ICAO in developing regulations, or the regulatory efforts of the FAO/WHO Codex Alimentarius may conflict with regulations negotiated by such a group as IMCO to control ocean dumping.

In summary, measures required to control various pollutants will depend on a variety of factors such as the medium involved, dose-effect relationships, and the resident time in the medium as well as the existing institutional framework. Given these complexities and the realities of international organizations, any suggestion of a single overall international pollution control agency must be viewed with great caution. Alternatively, it would seem best to work within the charter of existing agencies. For technical and regulatory issues of global concern the best place for action is a UN specialized agency. Since the problem of overlapping jurisdiction is bound to arise, a small coordination group at the secretary-general level could serve a useful function. Many environmental problems are of a strong regional character. For these such existing groupings as the ECE would be most appropriate for development of consistent regulatory practices though the very nature of the specific environmental problem (e.g., sulfur dioxide) may suggest a special grouping of countries. In any case responsibility for enforcement will continue to be a national responsibility with international organizations providing an oversight and review function.

Economic Consequences of Environmental Measures

The pollution control measures discussed above will require expenditures; in some industries these will be substantial. The additional cost of production due to pollution control measures will be reflected in the price of the goods. If the goods enter into international commerce, national environmental measures can lead to commercial advantages or disadvantages. Clearly, if the disruption to international trade is to be kept at a minimum, international mechanisms must be developed whereby the commercial consequences of environmental policies are not only understood but the basis is also provided for reaching needed agreements.

Environmental and economic policies cannot be separated. For example, in the United States many environmental problems stem from the fundamental failure of the economic system to take into account real environmental costs. Consumer demand for various products, for instance, is shaped by the prices of the products. When full production costs are included in the prices of the final products, the market, at least in theory, will allocate resources efficiently. However, if all the costs are not included (e.g., the cost to society of environmental degradation), the prices of products are consequently too low. This underpricing results in excessive consumption. Fewer of these products would be produced or bought if all costs were fully reflected in the final price.

Moreover, the common-property resources, such as air and water, do not enter completely into the market exchange. They are used as free "dumps" for the leftovers of production and consumption. Because there is little or no penalty attached to such dumping the environment is continually degraded. Yet this indiscriminate dumping is not in fact free. It extracts great social cost which comes at a high price to the country.

Basically, countries in the noncommunist world have three options. They can continue to permit relatively uncontrolled pollution. The resulting social cost, such as that associated with health services, would be borne by the general population either through increased taxes or increased personal expenditures. Economically, such a policy would lead to an inefficient use of resources as goods produced would not bear the full costs of production. A second policy option would be for governments to subsidize industries directly by providing grants for pollution control equipment. Such a policy would require higher levels of taxation, only part of which would fall on the polluting industry. The price of goods would reflect only in small part the total cost. Finally, governments could require that the polluter pay the total cost either by requiring unsubsidized control equipment or by charging for the previously free use of air, water, and land resources. In fact, governments of Western industrialized countries today follow policies that combine the notions of free dumping, subsidy, and payment by the polluter. In the United States the major burden falls on the polluter in that he has to install equipment to meet standards, but there are provisions for fast depreciation of equipment and exemptions for certain sales and land taxes. One can imagine rapid amortization and investment credits for research and development on new pollution control processes, as for equipment or services needed to encourage recycling. These are subsidies even if partly hidden. Further, there are still overall social costs being carried by the general public in the form of taxes for increased social services required by pollution and personal expenditures. The basic issue, however, is the mix of these policies. A country following the pure subsidy route would in effect have an export subsidy with respect to countries that adopt primarily the polluter-should-pay principle.

The United States has been attempting through the OECD to achieve agreement on the assignment of environmental use costs. The OECD brings together the major Western industrialized countries, the major trading partners, and, not coincidentally, the major polluters. Not only is Western Europe represented but also Australia, Canada, Japan, and the United States. Further, the OECD has earned for itself the reputation for serious work in bringing together governmental administrators and experts to exchange information on national policies and research programs. Through the creation of an Environment Committee it has strengthened itself to deal with the economic aspects of environmental issues. The OECD thus seems well suited for dealing with environmentally related economic issues of concern to Western industrialized countries. Such an assignment of responsibility leaves open the problems of trade involving less developed countries (LDCs) and the communist bloc, points to which I will return.

It should be recognized that even if there is general international agreement that product prices shall reflect environmental use costs, shifts in international trade patterns will only be reduced but not eliminated. Countries will in all probability continue favored tax treatment for pollution control costs and will adopt other economic policies favoring the reduction of social costs. Mechanisms should be developed, preferably through the OECD, to notify trading partners of such practices. A country which believes it is disadvantaged through these practices could then raise the issue either directly with the country involved or through the General Agreement on Tariffs and Trade (GATT). In this way serious discrepancies in policies could be identified at an early stage and long-term problems avoided.

Trade patterns will also be influenced by the fact that different countries will have, for a variety of reasons, differences in product mix, absolute levels of production, climatological and topographic factors, and different environmental use costs for the production of goods traded internationally. Therefore, the terms of trade for products that involve pollution will turn in favor of countries with low environmental use costs. The resulting arrangement of trade and investment would tend to concentrate production where environmental use costs are lowest. This arrangement would be economically efficient provided individual countries do not attempt to artificially protect domestic industries adversely affected by adopting such measures as export subsidies and import taxes. The institution of such protective measures could be minimized through regular consultation in the OECD.

Because of the greatly differing environmental and institutional conditions existing within states it is unlikely that agreements can be reached on international standards whether these be limitations on effluents or ambient standards of quality of air and water. For example, the enforcement of high standards in a country with high absorptive capacity for pollutants, or little polluting activity, may be extravagant in the sense that the same resources applied in another country would produce greater benefits. Yet, even if agreement is reached on the general assessment of environmental use costs and a notification procedure developed for exceptions, distortions in trade could result if trading partners instituted radically different national standards. The chances of this happening can be minimized through consultation and agreement on what in the United States are called criteria. Criteria documents describe the scientific evidence on dose-effect relationships of specific pollutants, the methods of sampling and measurement, the required monitoring system, etc. International agreements on criteria updated in time could be used by states in setting national standards. In this way possible trade distortions that might arise, for example, from differing methods of measuring sulfur dioxide in the atmosphere, could be reduced. Active work toward reaching internationally agreed upon criteria is underway in the WHO and in the Committee on the Challenges of Modern Society (CCMS) of the North Atlantic Treaty Organization (NATO). This effort could be complemented by a similar undertaking in the OECD, drawing on the work of the CCMS and the WHO, with a particular emphasis on understanding the economic consequences of varying standards based on agreed upon criteria.

International trade questions are raised when final products that produce pollution enter into international commerce. When the use of the products involves pollution and the price of the goods incorporates the relevant environmental use costs, international differences in these costs will give rise to changes in international trade and investment patterns. First, the price of the product or, more accurately, the consumer's cost of using it will change by different amounts in the various countries. Second, countries which produce the goods may differ in their ability to adapt to any given change in costs; for example, one country may be able to produce auto exhaust devices more cheaply than another. The prospect of such changes in international trade patterns may induce countries to create trade barriers or distortions. These may include subsidies to adversely affected export industries and tariffs on imports that meet use standards more cheaply than do domestic products. In these cases the same problems for international trade policy are raised as for production process pollution, namely, whether international agreement to forestall such trade barriers is desirable. The problem is intensified by the fact that

GATT inadequately covers nontariff distortions. One problem that may be particularly important in the case of consumer goods concerns the use of product standards as disguised nontariff barriers. For example, one country may impose a standard more easily met by home producers than by foreign producers. Indeed, some representatives of foreign automotive industries have voiced concern that the congressionally mandated United States automotive emission standards are disguised barriers since the larger American engines may have an easier time meeting the standards. As long as a standard is applied uniformly to both domestic and foreign products and is designed to minimize use costs, the barrier it creates to imports would not appear to create an artificial distortion in trade patterns. However, an excessively strict standard might be introduced largely to cut off imports. The problems for trade policy here would be how the substantively discriminatory standard could be distinguished from the nondiscriminatory standard and how an international trade policy that sought to forestall trade barriers could be adapted to the prevention of the discriminatory standards.

Again it would appear that the OECD with its more homogeneous membership could provide the institutional base for a notification procedure on product standards. As possible distorting measures are identified, negotiations could be entered into between the affected parties, probably under the aegis of GATT. If a new round of GATT negotiations is entered into, specific attention should be paid to nontariff trade barriers and particularly environmentally related barriers.

Environmental measures other than those involving strictly product standards or process standards can have an international economic impact. An important example is the decision taken by the United States automotive industry to produce low-compression engines capable of running on low-octane gasoline that does not require a lead additive. Technical developments make it appear that control devices required to meet the 1975-1976 emission standards will be poisoned by leaded gasoline. This implies that for cars beyond model years 1974, or possibly earlier, nonleaded gasoline must be available if the car is to operate. The United States petroleum industry is in the process of providing refining and distribution facilities to make nonleaded gas available. The problem arises in neighboring countries. For example, unless unleaded gas is made available in Mexico through the national company, Pemex, tourist travel in American automobiles will be discouraged and eventually made impossible. Thus, a policy decision made in one country can have serious economic repercussions in another. In this case the United States government opened discussions on a government-to-government basis with a view to presenting the rationale of the American policy as well as the expected longer term implications. In Europe, with its closer borders and the possibility of many states taking measures that are incompatible, the problem is far more serious. Here it would appear that the ECE might very well be the appropriate forum to initiate discussion leading to the adoption of comparable policies. The ECE has made progress in both Western and Eastern Europe toward adoption of common highway signs, and discussions within the ECE have been helpful in standardization in other areas.

The problem of lead in gasoline is not limited solely to transboundary automobile traffic. The United States measures will lower the overall demand for lead in the international market. The balance of payments of certain LDCs, Bolivia for example, will be adversely affected. In issues of this sort the UN regional economic commissions could play a role in providing for consultations or discussions of the economic consequence of environmental measures. Unlike the OECD and the ECE, the other regional commissions bring together countries with greatly differing levels of economic development, institutional bases, and interests in foreign trade. Despite these impediments the regional commissions could play a very helpful role in identifying problems at an early stage and providing for discussions between LDCs and the more industrialized countries. Alternatively, other regional organizations, for example, in the Western Hemisphere the Inter-American Economic and Social Council (IA-ECOSOC) of the Organization of American States (OAS), could play the leadership role in addressing the difficult issues linking environment with international trade.

I have discussed the economic consequences of environmental measures in some detail both because of the intrinsic importance of the subject to international affairs and because of the need to emphasize the pervasive nature of environmental measures. Environmental actions taken at a national level can have far-reaching international implications that may not be clearly perceived at the time of the action. Because of this and the inherent complexity of environmental economic issues it is essential to maintain a diverse and flexible institutional approach. Assignment of overall responsibility to any one organization would certainly be premature if not basically unsound. For special problems that might arise between two major trading states, for example, the United States and Japan, bilateral discussions at an appropriately high level, such as have been instituted between these two countries, would seem most appropriate. For economic issues affecting the important trading states of the noncommunist world the OECD, in terms of both representation and capabilities, forms the most important forum. Issues such as assessment of pollution control cost, the development of internationally agreed upon criteria, and nontariff trade barriers arising from product standards could all be productively discussed within the OECD. Specific trade issues could be taken to GATT, and certainly any future round of negotiations on tariffs and trade should include references to environmental measures. On economic questions involving East and West the ECE would appear to offer a suitable forum for discussion, and the other regional commissions could play a role in furthering consultations between the industrialized world and the LDCs. While such a broad assignment of responsibility may fail to achieve organizational neatness, it is important to maintain a responsive and flexible approach to the complex economic problems which we only imperfectly understand.

Natural Resources

The issues linking the development of natural resources and the environment are even more complex and controversial than environmental economic issues. Further, the institutional basis for action in the international arena is a good deal less adequate. In part the complexity arises from the traditional view that a country's resources are part of the national heritage to be used in advancing national purposes. Exploitation of natural resources is for the most part the responsibility of either nationalized enterprises or giant private corporations which wield great political power. The worldwide petroleum industry well illustrates the problems inherent in achieving international agreements with regard to natural resource management. The LDCs together with the large land-mass countries—Australia, Canada, and the United States—provide the noncommunist world's bulk of natural resources. In the past there has been relatively little international consideration of resource management problems. However, it would appear to be in the interest of both the LDCs and the industrialized world that the world's natural resources be managed in an environmentally sound fashion. The economic development of many of the LDCs depends on the wise exploitation of their natural wealth while the industrialized countries must, for the most part, rely on the LDCs for needed raw materials.

Natural resource problems can usefully be discussed under the headings of changing resource needs as a result of environmental measures, the planning for and the exploitation of natural resources, and the role of national and international assistance agencies. The first largely involves economic issues while the latter two are closely related in that assistance agencies have played an important role in the exploitation of the developing world's natural resources.

Environmental measures undertaken nationally are sure to influence trade and investment in resources and resource development. I have already noted the example of the gradual phasing out of lead in gasoline and the possible impact on the world's lead market. Of even greater potential importance are the limitations being placed by various countries on the emissions of certain pollutants, particularly sulfur dioxide. In the United States two federal measures and a variety of local ordinances illustrate the controls being exercised. The administrator of the Environmental Protection Agency, under the National Air Quality Standards Act of 1970, has set a national ambient air standard for maximum levels of sulfur dioxide. Under the same act the administrator also has set effluent limits of sulfur dioxide at new electric power plants. At the same time localities have taken action to limit the sulfur content of fuels burned within their area of jurisdiction. Japan, Sweden, and other industrialized countries are taking similar regulatory steps. These actions will put increasing pressure on the supply of low-sulfur residual fuel oil and natural gas; the removal of sulfur dioxide from the stack gases is still in the developmental stage as is the large-scale desulfurization of coal, and low-sulfur coal is in short supply.

Residual fuel oil is what is left over after refining crude oil to make gasoline, jet fuel, and other light distillates. Low-sulfur residual is particularly attractive to power-plant operators since it can be used directly or after partial desulfurization. However, because of the higher profitability of the lighter fuels United States production has supplied a decreasing percentage of residual, the vast bulk of heating oil being imported. International problems arise both because of the overall demand for low-sulfur fuels and because the sulfur content of the crude and the residual varies with geographic area. Indonesian, North African, and Nigerian oil is low in sulfur while that from the Persian Gulf is higher. Venezuelan oil is quite high in sulfur. In the past Venezuela has supplied about 40 percent of the residual demand in the United States. Even with construction of additional desulfurization facilities for Venezuelan oil this percentage will almost certainly decrease as the demand for low-sulfur residual continues to grow.

Another alternative to low-sulfur residual is natural gas. Limitation of domestic supply probably does not make it a viable alternative for the United States; consideration is being given to a major import program of liquified natural gas from such countries as Algeria.

A number of policy issues are raised as the pressure for low-sulfur fuels increases. For the United States an important issue is that of the import quotas and the ways in which they should be altered in view of new demands regarding this resource. A more general issue is how disruptions to patterns of trade and investment can be minimized as more countries follow disparate policies with respect to the use of lower sulfur fuels. The issue is complicated by the fact that many of the producer companies in the LDCs are subsidiaries in whole or in part of companies in the consuming states. Two approaches would seem worthwhile. Consultations between the consuming states as to extrapolated requirements and planned sources of supply may lessen the possibility of gross distortions. For example, Japan has an extensive program for contracting for its raw materials as much as 25 years into the future while the United States has no overall plan to meet its future resource needs. Another problem in which consultation within the regional economic commissions may be helpful is that the higher sulfur fuels may be channeled into the more rapidly developing LDCs because of the lower price of such fuels and the lack of regulatory mechanisms in the LDCs. Heavy use of such fuels could put additional burdens on the health services of the countries using high-sulfur fuels. A second approach would be the development of cooperative research efforts among the industrialized countries in such areas as stack gas removal and desulfurization of fuels. Intensive activities are underway in a number of countries, and coordinated efforts could reduce the time in which the reliance was principally on fuels naturally low in sulfur.

The resource implications of sulfur dioxide controls are not confined to petroleum, coal, and natural gas. For example, the United States and Mexico have substantial industries producing elemental sulfur by the Frasch process. As sulfur is produced in very large quanties as a by-product of stack gas cleanup and fuel desulfurization, the competitive position of elemental sulfur production will be put at a disadvantage. Again, early consultation between affected countries can go far to ease transitional problems.

The problems of solids disposal and the need to conserve energy and water resources will in the future lead countries such as the United States to policies that promote the recycling of more materials. At present, in the United States the reuse of waste materials is discouraged by tax policies, particularly the depletion allowance which encourages virgin material exploration and extraction. This tax advantage allows a direct offset against gross sales at a fixed percentage rate independent of the actual cost associated with the production of the virgin materials. In most cases this depletion far exceeds the cost depreciation which would be allowed without this special provision.

The substitution of waste materials for virgin materials has a number of indirect effects as well as the direct effect of reducing the social cost of solid waste collection and disposal. The shift, for example, from iron ore to scrap metal will result in savings in water use and energy as well as reductions in airborne pollutants and solid waste. Because of these savings the United States will be adopting tax and other policies which will place waste materials in a competitive position with respect to raw materials. Even today, without special provision for waste materials, increasing fractions of such metals as copper and lead are recycled. As new measures come into effect, there will be decreased demand for resources that go into the production of steel, paper, textiles, glass, and rubber. Transitional disruption can be minimized through advance consultation either directly with the countries involved or through the regional economic commissions.

Sulfur oxide controls and recycling are but two of a number of environmental improvement policies that can have a substantial impact on resource development around the world. What is needed to avoid confrontation is an understanding of these interrelationships and the development of appropriate mechanisms of consultation. The regional UN economic commissions could play an important role. For example, the Economic Commission for Latin America (ECLA) has undertaken a study of the energy needs of Latin America. The study, however, follows classical economic lines and does not take up environmental issues. Regional commissions, if they are to take the lead in this area, will have to develop increased awareness and expertise on the many links between environmental, resource, and economic policies.

Even without new pressures on resources growing from environmental measures the ever-increasing demand for traditional supplies will result in new emphasis on resource management. For example, within two or three decades the world must double its production of forest products from a declining land area. Yet improper management methods can lead to a long-term decrease in productivity, irreversible alteration of soil conditions, and increased erosion with consequent rapid siltation of water resource projects. Similar needs and potential attendant environmental problems eixst in other resource areas such as fish, water, land, and minerals. Many of the environmental problems arising from resource development can be avoided or at least mitigated by improved planning. Man-made changes in the environment do not occur in a vacuum but are likely to produce a series of ecological adjustments in their wake. The usual examples are projects in the developing world, but the industrialized world has more than its share of projects whose overall social costs have substantially reduced the anticipated economic benefits.

The construction of the St. Lawrence Seaway has contributed

significantly to the economic growth of the Great Lakes region, both on the United States and the Canadian sides. Yet it has done so at a high and largely unforeseen cost to the environment and, as a result, to the economy. The completion of the Welland Canal let the predatory sea lamprey into the lakes. The lamprey proceeded to decimate the commercial fish, particularly the trout. With the disappearance of the trout the alewife population exploded. In some cases the alewife became so numerous as to die in large numbers and create a public nuisance reducing the recreational value of the lakes. Eventually, lamprey control measures and the stocking of the lakes with salmon partially restored commercial fishing and controlled the alewife problem.

The lesson to be learned from the St. Lawrence Seaway and similar experiences is not that such projects should be stopped. Rather, the consequences of such resource development projects need to be carefully studied in advance. Such planning can lead to more efficient economic development. In the United States the National Environmental Policy Act of 1969 has provided the institutional base for such planning. The act requires that before any agency of the federal government undertakes any major action significantly affecting the environment it must prepare a detailed environmental report. Since permits, licenses, and legislative proposals are covered as well as actual projects, most major resource development projects would require such a comprehensive study. These studies cover not only the direct effects of the proposed project but also examine possible alternative courses of action. The principal function of such studies is to provide guidance for the decisionmaker on the environmental aspects. Environmental impact studies are designed to insure that environmental as well as technical and economic considerations enter into decisionmaking. The adoption of this or a similar system of environmental planning in other countries would require a marked upgrading of environmental sophistication.

It would appear to be in the interest of both the developing and the industrialized worlds to enhance the capabilities of the LDCs in planning and management of resource development since both depend economically on this development. At present in too many countries the administrative and technical capacities of governments are inadequate to deal with the giant international combines that have obtained concessions for resource exploitation. National governments have great difficulty in facing real problems such as controlling deforestation.

An institutional innovation that could provide assistance to governments is the establishment of regional environmental institutes. Countries having similar geographic and climatological conditions often face similar problems. For example, Indonesia, Malaysia, the Philippines, and Thailand possess some of the world's richest forest resources. These are currently being exploited in a way that will markedly lessen their value in the future. Yet the countries involved do not have the tools to manage these resources effectively, and the special conditions, both natural and institutional, make it unlikely that the problems could be solved by simple importation of techniques developed in the Western world. What is required is the development of an understanding of the nature of the problems and the creation of control measures appropriate to the institutional base. Small environmental institutes conducting research, providing training for technical experts, and having the responsibility for the provision of information could substantively aid governments in their management of natural resources.

An example of a successful regional institute is the International Rice Research Institute (IRRI) located in Los Banos, the Philippines. Originally funded by the Ford Foundation, the central goal of the institute was to discover ways of increasing rice production in the Philippines. Research succeeded in creating varieties of rice which with proper application of fertilizer, pesticides, and water greatly increased yields per hectare and made double cropping possible in areas which previously had been single cropped. The success of the IRRI quickly became known in neighboring countries. With the development of a training program and the founding of an information dissemination system the IRRI rapidly became an essentially regional institute. The ministries of agriculture in neighboring countries such as Malaysia financed projects which successfully applied the techniques developed by the IRRI. National governments, the FAO, foundations, and developed countries' aid programs have all contributed to the IRRI through the provision or support of technical experts from Southeast Asia.

It would appear from an examination of the operation of the IRRI and similar regional institutes that several features are key to success. First, governments in the region must be firmly convinced that a problem to be dealt with exists and is important for their future development. The governments are the basic consumers of the research results produced by the institutes; if they are not interested in applying the research, the activities of the institutes would quickly become academic. Financial support, at least in part, by participating governments would seem to be a prerequisite though additional funding through international agencies should certainly not be ruled out. Second, the goal of such an institute should be narrowly prescribed. The temptation would be great to deal with the vast array of environmental issues with a resulting dissipation of resources. Third, the staff of any such institute should originate at least in part from the region and also in part on detail from governments. Actually, all of the necessary expertise will probably not be available in the area, but it is essential that the expertise be developed that will translate research results into national policy. Experts from other regions and from developed countries will be needed initially, but they should not be allowed either to dominate the staff or to impose solutions developed for similar problems in other contexts.

The development of research institute activities, for example, an increasing productivity of arid land in the Middle East, could be fostered by the existing UN regional agencies. The institutes should not be viewed as competitive to these organizations, which should focus more on the economic aspects of environmental and resource development policies. Participation in financing probably would be required by both international agencies and national assistance agencies.

International financing agencies such as the International Bank for Reconstruction and Development (IBRD) and the Inter-American Development Bank (IDB) as well as developed countries' assistance agencies have over the years influenced resource development within the LDCs. In the past the decisions on grants and loans were based in most part on how the proposed project would contribute in a direct, visible way to economic development. Less attention was devoted to the potential social cost associated with development. The United States Agency for International Development (AID) adopted procedures in 1971 for analyzing the environmental impact of capital assistance projects that closely parallel the domestic environmental impact statement procedures referred to above. The intent is to provide both the AID and the assisted foreign country with a thorough environmental review so that in the bilateral decisionmaking process these considerations receive appropriate attention. In this way the overall most efficient economic solution can be identified even if another solution is chosen later.

There is no intention that through this procedure United States standards, priorities, or solutions will be imposed on foreign governments. This is an important point since developing countries are reportedly concerned that donor countries may seek to apply their own environmental standards in the establishment of development assistance priorities and in the approval of projects and fail to take into account the particular circumstances of each development assistance recipient. The LDCs fear that environmental measures might increase project costs and lead to alterations of their development plans. The LDCs are also worried that increasing donor concern over environmental matters will impede the developmental process itself. The United States view is that environmental analysis will provide both the donor and the recipient with cost-benefit analysis, including social cost, of various alternatives and will identify measures that could minimize environmental side effects while maximizing environmental benefits.

Among the multilateral agencies the IBRD has perhaps gone farthest in incorporating environmental considerations into planning and operations. It has instituted a procedure aimed at uncovering both environmental problems associated with a given project and opportunities for enhancing environmental quality. Incorporation of any subsequent environmental safeguards and controls are negotiated with the prospective borrower on the basis of studies carried out by experts. The United States, as a major donor, will be working within other assistance organizations such as the United Nations Development Program (UNDP) and the regional banks toward the adoption of similar policies and procedures that will guarantee an environmental examination of major projects.

Despite the progress to date the general situation with respect to assistance leaves much to be desired. Some donor countries and multilateral agencies have not adopted any policy with respect to environmental matters, and the policies eventually adopted may not be consistent. Since all developmental agencies have the common objective of furthering economic development, it would seem appropriate that they adopt consistent policies with respect to environmental considerations. The most appropriate forum to consider these issues is probably the Development Assistance Committee (DAC) of the OECD. On DAC are represented all the major donor countries of the noncommunist world. DAC has had a history of successfully developing aid policy in other areas. A possible weakness of using DAC is that the recipient countries are not represented. Any considerations within DAC should, of course, be supplemented by direct discussions with the LDCs.

In summary new environmental measures promulgated by the industrialized world as well as continually increasing demands will generate changing pressures on the world's natural resources. In order to avoid disruptions in trade and investment it is essential that these problems be anticipated. The regional economic commissions of the UN could play an important role both in developing an understanding of the longer term economic consequences of environmental controls and in fostering needed consultations. The wise use of global resources will require vastly improved management methods particularly in the LDCs. A system of regional institutes working on specific problems of regional concern could provide for a research base, training, and information dissemination. The financial support of such institutes should come in part from the countries of the region, from assistance agencies, and perhaps from private foundations. Incorporation of environmental considerations in the decision-making process of assistance agencies can also help develop an environmental awareness in the developing world. The institution of formal procedures by the AID to examine environmental aspects of capital assistance programs and the actions initiated by the IBRD are important first steps. DAC could play a prominent role in developing common policies toward assistance programs among the major donor countries.

Land Use and Urbanization

For many years, but increasingly in the last two decades, the cities of the world have drawn men from the countryside with the promise, often unfulfilled, of better jobs, better services, improved living conditions, and a more stimulating way of life. In the United States, for example, there has been a great northward movement of the rural poor from the southeastern part of the country to the cities of the midwest and the northeast. This influx has contributed to a wide range of difficult problems, including high unemployment, inadequate housing, poor schools, lack of medical services, and a general attitude of hopelessness. In the developing world the internal migration from countryside to city has been even more dramatic. More than 200 million people have moved from the rural areas to the cities of Africa, Asia, and Latin America during the last decade. Rates of urban growth have been particularly explosive in Latin America, but elsewhere the rates of movement have also been increasing. In general it is evident that the pace of urbanization in most of the developing world is outstripping the capacities of countries to supply the essentials of food, shelter, and health as well as other services.

Unlike other problems considered above the problems of urbanization and shifts in patterns of population distribution do not have direct international consequences through effects on trade or on transnational pollution. The global implications arise from the potential instability associated with the growing rings of squatters suffering the indignities of what is at best a marginal existence. The feelings of insecurity and impermanence can give rise to political instability further draining the government's capacity to solve the very problems that create the shantytowns. It would appear to be in the best interest of the developed, as well as the developing, world to attempt to find solutions.

The complex of legal, social, health, economic, and political factors associated with urbanization has been so difficult to handle that the governments of some developing countries, while realizing the severity of the squatter problem, have turned to other priorities more easily achievable. Other countries have decided to attack part of the problem by undertaking programs which meet one or more specific needs. Still others have laid emphasis on indirect approaches through the provision of better housing and facilities in rural areas or through programs benefiting the next higher economic strata with the hope that at least some of the benefits will trickle down.

Assistance agencies have in the past probably contributed to the problem through failure to analyze the long-term consequences of their actions. For example, a loan to Bogotá for the provision of an enlarged supply of drinking water will aid the urban population. But the very provision of additional services makes Bogotá that much more attractive to the rural poor. An alternative program for developing drinking water supplies in the rural regions of Colombia might reduce the net migration, but such a program would not only be less glamorous than the provision of a large new facility but also far more difficult to administer. What is needed is the kind of analysis that would focus on the second- and higher-order effects of particular projects or programs and ensure that assistance projects do not exacerbate existing problems or create new ones. The provision for environmental analysis of proposed projects by the assistance agencies can go far to identify potential environmental problems.

A second approach might be through creation of regional institutes of the type considered above but devoted to the study of urban problems. A regional approach would seem appropriate for a variety of reasons. While the squatter problem is virtually worldwide, each country is attempting to develop its own solutions. Within any given region institutional bases are more nearly similar than they are interregionally. The problems facing Santiago are more nearly like the problems of Mexico City than like those of Djakarta. There is a need to recognize common elements while at the same time respecting individual cultures. At present comparative studies on urban settlement problems in the developing countries are limited. Many governmental officials have no mechanism to learn of the experiences of the city next door, to say nothing of those of neighboring states or the region as a whole. In Africa, for example, communication tends to flow to the capital cities of prior colonial powers so that an urban planner in an ex-French colony knows more of the experience of mainland France than he does of the ex-British colony next door. Dissemination of the relevant experiences of others, coupled with an active program of controlled experimentation, would provide valuable new sources of policy direction to governmental officials of participating countries.

There is the basic requirement of an understanding of the phenomena of organization. For example, research is badly needed on property and landlord-tenant law and tradition in developing countries in order to pinpoint the factors preventing migrants from obtaining title or at least some form of tenancy. The situation with respect to research into the service infrastructure is well illustrated by the need for the treatment of sanitary waste. Typically, today the problem is approached by a large city, such as Bangkok, by contracting with a Western engineering firm for a study, usually financed out of assistance funds. The engineering firm will recommend the construction of a Western-style system of sewers, interceptor sewers, and sewage treatment plants for a city where few drains exist. The costs are, of course, astronomical, and the city uses its limited funds for other purposes. This does not mean that health is not imperiled by the lack of sanitary services but only that a traditional Western solution to the problem is far too costly when viewed against other needs. What is required is an understanding of alternative means of dealing with the problem, means that may fall short in terms of United States standards but that will provide increased health protection for the urban dwellers.

The establishment of regional urban institutes for the developing world to study the phenomena of urbanization, to develop programs, to upgrade techniques of public administration, and to devise innovative technical approaches to problems of services would seem to be of high priority. As in the case of resource-oriented institutes, their creation might be fostered by the UN through the regional economic commissions.

II. OTHER INSTITUTIONAL DEVELOPMENTS

I have touched only briefly on two developments to which the United States government assigns high priority: the Committee on the Challenges of Modern Society and the United Nations Conference on the Human Environment, scheduled for June 1972. Both the CCMS and the Stockholm conference have played and will play a special role in developing international environmental awareness.

An initiative by President Richard M. Nixon led to the establishment of the CCMS under NATO though several of the allied countries expressed serious reservations about including purely civilian activities under the umbrella of a defense organization. Since its establishment the CCMS has commissioned a number of national pilot projects on both the social and the physical environment with the view of stimulating national or international action. These projects include air pollution, disaster relief, health services, road safety, inland water pollution, open water pollution, job satisfaction and productivity, transmission of scientific knowledge into the decisionmaking process, and the strategy of regional development. Because of its limited membership, the attention the alliance gets from high political officals, and the long experience of cooperation between members it is expected that the CCMS projects can lead to rapid action either at the national or the international level.

A good example of the spin-off of a CCMS project into a broader forum was the United States proposal with respect to the intentional discharge of oil and oily waste into the oceans. While spectacular blowouts and accidents have attracted great public attention, the flushing of ballast and other waste by tankers deposits the vast majority of the oil that reaches the oceans. As a result of the strong United States interest in the subject the CCMS convened an oil spills conference in 1970. At the conference the United States proposed the goal of ending all deliberate discharges at sea by 1975. The conference adopted a resolution urging a special session of the IMCO assembly to take such measures as necessary for the drafting of an appropriate convention. The NATO Council of Ministers endorsed the resolution, and later the Maritime Safety Committee of IMCO approved the holding of the conference to draft an agreement dealing with the discharge of oil and other noxious substances into the ocean.

Two features of this experience are worth noting. The CCMS acted swiftly and prompted swift reaction from IMCO. There is every expectation that the 1973 IMCO conference will produce a negotiated treaty governing the deliberate discharge of oil at sea. Second, non-NATO states, including the Soviet Union, have participated in the follow-up of the CCMS initiative within IMCO.

The Stockholm conference will for the first time bring together members of the United Nations to consider a broad range of environmental problems, both physical and social. Public expectation runs high that the actions taken by the conference will lead to dramatic advances in environmental improvement. I take a more cautious view as to the actual accomplishments at the conference because of potential political problems. First, the participants will bring with them a very wide range of sophistication about the environment. Despite efforts before the conference there are sure to be feelings among the LDCs that strong action in environmental matters will be to their disadvantage. In addition to the tension between the northern and southern countries it appears that participation by the communist countries is in doubt. The Soviet Union has pressed very hard for full participation by East Germany in the conference. This has been opposed by West Germany and its NATO partners. The UN General Assembly adopted the so-called Vienna formula for participation in the conference, that is, all UN members plus members of UN specialized agencies. Under this formula non-UN countries such as West Germany and Switzerland could participate but East Germany would be excluded from full participation. Because of this action the Soviet Union has reconsidered its role in the conference, as has the East European bloc. Finally, because of political sensitivities such key issues as population policy and environmental economics will not be taken up, at least in any detail, at Stockholm.

Whatever fate awaits the Stockholm conference, the preparatory activities have had signal success in stimulating environmental awareness in many countries in which the problems were only dimly perceived. The requirements of preparing country reports, the many preparatory conferences, and the visits of the conference secretariat have forced countries to recognize problems, and many have to take actions such as governmental reorganization, enactment of legislation, and promulgation of regulations. Thus, while the international accomplishments of the conference may fall short of expectations, the overall impact of conference-related activities has been considerable.

III. SUMMARY

Environmental problems are many-faceted ones. If these are analyzed, few are truly global issues requiring worldwide action. The pollution of the oceans or the stratosphere can affect all countries, and these questions must be dealt with through organizations of the United Nations so that a broad participation in the decisionmaking is assured. For the most part environmental problems can best be dealt with at the national level. The lack of a tradition and capabilities of enforcement by international organizations argues for strong national legislation, standard setting, and enforcement. There is much to be gained by exchanging information and experience with respect to environmental control measures, but truly international action would seem to be appropriate only for transnational pollution or pollution of the international regions. Environmental measures can have important economic repercussions. If distortions in trade and investment are to be minimized, consultation between trading partners is essential. For the industrialized countries the OECD provides the best forum both for arriving at an understanding of the economic impacts and for promoting early consultation.

The classical pollution problems of the developed world are not yet serious in much of the developing world except in the teeming cities. However, the pressures for developing national resources pose serious environmental problems for these countries. It would seem that regional cooperative efforts between LDCs in their development would be most fruitful. In particular, the establishment of problem-oriented regional institutes with responsibilities for research, information dissemination, and training would seem particularly valuable in upgrading national capabilities for environmental management. This process can be aided by efforts on the part of assistance agencies, both national and international, to undertake environmental analyses of programs and projects and to make such analyses available to the recipient countries.

ENVIRONMENT AND DEVELOPMENT: THE CASE OF THE DEVELOPING COUNTRIES

Joao Augusto de Araujo Castro

JOAO AUGUSTO DE ARAUJO CASTRO is the ambassador of Brazil to the United States. A career foreign service officer, he earlier was his country's permanent representative to the United Nations. The author wishes to stress that this article reflects a personal contribution to the understanding of an ecological policy as envisaged by developing countries. It should not be interpreted as necessarily reflecting the position of the government of Brazil.

I. INTRODUCTION

Interest in the field of ecology, which is centered in the developed countries, has recently increased due to the sudden discovery of a possible imbalance between man and earth. Resulting from the population explosion and the misuse of existing and newly developed technologies, this potential imbalance could bring about an environmental crisis menacing the future of mankind. In several countries the emergence of an interest in ecological problems has not been confined to the realm of the scientific community. It has aroused public concern which has expressed itself, although sometimes vaguely, in such initiatives as Earth Week, celebrated in the United States in April 1970, and the mushrooming of a specialized literature.

As would be expected, the methods envisaged to resolve on a world basis the so-called environmental crisis were inspired by the realities of a fraction of that very same world: the family of the developed countries. Furthermore, the bulk of the solutions in hand, mainly of a technical nature, seek primarily to make healthier the consequences of the Industrial Revolution without necessarily providing a tool for a further distribution of its benefits among states.

This study seeks to introduce some neglected aspects of the interests of developing countries into discussions about a world ecological policy. The working hypothesis is that the implementation of any worldwide environmental policy based on the realities of the developed countries tends to perpetuate the existing gap in socioeconomic development between developed and developing countries and so promote the freezing of the present international order. As the environmental issue has been only roughly scrutinized in all its implications, this study will seek to do no more than to present a broad outline of the elements involved from the viewpoint of developing countries. Crucial to this sketch is the relationship between environment and development and its influence on the future dialogue between developed and developing countries.

II. DEVELOPED COUNTRIES

Although there does not yet exist a systematic body of doctrine, the new ecological policy of the developed countries contains several elements that have already stimulated important developments in academic thought, as indicated by the growing literature on the matter, and attitudes of governments and private sectors in these countries, mainly in their relations with the developing countries.

A short historical digression may help in analyzing the rationale of this ecological policy. As a localized phenomenon in the countries of the Northern Hemisphere, the Industrial Revolution of the eighteenth century was not brought about by one single factor. It was not, for instance, the result of inventions or the coming into operation of new machines. As in the case of other major movements in history, it was the result of the interplay of many factors, some obscure in themselves, whose combined effort laid down the foundations of a new industrial system. Growing organically, cell by cell, new patterns of industrial organization were soon translated into the establishment of a new international order. Around the group of countries enjoying the benefits of the Industrial Revolution there existed an increasing family of countries, trying, mostly unsuccessfully, to modernize their own means of production.

This new international order and the relatively uneven distribution of political power among states, based on the use and monopoly of advanced technologies, may be considered one of the most enduring effects of the Industrial Revolution. And since then, as a normal corollary of the new order, the technologically advanced countries have been endeavoring to maintain their political and economic position in the world while the technologically less endowed countries have been seeking to alter, through development, this global status quo.

This permanent struggle between the two groups of countries persists in the present days and it is unlikely that it will cease in the near future. For this to happen one would have to assume a perfectly homogeneous world community whose conflicts would have been eliminated through a perfect satisfaction, on a homogeneous basis, of all human needs. This condition is most likely to be found only in the realms of utopia. The struggle, however, may not necessarily become apparent through direct confrontation between countries as the war hecatombs that have been devastating mankind for centuries. Rather, it may assume subtle forms, hardly detected by the common observer and sometimes only fully understood when its concrete effects become irreversible.

According to a helpful image taken from academic and governmental sources in the developed countries our planet could be visualized as a "spaceship earth," where life could only be sustained, nay simply possible, through maintenance of a delicate equilibrium between the needs of the passengers and the ability of the craft to respond to those needs. Undisturbed until recently, this equilibrium would now be menaced by an excess of population and the consequences of the use of both previously existing and newly developed technologies. Elaborating the same image, "spaceship earth" would be divided into two classes of passengers, the first coincident with the technologically advanced countries and the second representative of the technologically less endowed countries, which would necessarily have to trade off positions with a view to maintaining the equilibrium of the vessel.

As regards population the problem is then focused on the amazingly growing number of the passengers, which may amount to four billion in 1975 and some eight billion by 2010. These figures would be reached chiefly by the rate of population growth in the second-class section in which, at the same time, the resources would be less abundant. To solve the problem it is proposed to adopt either a policy of the enforcement of rigid policies of birth control or the implementation of techniques directed to augment the resources needed for the survival of both classes. However, it is then assumed that, even if applied simultaneously, population control and new techniques of production would hardly cure the patient's sickness and the vessel would certainly succumb to the passenger overload.

The existing technological problem (the result of, e.g., combustion engines and present-day agricultural and industrial processes) would be mainly localized in the first class and its cumulative effect is determined by each passenger in the vessel. This newcomer, by requiring increasing levels of production through the addition of new capital equipment, ultimately causes a pattern of a mounting physical and chemical transformation in the industrial process. The strain would then arise from the inability of the natural elements (soil, water, and atmosphere) to absorb, at adequate rates, the harmful by-products of the growing industrial process.

Among the newly developed technologies nuclear radiation, pesticides, and fertilizers have been viewed as the most threatening factors of imbalance. While nuclear radiation is still a monopoly of the first-class passengers, and is only likely to be delivered in the event of devastating wars, the hazardous consequences of the use of pesticides and fertilizers for man are already felt by both classes through the constant contamination of food supplies.

In order to maintain the equilibrium of the vessel the problems created by population explosion and the use of both previously existing and new technologies should, in the view of developed countries, now be dealt with globally, irrespective of the unequal distribution, on a world scale, of the benefits and related destructive effects on the environment engendered by the Industrial Revolution. Germane to such a global ecological policy is the need for world planning for development which, to be successful, might purposely aim at freezing the present relative positions of the two classes inside the vessel.

Provided that the first class already enjoys low average rates of population growth and is unlikely to opt for a slower rate of industrial growth for the sole purpose of guaranteeing a purer atmosphere or cleaner water, the new ecology-saving policy would be more successful if applied in the areas where the environmental crisis has not yet appeared, even in its least acute forms. Actually, these areas would mainly comprise the territory of the second class. Thus, the second class should be taught to employ the most effective and expeditious birth control methods and to follow an orderly pollution-reducing process of industrialization. In the case of industrialization, the mainstream of socioeconomic development, the lesson must be even harsher: The second class must organize production in accordance with environment-saving techniques already tested by the first class or be doomed to socioeconomic stagnation.

Complex by its nature, the subject of the effects of population explosion and technological progress on environment tends to become a *chasse gardée* of the most industrialized countries which favor its discussion and consideration on a technical rather than on a political level. These countries maintain that environmental problems should not be the concern of diplomats and official representatives but should be dealt with by experts and wise men who affirm that in the beautifully imaginative "spaceship earth" the developing countries are condemned to live forever as second-class passengers. According to these experts technological progress and the so-called population explosion are responsible not only for terrifying damage to the environment but also for a tremendous strain on available natural resources. Granted that this strain is localized mainly in the developed countries, it should be only natural that the developing countries, for the well-being or survival of the first-class passengers, should become a vast "Kruger Park."

Nowadays some ecologists do not hesitate to say that the developing countries can never hope to achieve the consumption patterns of the developed countries. Some seemingly appalling calculations are offered as proof of this. To raise the living standards of the world's existing population to American levels the annual production of iron would have to increase 75 times, that of copper 100 times, that of lead 200 times, and that of tin 250 times. Were a country such as India to make use of fertilizers at the per capita level of the Netherlands, it would consume one-half of the world's total output of fertilizers. Clearly, the parity of the developing countries with the developed ones is no longer compatible with the existing stocks of natural resources. Again, according to those wise men, the increasing expectations in developing countries, which are sometimes associated with something approaching a revolution, are nothing more than expectations of elites and therefore must be curbed. Most of the population of these countries, it is claimed, do not have an ambition to reach Western standards and do not even know that "such a thing as development is on the agenda."

Now, the alleged exhaustion of natural resources is accompanied, in general, by forecasts of the fateful coming of formidable ecological hecatombs. The continuing progress of developed countries would require an economic lebensraum in the Southern Hemisphere. In the name of the survival of mankind developing countries should continue in a state of underdevelopment because if the evils of industrialization were to reach them, life on the planet would be placed in jeopardy. A particularly dramatic circumstance suffices to illustrate this possibility. The increasing carbon dioxide content of the air, resulting from the growth of industrial combustion, is steadily raising global temperatures. These climatic changes may entail the melting of the Arctic ice floes and generate a new ice age, or they may start the slumping of the Antarctic ice cap into the oceans and generate a tidal wave that could wipe all passengers off the spaceship earth. To such cataclysmic disasters would mankind be doomed should the rich countries disregard the primacy of nature or should the poor countries insist on carrying out industrialization.

Very few reasonable people underwrite these fanciful ideas. Yet, it cannot be denied that the environment in developed countries is threatened and that it should be preserved. The difficulty in dealing with environmental problems nowadays is that they have become a myth, and this new myth has something in common with some extreme reactions that from time to time are raised in the United States concerning certain specific issues. It is interesting to observe, in this respect, the recurrent changes in public opinion in the United States on the desirable extent of United States involvement in foreign affairs. In this field attitudes vary from all-out commitments to isolationism, and intermediary positions or conciliatory opinions have no widespread support. What is happening with environmental issues is not essentially different. From an uttermost neglect of ecological problems public opinion in the United States has swung to an outright "geolatry." The environment has been rediscovered and Mother Earth now has a week dedicated to her in the calendar. School children crusade to clean up the streets; college students organize huge demonstrations; uncivilized industries that dump their wastes in the air, in the water, or on the ground are denounced as public enemies.

At first opinion in the United States identified population growth as *the* cause of pollution and of the strains on natural resources. Even a modest increase in birth rates was deemed to be responsible for an irrecoverable depletion in the stocks of goods and natural resources. The implication was that the national goal should be to reach a zero growth in birth rates. It was then the high time for the rediscovery of Malthusianism. As the idea of Rousseau's "happy savage" has been reintroduced to try to convince the developing countries of the blessing of backwardness, century-old Malthusian ideas have once again been invoked in order to preserve the environment and alleviate the frightening burden placed on the earth's "carrying capacity."

Although this neo-Malthusian vogue has not passed away in the United States, emphasis has been put lately on other allegedly important factors affecting the environment. It is now being argued that growing affluence presents more danger to the environment than does overpopulation. The ecologist Wayne D. Davis has said, "Blessed be the starving blacks of Mississippi with their outdoor privies, for they are ecologically sound, and they shall inherit a nation."

As far as the United States is concerned, the prevailing argument now follows these lines: Polluted air and water, filthy streets, traffic jams, overcrowded schools, and many other related problems can be attributed to population growth, but it must be realized that rising incomes also add to these woes, perhaps even more than population growth. "If the United States were to double its GNP," says Princeton Professor Richard A. Falk, "I should think it would be a much less livable society than it is today." It cannot be easily understood how Rousseaunean and Malthusian theories are coupled together in defense of the environment. On the one hand, it is stated that population growth should be slowed down or eliminated so that a relatively smaller population could enjoy rising incomes and better consumption patterns; on the other hand, it is stated that rising incomes and better consumption patterns are undesirable because this would increase the pollution. A clearer understanding of the nature and origins of the present so-called environmental crisis is essential. The simplistic concepts that ecology is disturbed because there are "too many people" or because they "consume too much" must be discarded as nothing more than fallacies. There is abundant evidence that the earth is capable of supporting a considerably greater population at much higher levels of consumption. The simple fact that in half a century mankind found it possible to wage four major wars, with a terrible waste of wealth, is a clear indication that we are not after all so short of resources although we may be short of common sense.

Annual military expenditures in today's world are over $140 billion which means that each hour these expenditures amount to $16 million. Current military expenditures exceed the world's annual exports of all commodities and even exceed the combined gross national product (GNP) of Latin America, Asia, and Africa. One Atlas missile costs $30 million, or the equivalent of the total investment needed for a nitrogen fertilizer plant with an annual capacity of 70,000 tons. One ground-to-air missile uses resources which could produce 100,000 tractors.

Environmental problems not only pose a new and compelling argument for disarmament and peace but also call attention to the question of efficiency in the organization of production. It is widely known, but seldom remembered when the availability of natural resources is discussed, that in developed countries billions of dollars are spent every year to purchase so-called farm surpluses. Millions of tons of agricultural products have been regularly stored or destroyed to keep prices up in the world markets. By 1960, 125 million tons of wheat had been stored, an amount sufficient to provide food for every inhabitant in India for a year. These figures and these facts evidently do not agree with the superficial statements which have been made about the irreparable strain being put on natural resources.

Pollution of the air and water and related damages to the environment are loosely attributed, in general, to faulty technologies, but few have bothered to assess objectively the exact proportions of the problem. According to experts at the Organization for Economic Cooperation and Development (OECD) safeguarding the environment in the United States would require annual expenditures of about $18 billion, less than 2 percent of the American GNP. Clearly, there is no real cause for most of the fuzzy agitation about the environment. Put in their proper perspective, environmental problems are little more than a question of the reexamination of national priorities. And in this case nothing as dramatic as putting an end to the war in Southeast Asia has to be called for on grounds of the need to preserve the environment. By this time it should be clear that most of the existing pollution problems are simply noncomputed social costs of private activities. The social costs represented by the dumping of chemical wastes into a river are not included in the price of chemical products. Were the polluters liable for the damages they cause, incentives would be created to solve environmental problems. Provided that the costs of pollution are somehow paid for, what is left is simply today's empty rhetoric about pollution. As it has been aptly put, "eat the cake but pick up the wrapper, too."

When discussing the environment some ecologists and other wise men, as often happens in many other instances, try haphazardly to superimpose peculiar situations prevailing in developed countries onto the realities of the developing countries. Following this reasoning, if the developed countries are in an ecological crisis, the developing countries must also be in an ecological crisis. Of course, this has nothing to do with hardly sane ideas about shrinking spaceships in which the richer part of mankind is destined to become richer and the poorer part is doomed to become poorer, unpolluted by industry and untarnished by affluence. The point here is that the environmental conditions and myths prevailing in developed countries have been automatically transposed to developing regions of the world.

Among the reputed causes of pollution mention has been made of population growth, increasing incomes, and modern technologies. If the peculiarities of developing countries are taken into account, it will not be difficult to recognize that, in broad terms, they are still at a prepollution stage or, in other words, have not yet been given the chance to become polluted. First, it is necessary to examine the gross statistical manipulations that lead to fantastic figures on the future world population, especially in developing countries. These manipulations disregard the fact that in those countries there has been a desirable increase in life expectancy that accounts for most of their population growth. This increase in life expectancy has indeed been followed by a decrease in birth rates, so that there is obviously an automatic limit to population growth. This automatic limit to population growth arises from the fact that higher income tends to slow down birth rates. But the neo-Malthusian statistics do not take into consideration all the important factors that determine the growth of population. The opinion that more people means more pollution cannot be substantiated, not even in developing countries, where population growth is currently higher than in developed countries.

Yet, population control is preached not only as a way to defend the environment but also as a way to promote development. It is worth noting that per capita income has been taken lately, rather simplistically, as the sole standard for measuring economic growth and welfare. The policies now espoused by the developed countries in this respect are not aimed at increasing the dividend, that is, the national income of developing countries, but rather at immobilizing the divisor, namely, population. This is not only poor arithmetic but also poor economic logic.

But the fallacy that greater affluence leads to more environmental deterioration is even less acceptable than the idea that "too many people" disturb the ecology. The fallacy of affluence implies an anti-social policy of nondevelopment. The suggestion here seems to be to hold down incomes, after holding down population. The standard example to show that if people "consume too much" the ecological conditions worsen is that of a purchase of a second car. In a one-car-family community the purchase of a second car would double the burning of fuels, and, other things being equal, air pollution would double. However, in this prosperous one-car-family community the doubling of the harmful effects of air pollution may be offset by the utility gained with the second car. Would it not be expected that for those who do not own a car the utility of having one would be much greater than the disutility of increased air pollution? Consumption patterns can be roughly evaluated by the number of cars existing in one country. The 24 countries of Latin America, the least under-developed region in the developing world, have less than one-tenth of the total number of motor vehicles in the United States. Only a few ecologists and other wise men would say that Latin Americans should rather have fewer cars and cleaner air.

There is a pollution of affluence and a pollution of poverty. It is imperative to distinguish between the two lest some pollution be prevented at the cost of much economic development. Were it not for the dangers arising from the confusion between the two kinds of pollu-tion, there would be no need for calling attention to the precarious housing conditions, poor health, and low sanitary standards not to mention starvation in developing countries. The linear transposition of ecological problems of the developed countries to the context of the developing ones disregards the existence of such distressing social conditions. Wherever these conditions prevail, the assertion that less income means less pollution is nonsense. It is obvious, or should be, that the so-called pollution of poverty can only be corrected through higher incomes, or more precisely, through economic development.

The most sensible ecologists are of the opinion that the pollution levels can be attributed not so much to population or affluence as to modern technologies. In the United States the economy would have grown enough, in the absence of technological change, to give the in-creased population about the same per capita amounts of goods and services today as in 1946. The ecological crisis has resulted mainly from the sweeping progress in technologies. Modern technologies have mul-tiplied the impact of growth on the environment and, consequently, generated most of the existing pollution. Those who haphazardly trans-pose developed countries' situations to the milieu of an underdeveloped country repeatedly warn the latter against the dangers of modern technologies and rapid industrialization. "Don't let happen to your cities what happened to New York; keep your beautiful landscapes."

It is ironic that developed countries, which create and sell modern technologies, should caution developing countries against utilizing them. Is this done to justify the second-hand technologies that sometimes accompany foreign direct investments?

III. DEVELOPING COUNTRIES

A somewhat apathetic attitude on the part of the developing countries regarding the environmental issue does not imply negation of the relevance of the matter and the need for true international cooperation to solve the problem it poses for the survival of mankind. This apathetic attitude, however, clearly is derived from the developing countries' socioeconomic experience which differs, to a large extent, from that of the developed countries. Consequently, one has to bear in mind that, not having enjoyed the opportunity to experience their own Industrial Revolution, the developing countries have not been stimulated to think about the environmental crisis as posed in the present days. The phenomenon of urbanization in the Southern Hemisphere, even in the countries experiencing a considerable degree of progress, may raise questions about poor living standards in some areas but has not thus far led to industrial congestion.

As indicated in the elements of the ecological policy of the developed countries, the equilibrium of "spaceship earth" would depend on the enforcement of measures bearing on population and on the use of the previously existing and new technologies chiefly in the second class of the vessel or, in other words, in the territory of the developing countries. Even if applied to their full extent, those measures would not result at some foreseeable date in a single-class carrying vessel, preferably closer to the first steerage. This ecological policy, which aims primarily at the equilibrium of the vessel, could better succeed if the relative positions of the classes were maintained, for the emergence of one single class would presuppose a considerable change in the living standards of the first class, something that may not be attained in the light of present global socioeconomic realities.

An attentive analysis of the domestic and international aspects of the ecological policy advanced by the developed countries will not fail to persuade the developing countries to seek carefully and in their own terms possible solutions for the present environmental crisis. The population problem deserves first consideration in devising the developing countries' own interpretation of how to secure the equilibrium of the vessel. It is rather simplistic to apply uncritically Malthus's law of population growth to the so-called threat posed by the population explosion in the developing countries. These countries have at their disposal a wide array of technological improvements including better techniques of land use leading to increased food supplies, which were unknown in the time of the English economist. Besides the improvement in the methods of production the territorial space and habits of consumption in Malthus's thinking were those of the eighteenth century and can hardly be reconciled with the present environmental conditions.

It is undeniable that population grows at relatively very low average rates in those developing countries where there still remain large areas of foodstuffs produced through the simple use of present-day farm technology and domestic management skills. In this context the door is left open for the introduction of advanced technologies and management procedures which may appear as a further threat to Malthus's reasoning. This may explain the reluctance of the developing countries to adopt the linear concept embodied in the rule of a geometric growth of population accompanied by an arithmetic increase in food supplies.

On the question of the preservation of the environment the passenger's survival would call for the enforcement of a drastic decision, globally applied, to maintain a "green area reserve" which would have to coincide mainly with the territories of the developing countries. This step would safeguard, against complete exhaustion, the natural elements (soil, atmosphere, and water) still available on the planet just to provide some sort of counteraction to the spoilage of the same natural elements used up in the countries where the benefits of the Industrial Revolution were massively concentrated.

Besides the ethical question raised by this policy, as expressed in the ostensive imbalance between responsibility for the damage and obligation for repair, the developing countries, in abiding by its prescriptions, would make a commitment to conservatism rather than to conservation. Furthermore, the possibility of a widespread application of developed countries' ecological policy, theoretically conceived to secure the equilibrium of "spaceship earth," may risk transforming the Southern Hemisphere countries into the last healthy weekend areas for the inhabitants of a planet already saturated with the environment created by the Industrial Revolution. As a token of compensation the Southern Hemisphere countries could claim to have resurrected, and adequately preserved, the environmental milieu for the living and the survival of Rousseau's "happy savage." In expressing their concern over the environmental crisis the developing countries cannot accept, without further refinement, the ecological policy devised by the developed countries whose socioeconomic structure was deeply influenced by the unique phenomenon of the Industrial Revolution.

The first step toward the refinement of that policy may be the rejection of the principle that the ecology issue, taken on a global basis, can be dealt with exclusively through a technical approach, as suggested by the developed countries. Given the implications for the international order, including the freezing of the status quo, any environment-saving policy must necessarily be imbued with a solid and well-informed political approach. This would provide an opportunity for the developing countries, by preserving their national identities, to join safely in the effort of the international community to preserve the equilibrium of "spaceship earth."

As a normal corollary of the political approach, ecological policy should not depart from the broader framework of socioeconomic development. In this regard a second step of refinement would require a corresponding universal commitment to development if the task of preserving the environment is to be shared by the world community. As a last point of refinement the political and socioeconomic development approaches, working together, may be helpful in understanding that a meaningful ecological policy will have to consider man and earth in perspective and avoid any simplistic form of "geolatry" as embodied in the measures designed to preserve nature for nature's sake.

If the political questions concerning the environment are left to ecologists, chances are that they will elaborate a general and overall city planning scheme for the world, allowing for some irreducible minimum of parks and green areas for summer and holiday relaxation in the developing countries. This would be done to control or eliminate the isolated islands of the so-called pollution of affluence that exist in some developing countries. Yet, this represents a local problem without any national or international significance. The pollution of poverty is the one that, nationally and internationally, is of real significance for those countries, and it can be eliminated precisely through population growth, higher incomes, and modern technologies, the factors that ecologists generally consider to be the causes of pollution of affluence.

Environmental deterioration, as it is currently understood in some developed countries, is a minor localized problem in the developing world. Nobody should expect to find an environment devasted by industrial activity where industries are so few and, more often than not, primitive. Evidently, no country wants any pollution at all. But each country must evolve its own development plans, exploit its own resources as its thinks suitable, and define its own environmental standards. The idea of having such priorities and standards imposed on individual countries or groups of countries, on either a multilateral or a bilateral basis, is very hard to accept.

That is why it is disturbing to see the International Bank for Reconstruction and Development (IBRD) set up its own ecological policy. Repercussions on the environment, defined according to IBRD ecologists, have become an important factor in determining whether financial assistance by that institution should be granted for an industrial project in developing countries. It seems reasonable that the preservation of the environment should not exclude the preservation of national sovereignty. Ecological policies should rather be inserted into the framework of national development.

It is perhaps time for the developing countries to present their own views on the framing of an environmental policy in spite of the fact that the developed countries have not yet ended their own controversial debate or furnished definite and convincing data on the issue. In adopting a position the developing countries recognize the existence of environmental problems in the world and the possibility of finding solutions through both national efforts and international cooperation.

The first point to be touched on concerns the question of national sovereignty. In this regard any ecological policy, globally applied, must not be an instrument to suppress wholly or in part the legitimate right of any country to decide about its own affairs. In reality this point would simply seek to guarantee on an operational level the full exercise of the principle of juridical equality of states as expressed, for instance, in the Charter of the United Nations and in Hobbes's formula that a state bears no sovereignty in vain: *Non est potestas super terram quae comparetur ei.* Sovereignty, in this context, should not be taken as an excuse for isolationism and consequently for escapism in relation to international efforts geared to solving environmental problems. For the developing countries it is crucial to consider, in the light of their own interests, nationally defined, the whole range of alternative solutions devised or implemented in the developed countries. Naturally, it is assumed that all countries can act responsibly and that none is going to deliberately favor policies that may endanger the equilibrium of "spaceship earth."

Closely linked to the problem of sovereignty, the question of national priorities calls for an understanding of the distinction between the developmental characteristics of developed and developing countries. As has been previously pointed out in this article, while the ecological issue came to the forefront of public concern as a by-product of postindustrial stages of development, it is not yet strikingly apparent in the majority of the developing countries. And different realities, of course, should be differently treated or, at least, given the fittest solutions.

In the developing countries the major concern is an urgent need to accelerate socioeconomic development, and a meaningful ecological policy must not hamper the attainment of that goal in the most expeditious way. Accelerated rates of socioeconomic development designed to equalize the status of the two sections within the vessel, however, do not blossom spontaneously in the present days: They presuppose careful planning for development, and for a successful accomplishment of this sole task, extremely demanding in itself, several qualifications are required from the outset.

Conceptually, the purpose of development in developing countries is to create the conditions for the establishment of the first modern patterns of production aimed at enhancing the desperately low levels of socioeconomic welfare. By contrast, in the developed countries, which already enjoy modernized means of production, the chief developmental objective is to universalize an already advanced socioeconomic welfare by making more efficient the existing industrial structure. In this context the developing countries, while rejecting the implementation of any ecological policy which bears in itself elements of socioeconomic stagnation, could only share a common responsibility for the preservation of the environment if it was accompanied and paralleled by a corresponding common responsibility for development.

Operationally, the developmental task and the preservation of the environment, which are closely associated in the developing countries, call for a brief discussion of the institutional framework necessary to formulate and carry out policy decisions. In a market economy the price system is supposed to play the crucial role of allocating resources and guiding the entrepreneur's rational decision in the production of goods and services. The price system, however, basing itself mainly on the quantitative aspects of the use of money, for which rationality and exactness constitute the departing points of analysis, fails to account for all aspects of monetary transactions. As recognized even by the academic community of the developed countries, the price system fails to account appropriately for the benefits and costs distributed among those not party to the transaction. These extraparty costs and benefits are elegantly called by the economists the "externalities." While recognizing the existence of such externalities economists have long considered them as side effects of indefinite magnitude rather than as major points of interest. Generally, these externalities are not expressed in monetary terms because the instrument to effect this evaluation — the price system — does not include them.

The market's malfunctions are apparent not only when it fails to reflect the costs borne by those that are around but outside the productive process but also when the active participants act only in accordance with their individual interests. The reasoning makes obvious the conclusion that, to the extent that welfare maximization is based on the assumption of the consumer's perfect knowledge of all market conditions, people normally acting without adequate knowledge prevent market transactions from maximizing human welfare.

This divergence between private and social costs, a by-product of the previously existing and newly developed technologies operating in a market economy, suggests that the hand of the public authorities in the developing countries should become less invisible and provide a set of criteria, defined in the light of the interests of national development, for the "internalization" of the social costs generated by the industrial sector with special treatment accorded to genuine national productive concerns. This exception would serve to help technology within a country reach the degree of modernization prevailing in industrial countries. Additionally, if an ecology-saving policy calls for the development of new technology, an exclusive or outstanding role should be reserved for the employment of local technical, managerial, and material resources.

The population issue in developing countries, taken with all the implications of preserving the quality of life indispensable for a sound, ethical, and productive society, cannot be exhausted through the exclusive means of economic rationality in its highest expression: the market system analysis. While a population control policy may bear quick results for securing, in the short run, the equilibrium of "spaceship earth," as ascertained by developed countries, it does not necessarily bring about an equilibrium of the socioeconomic status of both sections of the vessel. Furthermore, uninhabited areas in the developing countries are not only a statistical fact; in qualitative terms they represent an invaluable asset of a productive factor, generally abundant in developing countries, ready to be combined with additional efforts on the part of man and so effectively to contribute to the expeditious attainment of developmental goals. Both reasons substantiate the refusal of the developing countries to adopt a policy of population control which emphasizes, on a mere technical basis, the attainment of better levels of socioeconomic welfare through limitations imposed forcibly on the number of income earners rather than through an increase in the total social product.

IV. CONCLUSION

This study has probed very briefly some aspects of an ecological policy in the light of the interests of the developing countries.

For the sake of presenting the matter within an orderly framework, and not with a desire to make any intentional contribution to methodology, the subject has been divided into three main topics. First of all, a tentative characterization of a model of an ecological policy of developed countries has been briefly outlined with a central focus on the aspect of the concentration in those countries of the benefits as well as of the hazardous consequences of the unique phenomenon of the Industrial Revolution.

Second, emphasis has been laid on the undesirability of transposing, uncritically, into the realities of the developing countries the solutions already envisaged by the developed countries to eliminate or reduce the so-called environmental crisis to the extent that those solutions may embody elements of socioeconomic stagnation. At this point all arguments sought to demonstrate the need to approach differently environmental crisis generated by persistent levels of poverty, as is the case of developing countries, and that related to affluence, as present in the majority of the developed countries.

Finally, a preliminary and broad picture of a position of the developing countries has stressed the relation between preservation of environment and the urgent need to speed up socioeconomic development and the desirability of a common world effort to tackle both these aspects simultaneously. This common effort, however, should not preclude or trespass on national interest as a departing point for the setting up of concepts and operational guidelines of an ecological policy for the developing countries.

In conclusion, a discussion of any meaningful ecological policy for both developed and developing countries, which hopefully will take place during the upcoming 1972 United Nations Conference on the Human Environment in Stockholm, would better reflect a broad socioeconomic concern, as tentatively suggested in this article, rather than confine itself to a strictly scientific approach. Man's conceptual environment, and nothing else, will certainly prevail in shaping the future of mankind for the preservation of the environment presupposes a human being to live in it and a human mind to conceive a better life for man on this planet. From the point of view of man — and we have no other standpoint — Man, Pascal's "roseau pensant," is still more relevant than Nature.

PART IV

SALIENT ISSUES FOR THE FUTURE

ENVIRONMENTAL QUALITY AND INTERNATIONAL TRADE

Ralph C. d'Arge and Allen V. Kneese

RALPH C. D'ARGE is associate professor of economics, University of California, Riverside, and ALLEN V. KNEESE is director, Quality of the Environment Program, Resources for the Future, Inc., Washington. The authors would like to express their indebtedness to E. Brook, O. Bubik, S. Follmer, T. Munnecke, and W. Schulze.

I. INTERNATIONAL ASPECTS OF ENVIRONMENTAL PROBLEMS

The Nature of International Environmental Problems

Environmental problems are currently a matter of international interest and concern for a wide variety of reasons ranging from those which are rather general and even vague to others which are concrete and sometimes very pressing.[1] There are, hopefully, more than a few people who are concerned about the welfare of their fellow man wherever he may be; moreover, there is an evident feeling of "one-worldness" resulting from an increasing degree of interdependence in several spheres, including the economic and the cultural. Further, the developed countries feel that they can learn useful lessons from one another about how to cope with environmental problems which are quite similar from country to country. These problems usually result from high population densities combined with large and rapidly growing per capita production and consumption which are often brought about by the use of technologies that generate large amounts of destructive residual materials. There is also an almost universal absence of satisfactory institutions for collective management of a number of "common property resources" including the air mantle, watercourses, and other large ecological systems. Interest in study-

---

[1] The matters passed over lightly in this section are discussed in some detail in Clifford S. Russell and Hans H. Landsberg, "International Environmental Problems—A Taxonomy," *Science*, June 25, 1971 (Vol. 172, No. 3990), pp. 1307-1314; Marion Clawson, "Economic Development and Environmental Impact: International Aspects" (Paper prepared for the Symposium on Political Economy of Environment—Problems of Method, Ecole Pratique des Hautes Etudes, Paris, July 1971); and William Baumol, *Environmental Protection, International Spillovers, and Trade* (Wicksell Lectures 1971) (Stockholm: Almquist and Wiksell, 1971).

ing these problems in a cooperative manner and exchanging information about them is evident in much of the current activity of the World Health Organization (WHO), the Economic Commission for Europe (ECE), the Organization for Economic Co-operation and Development (OECD), the North Atlantic Treaty Organization (NATO), and other international institutions, and, no doubt, the 1972 United Nations Conference on the Human Environment will occupy itself considerably with them.

Another primary source of concern is the pressingly evident fact that economic activities in one country are producing direct "spillover" or, in economic terms, "external" effects on one or more other countries. Examples are legion: the salt pollution of the Rio Grande in the United States which adversely affects agriculture in Mexico; the virtually unrestricted discharge by many countries of residuals into the Baltic Sea which is already in a most precarious ecological state; the progressive and accelerating degradation of the Rhine; and the discharges of sulfur oxides in the Ruhr area and elsewhere in northern Europe which are causing "acid rain" in Scandinavia. One of the most distressing features of the present world condition is that although many of these are clear and pressing problems, advanced countries seem totally unable to develop effective international measures to deal with them. This itself should not be very surprising, however, since many of those advanced countries appear incapable of coping even with their internal environmental problems.

While many specific regions of the world are afflicted with more or less uncontrolled pollution problems, there are some truly global problems which exist either in fact or at least as potential problems. The possible climatic effects of man's already detectable alteration of the atmosphere's chemical properties have been amply publicized although they are not well understood scientifically. More pressing are the disturbances associated with the introduction of "exotic" and very persistent substances into large ecosystems: DDT, mercury, and other substances have already aroused concern.

These are all salient and important reasons for trying to achieve international monitoring and information exchange and for working toward agreements on the management of substances actually or potentially deleterious to both regional and global natural environments.

Other more subtle international problems related to the natural environment result from demands (or preferences) for goods produced in one country on the part of another country's citizens. Sometimes these linkages are not expressible through markets; for example, substantial numbers of people throughout the world may feel quite unhappy if a unique natural feature like Lake Baikal is irreversibly changed or if an animal species is driven to extinction, even though these events occur wholly within another country. In instances like these discontent is not individually expressible through markets. If people's preferences are to count at all in these cases, they must be expressed through collective action and international agreement. In a vast number of other cases the preferences for goods produced in one country on the part of citizens in another, and vice versa, are both expressible and expressed through markets. These preferences may result from qualitative or price differences with respect to domestically produced goods, and the result of the expression of those preferences is, of course, international trade.

This discussion shows that both environmental preferences and dispersal of residuals into the environment may occur on an international scale. We do not intend to treat transnational and global residuals problems in any depth here. Rather, we will deal rigorously and empirically only with those problems (or apparent problems) associated with the influence on international trade of environmental controls instituted within a country. Also, we limit our consideration to pollution control or "residuals management" problems although our general approach and conclusions apply to other types of environmental disruption. We appreciate not only that this is but a part of the problem but also that many countries and industries regard it as an extremely important one. We comment about other aspects of environmental controls only in general terms.

Impact of Environmental Controls on International Trade of Major Trading States

The major trading states are clearly concerned about the effect that environmental controls in their own countries or in other states may have on their international trade position, on their national income, and on the prosperity of specific industries in their economies. This set of issues was at the center of discussion during the January 1971 Atlantic Council meetings.[2]

One fear is that cost increases which home industries may have to sustain because of environmental controls will adversely affect both the industry's and the state's international trade position, the level of real national income, and long-term comparative advantage. This fear becomes particularly acute when it is suggested that one trading country move to curb environmental degradation without coordinate action by others or when it is thought that other countries will subsidize the environmental controls instituted by industry while

---

[2] See Allen V. Kneese, Sidney E. Rolfe, and Joseph W. Harned, eds., *Managing the Environment: International Economic Cooperation for Pollution Control* (New York: Praeger, 1971).

the country in question will not subsidize but perhaps even charge or tax them for any environmental disruptions.

The latter possibility is rapidly becoming a genuine problem in the United States and a few other countries. There is now a substantial theoretical and empirical literature in the United States which concludes that from the domestic economy's point of view "effluent charges" or taxes are the most effective and efficient means for achieving control of industrial residuals discharges.[3] Moreover, and politically much more important, the "conservation" groups, which previously opposed the effluent charges technique, are now solidly behind it.[4] There are also proposals to tax particular commodities which cause notable environmental problems; a tax on containers which are particularly resistant to reuse is an example.

Other impacts on international trade may result from direct controls imposed in the interest of environmental protection on either emissions of residuals or on the qualitative characteristics of commodities. For example, if the conventional internal combustion engine remains the power source for new automobiles, it appears that foreign manufacturers, who typically use small engines in their cars, will have a disproportionately difficult time meeting increasingly strict emissions standards relative to the problems associated with large understressed engines in American cars. Moreover, they may be faced with the problem of producing different cars for different markets with relatively short production runs of each type. Such disproportionate effects raise both the possibility and the fear that alleged environmental controls may be used as restrictive trade practices. A related example is provided by quality control on pharmaceuticals in France. The French require inspection of production processes and by this means have effectively frozen foreign manufacturers out of the market. We discuss the various policy options which a country might adopt in domestic environmental protection further in section II.

Some Special Concerns of the Developing Countries

Developing countries may also have some special cause for concern. Due to the costs of residuals disposal in developed countries pressures for more efficient materials use through increased recycling and other means may affect the developing countries' economic development adversely if they are still heavily dependent on the export of

---

[3] See Allen V. Kneese and Blair T. Bower, *Managing Water Quality: Economics, Technology, Institutions* (Baltimore, Md: Johns Hopkins Press [for Resources for the Future], 1969), chapters 5, 6.
[4] United States Congress, Subcommittee on Priorities and Economy in Government, Joint Economic Committee, *Hearings, Economic Incentives to Control Environmental Pollution*, 92nd Cong., 1st sess., July 12, 1971.

basic resource commodities. It appears somewhat doubtful, however, that the efficiency of materials used in developed countries could grow to such an extent that the international demand for these commodities would actually be reduced, at least in the next few decades. But it is quite plausible that the demand might grow at a lesser rate than now anticipated.

There are other fears in developing countries that environmental policies in developed countries will adversely affect their trade positions, international assistance, and the transfer of technology.[5] One aspect of this thinking is a fear that cost increases for environmental controls in developed economies will give rise to "neoprotectionism" as a means to protect home industries from those in developing countries whose environmental standards are lower. Agricultural products might be especially vulnerable. For example, nontariff barriers may be erected against developing countries' products carrying some small environmental hazard which is unacceptable to the developed country; the banning in some European countries of fruits and vegetables carrying traces of DDT is one such case. Another aspect is the thought that government subsidies for pollution control in developed countries will reduce funds for foreign aid. Further, there is concern that in providing aid the developed countries will unfairly or unthinkingly press their own environmental standards, instituted for domestic environmental protection, onto developing countries. Finally, there is concern that the kind of technology transferred from the developed to developing countries will be effected in a manner adverse to development in more economically primitive circumstances. For example, technology might develop in the direction of engine types in which considerable cost is incurred to keep emissions low for domestic purposes but lower than developing countries would find optimal.

There are, of course, possible influences of environmental concerns in developed countries favorable to developing countries. For instance, the concern for global pollution may help to stimulate a "one-world" feeling which could extend to a concern for poverty all over the world and which might lend support to projects and programs in the human resources sector which have been rather neglected in aid programs. Suspicion or demonstration of the pollution effects of synthetics may rebound to the benefit of natural resources products of some developing countries. Perhaps most important of all, controls on high residuals

[5] These issues are examined to some degree in a draft report *Development and Environment,* submitted by a panel of experts convened by the secretary-general of the United Nations Conference on the Human Environment, Founex, Switz., June 4-12, 1971. (Mimeographed.) Our summary here is based largely on this report. A discussion of the impacts of environmental controls on the balance of payments and the national income of developing countries is offered in section IV.

industries in developed countries will tend to stimulate their growth in developing countries where controls are less strict. This relates to basic materials as well as processing industries. For example, present technologies used in the production of basic copper generate sulfur oxides almost pound for pound with copper, and control technologies are costly. Emissions controls or taxes in the developed countries would tend to stimulate the copper market in the less developed countries. This raises the issue of "exporting pollution," discussion of which has so far generated a lot more heat than light. Many of the fears, concerns, and positive possibilities surrounding relationships between environmental policies in developed countries and rates of development in less developed areas are so ill formed and vague that little more can be said about them. Our further analysis will have some bearing, however, on the influence of environmental controls on trade patterns, and we will have more to say on the "exporting pollution" issues.[6]

Analysis of International Trade Impacts at the Macroeconomic and the Microeconomic Levels

The two levels at which international trade impacts of environmental controls may appropriately be considered have already been implied by the above discussion. On the one hand, it is pertinent to consider the "macroeconomic" effects on the balance of payments, national income, and employment. On the other, impacts on specific industries are of concern both to the industries themselves and to the government of the states in which they manufacture. It should be pointed out that there is no sharp distinction between macro and micro since what occurs cumulatively at the micro level determines the extent of macro adjustments. Our primary focus in this article is on the macroeconomic level, but we will also have some comments to make about the microeconomic level and comparative advantage in the next section.

[6] Another broad question, of course, is whether environmental protection really deserves the low status the developing countries are giving it in their domestic priorities. Our view is that in many instances it does not. Developing countries, especially in the western hemisphere, exhibit great diversity internally from region to region. In addition to economically primitive backcountry with poor environmental conditions related to extreme poverty and often ignorance of even basic sanitation they also have the dubious distinction of being centers of some of the worst environmental pollution in the world: Sao Paulo and Mexico City are excellent examples. Moreover, one of the most important characteristics of these situations is the rate at which they are deteriorating. Some measure of this is given by rates of population growth for these cities which range up to 500,000 people, net, per year. It seems that these facts are neglected by those persons in developing countries who claim that "this is not a problem for us." On the contrary, inclusion of environmental considerations in development planning appears to be a matter of some urgency.

In section III we turn to 1) a discussion of an econometric model which has been constructed to assist in the analysis of macroeconomic effects for several countries and 2) a presentation of some numerical results obtained from using the model in connection with various assumptions concerning domestic environmental policy. Measures of macroeconomic impacts are made when unilateral action on environmental controls is undertaken by a particular country (which raises costs in its export industries) while no other countries take action. We also experiment with various combinations of multilateral action. We conclude with discussions of ways to mitigate adverse effects on domestic industries resulting from losses in competitive international advantage and problems of separating legitimate governmental actions directed toward improving environmental quality from those that are taken for other objectives.

II. NATURE AND MAGNITUDE OF IMPACTS AT THE MICRO LEVEL: POSSIBLE EFFECTS ON SPECIFIC INDUSTRIES AND COMPARATIVE ADVANTAGE

Domestic Civil Costs of Residuals Discharge

In the introductory section we indicated, in general terms, the relationship between the common property characteristic of resources like the air mantle, watercourses, and ecological systems and the problem of environmental pollution. These resources have not been and in many cases could not be converted to private property which could be exchanged in markets to establish its value in alternative uses. Accordingly, unless some sort of public policy prevents it (and we consider later what sorts of public policies might do so) these resources are the recipients of residuals from extractive, processing, and consumption activities that are discharged without regard to their destructive effects. A residual's discharge may have a highly degrading effect on the ability of a watercourse to support a valuable ecological system or on the air's life-support capacity. But since these services of the common property resource are not priced, the residuals discharger does not have to pay for his discharge; in fact, he has no incentive to even take them into account. Thus, a kind of real cost goes unmet. It is called variously, in the literature, an external diseconomy, an external cost, or a social cost. Several results follow from this situation: Too much residual is discharged, too much residual is generated which is either treated or controlled too little, and the price of the good which is finally sold to consumers is too low. A public policy must be devised to cancel these effects if we are to have an efficient economy in which all social costs are met when a decision is made to undertake an extractive, processing, or consumption activity.

The distinction between extractive and processing industries, on the one hand, and consumption activities, on the other, is important in connection with international trade issues. If a consumption activity gives rise to external costs, it is the external cost-generating aspect which must be controlled or managed, and it is a matter of indifference whether the good whose services are being consumed is of foreign or domestic origin. For example, restrictions on automobile exhausts imposed by a given country or region within a country would apply equally to automobiles of foreign or domestic manufacture. Another example is a "disposal charge" levied on automobiles. Again, any distinction made would not be contingent on whether the automobile is foreign or domestic. Moreover, if an automobile is exported, domestic emission standards should not govern, nor should the disposal fee be imposed on it for, in this case, the external cost associated with its use will occur in the destination country which may or may not wish to control it. Thus, controls on consumption-related externalities are simliar to excise taxes levied for domestic purposes. They apply equally to foreign and domestically produced items and should not be levied on exported items. Only when an externality-producing good is imported but not produced domestically would a tax or other control on it come to resemble a tariff in the trade-restrictive sense. But, as long as this restriction reflects a genuine domestic environmental objective, the resemblance is only superficial for what is involved is simply an effort to equate domestic social and private costs.

The situation is quite different in the case of an external cost associated with an extractive or processing activity. When these costs are made internal, they become "embodied" in the price of goods to which they furnish material or component inputs, and an effort to isolate those costs which are "attributable" to environmental protection resembles unscrambling an omelet. But the difference is deeper than the mere difficulty of isolating a cost component. The incidence of the external or social costs in this case is where the goods are produced and not where they are consumed. Thus, for example, external costs associated with the discharge of biologically active or chemical residuals from a pulp and paper plant or costs associated with reducing such discharges are social costs in the country where the paper is produced whether or not it is consumed domestically.

From this discussion we see among other things that a tariff-like, excise-type levy on a foreign-produced good as it enters the country (one not applicable to a similar domestically produced good) would be an appropriate environmental protective device only in rare instances. This would only be true if a similar good were not produced domestically, if it were not possible to tax or otherwise appropriately restrict the externality-generating activity itself (e.g., tax auto emissions rather than autos), and if the appropriate tax were uniform nationally. Thus, tariffs imposed with the nominal purpose of environmental protection should be viewed with suspicion as in fact being trade restrictions.

Effluent Charges, Standards, and Subsidies within a Domestic and an International Context

We have spoken in general terms about internalizing external costs, but now we must confront the question of how this might be done more directly. In doing this we neglect the matter of consumption-related externalities because, insofar as relationships to international trade issues are concerned, they have been adequately described above.

There are really two steps involved in approaching this question. The first involves the matter of how much environmental capacity is to be allotted to residuals discharge, and the second is the question of how this available supply is to be distributed among residuals dischargers. The process whereby the first is determined involves some sort of weighting of the costs of controlling residuals discharge against the external cost or damage which can be avoided by reducing it. In practice this process is usually crude, with a large intuitive or judgmental element.

Once a permissible amount of environmental capacity is allotted to residuals discharge, its distribution among actual and potential residuals dischargers must be determined. In general, economic efficiency demands that this capacity be distributed in such a way that those potential users to which it is most valuable are able to use it most. In other words, those that find it least costly (everything considered) to reduce their waste discharge should reduce it most and those who find it most costly should reduce it least. If we put aside many qualifications, the economic criterion is that the incremental costs of reducing residuals discharge must be equated for all dischargers.

It follows from this discussion that two major types of errors may occur in residuals management policy within a domestic or an international context: 1) Too much or too little environmental capacity may be allotted to residuals discharge; and 2) the available capacity may be ill distributed within and among countries. An extreme case of the former occurs when no environmental control is exercised. In this case all costs remain external and most of these are visited directly upon the populations as consumers — in the form of poor health, reduced aesthetic value of the environment, or lower productivity. The second type of error involves needlessly high costs of attaining the environmental standards and consequent unnecessary restrictions on the production of other goods and services. The international trade implications of these errors are discussed below.

As a means of diminishing the second type of error and at the same time reflecting the external costs of production in the various salient decisions economists have long advocated the use of publicly administered charges and taxes on external cost producing activities. The level of the charge would be set so that waste dischargers would have an economic incentive to cut back just enough so that the allotted environmental capacity would not be exceeded. This would have the effect of providing an incentive to those that can control residuals most cheaply to do so.[7]

Of course, other techniques can be used to limit the use of environmental capacity. In principle, a payment could be made to a waste discharger per unit of discharge withheld. This is a rather idealized subsidy scheme. The general conclusion is that informational and administrative problems make it virtually impossible to obtain an efficient result with this type of payment.[8] Omitting for the moment considerations of long-run adjustments and information-administrative costs associated with subsidies, we can make several statements with regard to effluent charges and subsidies within an international context. First, if subsidies are offered strictly for pollutant emission reductions, effluent charges and effluent subsidies or payments will achieve the same degree of short-run domestic efficiency in reduction of emissions.[9] The question of whether this result still holds when international trade is introduced is answered by a qualified yes. Since the firm is presumed to view the subsidy as an opportunity cost of production, it will adjust production downward so that the marginal loss associated with waste residuals reduction is equated with marginal revenue gains from the subsidy for the reduction. If all firms within a country respond in this manner, however, the domestic industry's output will be reduced and prices will thereby rise. That is, prices will rise provided that the domestic industry produced more than an insignificant share of world consumption of the commodity. Thus, if the commodity is being produced domestically and exported, an outcome of increased domestic and export prices will occur which is identical in immediate impact to an efficient effluent charges system. The same result holds for domestic substitutes for imported commodities. Effluent subsidies will also increase domestic

---

[7] There is considerable economic literature on this. See, for example, Allen V. Kneese, "The Political Economy of Pollution," *American Economic Review*, May 1971 (Vol. 61, No. 2), pp. 153-166.

[8] See the discussion in Kneese and Bower.

[9] This has been demonstrated in ibid., chapter 5.

opportunity costs of producing imports with the same immediate impact on comparative advantage of producing the imported good domestically as with implementation of effluent charges. However, while the immediate theoretical impact is identical, long-run impacts are likely to be extremely different. This is due to changes in relative profitability of a particular industry between countries which will induce shifts in international investment and perhaps even international relocation of existing capital and labor.[10]

The effect of such differences in profitability that emerge, in the long run, from the use of domestic effluent subsidies rather than charges may be a serious misallocation of international investment, particularly if all countries did not adopt the subsidies approach. International investment would probably accumulate in those countries willing to continuously maintain a subsidy for such investment which may or may not have any direct relationship to productivity of capital, at the margin, between countries. Thus, long-run efficiency from the global viewpoint, by utilizing domestic subsidies which are geared to emission reductions, is conceptually infeasible.

A subsidy device frequently used is to meet part of the cost of constructing (and possibly operating) waste treatment plants from general public funds. This procedure has several severe drawbacks, including the fact that it tends to bias the discharge-reducing technology selected in favor of waste treatment plants even though other methods for reducing residuals generation would often be cheaper. More generally it makes it impossible to equate social and private costs, which we have already argued is necessary for efficiency in the domestic economy. Moreover, this form of subsidy does not by itself provide an incentive to reduce waste discharge. Even though the government pays part (say half) of the cost of a waste-treatment plant, it is still cheaper from the private viewpoint of the residuals generator to dump them into the "commons" without reductions. Thus, this system undoubtedly reinforces the inefficiencies inherent in schemes to enforce direct restriction on residuals discharge. Nevertheless, the combination of treatment subsidies and enforcement is now in (highly imperfect) use in the United States and is probably the most common single approach used elsewhere.

Enforcement of specified residuals discharge controls has suffered from great difficulties in practice. The legal processes used have been

[10] There is some evidence, though meager, that long-term direct investment flows are quite responsive to short-term changes in relative profitability. See R. C. d'Arge, "Customs Unions and Direct Foreign Investments: A Correction and Further Thoughts," *Economic Journal*, June 1971 (Vol. 81, No. 322), pp. 352-355.

cumbersome, expensive, and very time-consuming.[11] Even if these problems could be largely overcome, efficient allocation of permissible environmental capacity would tend to be precluded by other factors. Problems of information, administrative complexities, and equity usually push this approach in the direction of applying uniform discharge standards to all dischargers. This effectively forecloses an efficient allocation of permissible capacity for reasons we have discussed above. We briefly consider the international trade implication of this problem in the succeeding sections.

Some Observations on Externalities, Welfare, and International Trade

One of the most important welfare propositions in the international trade literature is that given a world composed of sovereign states independent of each other except through international market exchanges, world welfare will be maximized if domestic and international prices fully reflect the social costs of production and consumption for all states.[12] This proposition is central to the often-stated belief that tariffs are undesirable. Tariffs have the effect of distorting the relationship between prices and costs of production for individual countries. Such distortions do not allow either domestic or international markets to establish prices which reflect production costs. Consequently, resources such as labor, capital, and land may be used in the domestic production of commodities that are protected by tariffs and which could be produced more cheaply abroad. With full employment of all resources worldwide, domestic resources, if reemployed in producing nonprotected domestic commodities or exports, could yield a net increment to world output. That is, without tariffs foreign resources would be committed to producing those commodities for which they have a comparative advantage while domestic resources would be employed in producing commodities for export and domestic consumption which can be produced at least cost domestically. For example, if country x can produce commodity A at half the cost of resources compared with country y, but country x can only produce commodity B with equal resource costs as country y, country x has a comparative advantage in producing commodity A. Without tariffs x will obviously import commodity B and export commodity A. If x institutes a tariff rate of above 100 percent on commodity B and places no restrictions on domestic producers as to the mix of domestic production between A and B, and y does not retaliate with its own

---

[11] See *Water Wasteland* (Report of Ralph Nader's Task Force on Water Pollution) (Washington: Center for the Study of Responsive Law, 1971).

[12] See P. A. Samuelson, "The Gains from International Trade Once Again," *Economic Journal,* December 1962 (Vol. 72, No. 288), pp. 820-829.

tariffs, then producers in x will shift resources to production and export of commodity B and attempt to import commodity A. The net result will be that the combined output of x and y in producing A and B will fall. In the extreme case in which all resources in country x are transferred to the production of B and all resources in country y are utilized in producing commodity A, and each country contains an equal endowment of resources, world production of B will remain constant but production of A will decline by 50 percent. While extremely simple, this example illustrates how tariffs distort the global allocation of resources and thereby reduce the level of global output.[13] In reducing global output and efficiency of resource use tariffs are presumed to also reduce world welfare since world output could be increased and distributed by tariff removal in such a way that no country would be made worse off while at least one country would be made better off.

External diseconomies associated with waste residuals are like tariffs in creating distortions in international markets and thereby in affecting world output and welfare. A domestic external diseconomy which has not been internalized yields a separation between private production costs and social costs meaning that the real production costs are not reflected in domestic or export prices. The effect of such a separation on world welfare is precisely the same as that of tariffs. Since resources are inefficiently allocated both domestically and internationally, at least one country can be made better off without harming others (given suitable redistribution of goods) by correcting for the external diseconomy. Note, however, that external diseconomies involve the production of "bads" which are unpriced by domestic or international markets. Therefore, unlike tariff removal, internalizing external diseconomies may result in reduced production and trade of commodities and therefore a *reduction* in world output. But this reduction is only in output of commodities already traded and not in output of such untraded goods as domestic air or water quality.

Tariff and Externality Distortions

Import tariffs or exports subsidies cause distortions in two ways:

---

[13] While tariffs tend to reduce global output and efficient utilization of resources viewed globally, tariffs may improve the welfare position of any individual country, especially if there is little or no tariff retaliation by other countries. As a simple example, if country x placed a tariff on comodity B and this action caused y to demand less of commodity A but pay more for it in terms of commodity B, i.e., inelastic demand for commodity B in country y, then country x may be made better off. This occurs because x receives in addition to the tariff revenue on B a greater amount of B per unit of A exported which is large enough to offset the loss in revenue from reduced exports of A.

1) They drive a wedge between domestic and international costs of production at the margin; and 2) they induce a distortion between domestic valuation of commodities and their foreign valuation by consumers. Domestic prices do not adequately reflect costs of production *or* consumer valuations abroad. Unlike monopolistic factor or product markets which only distort the production side of domestic and international markets, tariffs induce distortions from both production and consumption forces in domestic and international markets. International differences in productivity, factor availability, and technology are not allowed to be fully reflected in cost differences between states when tariffs are introduced. Consequently, the correct price signals are not available to domestic producers. The result is that domestic producers tend to produce smaller quantities of exports and larger quantities of commodities competing with imports than they would if tariffs were not imposed. Also, consumers responding to relatively lower prices of commodities produced domestically consume too small a quantity of imports and excessive amounts of the import-competing commodity produced domestically.

When external diseconomies arise domestically in the production of goods normally imported, the distortion in domestic production and consumption patterns is similar to that of tariffs. The major difference between tariffs and external diseconomies in domestic production is that tariffs affect price signals while external diseconomies affect cost signals to domestic producers. Domestic production costs of import-type commodities are lower since environmental services are unpriced domestically. This induces too high a rate of domestic production of commodities normally imported and too low a level of production of exports, which is identical in direction of effect to import tariffs. Likewise, because of lower domestic prices for imports domestically produced, domestic demand is too large. Further, because the external diseconomy results in unpriced damages to consumers, consumer patterns of consumption are distorted in the domestic economy. Thus, import tariffs and external diseconomies in domestic production of import-type commodities are similar in their effect in distorting both production and consumption patterns.

External diseconomies in the domestic production of exports (and not in imports) are similar to import subsidies or export tariffs in impact on production and consumption. Export prices due to non-priced environmental services used in their production will be lower than they should be both in domestic and in international markets. The result will be excessive production of exports and excessive domestic consumption of commodities which should be exported. In the case in which both imports and exports have identical external diseconomies associated with their domestic production, domestic production and consumption of both exports and imports will be too large. Finally, when external diseconomies arise in both domestic and foreign production processes, little can be said regarding excessive domestic production of export *or* import type of commodities without detailed information on the relative magnitude of the external diseconomies encountered both domestically and abroad.

The foregoing statements lead us to the conclusion that external diseconomies are structurally more like tariff distortions than other types of domestic distortions (e.g., the presence of monopolies in product or factor markets). This is because uncorrected external diseconomies, like tariffs, distort price and cost signals to both domestic producers and consumers whereas domestic distortions in factor and/or product markets distort domestic production patterns but not domestic consumer responses to competitively established international prices.[14] In addition, and perhaps most importantly, the distortions are likely to be more pervasive on the consumption side with external diseconomies than with tariffs. The reason is simply that receptors or parties damaged by waste residuals stemming from production are generally consumers, particularly in highly urbanized locations. In the absence of a suitable negotiating mechanism consumers are unable to register their preferences for less waste residuals through payments or other means. In consequence public "bads" go unpriced and thereby encourage excessive expenditure on other commodities. On the production side external diseconomies also may distort productive efficiency since, with one factor price (for environmental assimilative capacity) constrained to zero, factors of production will not be allocated efficiently. Unlike tariffs, unregulated external diseconomies induce distortions in the economy's efficiency beyond distortions in the amount of exports and imports produced.

Long-run Comparative Advantage, Externalities, and Cost Structure

Efficiency in the production of commodities by a group of trading

[14] In the economist's language there is distortion between domestic consumers' marginal rates of substitution between environmental goods and other goods which thus distorts marginal rates of substitution between other goods and domestic prices. Likewise, the existence of the externality in production means that producers' marginal rates of transformation are equalized with international price ratios but not with the social marginal rates of transformation for the domestic economy. Therefore, external diseconomies not only induce discrepancies in equality of marginal rates of transformation between producers in different countries but also marginal rates of substitution between consumers in different countries on traded commodities. The one case in which such consumer preference distortions would not occur is when no substitution existed between environmental "bads" and internationally traded commodities.

states requires that each country utilize its unique attributes in terms of productive resources to their best advantage. Unique attributes may include such things as special labor skills, relative capital abundance, soil fertility, and, of increasing importance, the environment's capacity to assimilate and neutralize waste residuals. Countries with relatively large environmental assimilative capacities (EAC) should, other things being equal, produce commodities with relatively high wasteloads per unit of production for export and import commodities with relatively low wasteloads in their production. Also, such countries would consume relatively more commodities with greater residuals generated in consumer use (or in final disposal). Of course, these statements are predicated on the assumption that the citizens of countries with relatively high environmental capacity do not have a greater preference for environmental quality compared to countries relatively less well endowed. The introduction of EAC as another determinative factor for patterns of trade is likely in the long run to: 1) reduce the flow of trade in commodities with relatively high residuals generation in their production *and* consumption; 2) increase trade in commodities with relatively high residuals generation in production; and 3) reduce trade in commodities with relatively high residuals generation in their final disposal and use. Given variations in preferences of different countries for improved environmental quality, the resulting patterns of trade are not clearly identifiable without knowledge of each country's preferences and EACs.

There have been assertions that developing countries will prefer to adopt a lower level of environmental quality in order to achieve a higher and more rapidly growing domestic income. If this assertion is true, then in the long run there will be economic pressures for high residuals generating industries to relocate in developing countries with substantial natural EACs. Such relocations are desirable from a global efficiency viewpoint, since comparative advantage and differences in preferences are reflected, but may be harmful for some industrialized countries.[15] A fear has emerged that some developing countries may become "pollution havens" and thereby achieve a trade position superior to industrialized states with assumed higher emission or environmental quality standards. While in the short run particular industries in the developed countries may be placed at a competitive disadvantage, in the long run domestic factors of production will be shifted to more internationally productive uses pro-

---

[15] In this and later sections we have assumed that developing countries can and do develop adequate analytical procedures for assessing damages and monitoring waste flow as well as reasonable enforcement provisions. If this is not true, then the statements on global efficiency and comparative advantage may well be invalid.

vided domestic and international prices are allowed to reflect all costs including waste disposal costs. Several policy tools to mitigate the impact of loss in comparative advantage in the short run by particular domestic industries are discussed in section IV.

The shift in domestic and export prices accompanying implementation of domestic environmental controls depends crucially on the magnitude of control costs to domestic industries and on the structure of all production costs. Several estimates have been developed as to the likely extent of changes in production costs resulting from domestic environmental control programs. These estimates, although not strictly comparable, indicate that pollution control costs for the United States will increase total costs for producing exports in the approximate range of 2 to 8 percent.[16] However, for specific industries the *full* effect of changes in costs including the industry's own pollution control costs as well as pollution control costs for other industries which supply inputs to the industry may be much larger. For example, Wassily Leontief estimates that the range of increase in costs necessary for air pollution control (for products that enter the export sector) spreads from 0.2 percent for petroleum refining to 16.8 percent for primary nonferrous metals. Changes in domestic costs of these probable magnitudes may have a substantial impact on export prices and thereby comparative advantage, but the exact magnitude depends on the structure of all production costs.

The first question that may be posed regarding the connection between changes in domestic costs and changes in export prices is whether the export industry produces its products under conditions of increasing, decreasing, or constant costs per unit of product.[17] If the domestic pollution industry produced under conditions of constant costs per unit of product, then export prices will be shifted upward by an amount equal to pollution control costs (including damages not ameliorated by pollution abatement if effluent charges are imposed) per unit of product. However, for industries with increasing costs per unit of production, as production expands a proportion of the pollution control costs will be paid for via lower profits

---

[16] See W. Leontief and W. Ford, "Air Pollution and the Economic Structure: Empirical Results of Input-Output Computations" (mimeographed), referenced in the General Agreement on Tariffs and Trade study cited below; Ralph C. d'Arge, "International Trade and Domestic Environmental Control: Some Empirical Estimates," in Kneese, Rolfe, and Harned, appendix F; and "Industrial Pollution Control and International Trade," *GATT Studies in International Trade* (Geneva: General Agreement on Tariffs and Trade, July 1971), p. 26.

[17] In this discussion we implicitly presume that pollution control costs or damages are not so pervasive as to cause a basically decreasing-cost industry to become an increasing-cost industry or vice versa.

to the industry, and export prices will increase by less than the domestic pollution abatement costs and damages, when these are added to other production costs which increase prices but in so doing induce a reduction in sales. The reduction in domestic and export sales raises the average cost per unit of production in decreasing-cost industries, creating a greater adjustment in prices than the cost of pollution including abatement and damages. Thus, countries with decreasing-cost industries in the export sector will tend to have relatively larger adjustments in export prices stemming from pollution abatement costs.

In the United States a substantial proportion of exports (very crudely more than 50 percent) are produced by industries with estimated increasing returns to scale which implies decreasing costs. Perhaps it can be inferred that this is true for other developed countries. Alternatively, agriculture and raw materials industries tend to be subject to constant or decreasing returns which on balance is suggestive that developing countries' exports may be produced under conditions of constant or increasing costs. In consequence it can be expected that developed countries will undergo export price changes in excess of domestic pollution control costs while developing countries' export prices, if these states institute domestic controls which are reflected in export prices and costs, will shift by less than pollution control costs. Of course, the above statements may not be applicable to any particular industry or country since scale effects or differences in technology could make an industry subject to increasing costs in one country and decreasing costs in another. What this brief discussion does illustrate, however, is that a simple one-to-one correspondence between pollution control costs and changes in export prices undoubtedly does not exist.[18]

Some Observations on Domestic External Diseconomies and Protection

So far, our remarks on comparative advantage have been directed

[18] In addition there is some slight evidence that decreasing-cost industries in the United States will have higher costs for pollution abatement. A correlation coefficient of .58 was obtained between measured returns to scale and air pollution abatement costs as estimated by Leontief and Ford, where both variables were transformed into logarithms. From this one might even infer that a proportion of the observed increasing returns to scale is "explained" by excessive utilization of the natural environment although the meager evidence at this point does not allow more than a casual hypothesis. Data on increasing returns to scale for the United States by industry was obtained from: George H. Hildebrand and Ta-Chung Liu, *Manufacturing Production Functions in the United States, 1957: An Inter-Industry and Interstate Comparison of Productivity* (Ithaca, N.Y: New York State School of Industrial and Labor Relations, Cornell University, 1965).

toward the effects on comparative advantage of effluent charges, emission standards, or any other control strategy in which costs are wholly reflected in domestic prices. We have also briefly discussed the connection between changes in domestic costs and changes in domestic and thereby international prices. However, questions regarding the use of domestic environmental control strategies which have no impact or a substantially different impact on the domestic and international price structure have not been posed or answered. Also, we have as yet not considered the effect of using tariffs or nontariff barriers to reduce the domestic impact of environmental control programs.

As was mentioned earlier, a trend appears to have emerged in developed countries toward the utilization of emission, effluent, and/or quality standards coupled with subsidies for the construction of particular types of waste treatment facilities. Of course, strictly enforced emission standards with no compensating treatment cost subsidies will have a similar impact on domestic costs and therefore export prices as effluent charges since domestic firms must incur costs to meet such standards. However, partial or complete subsidization through such means as investment tax writeoffs, special leasing arrangements, relocation costs of pollution-affected groups, or any payments strategy which is not reflected in higher production costs will cause domestic and international prices to be distorted. If all countries adopt a standards-subsidies approach, then only by chance will the resulting international trade patterns be efficient. In addition there will be pressures for countries, especially developing ones, to lower standards and pressures in the developed countries to increase subsidies. Consequently, little or no relationship will emerge between the types of goods a country exports and the country's natural endowment of environmental assimilative capacity or preferences for environmental quality. Pressures may also develop to equalize standards *and* subsidies between countries so that no particular country would be given a net advantage for location of relatively high polluting industries. But such an outcome would only be globally efficient if all countries had identical preferences, technologies, and natural endowments including waste residuals assimilation, a most unrealistic hypothesis since in that case there is no economic reason for trade. In consequence, in order to avoid such distortions and politically expedient but economically unsound retaliation between countries most, if not all, pollution control costs should be reflected in export prices. The possibility of pressures for individual countries to take remedial action in order to protect domestic industries would still be present but might be countered by the threat of retaliatory action by others. Trade patterns would at least be partially, if not completely, determined by comparative advantage.

If higher import tariff rates are adopted in conjunction with domestic environmental control programs which affect costs and prices, then the economy is simultaneously undergoing a reduction in one distortion while being confronted by an increase in another. The net effect may or may not be advantageous to the country. In the long run it is not likely to be advantageous if tariff imposition induces other countries to also implement protective tariffs. This is because the country will not be utilizing its domestic resources efficiently, *and* its trade will be reduced substantially by multilateral adoption of tariffs.

Nontariff barriers such as artificially high quality restrictions, quantitative restrictions or quotas, and quarantine requirements have the same impact as tariffs in distorting comparative advantage. However, in many cases regarding environmental protection it will be difficult to discover whether nontariff barriers are being used to protect the domestic environment or are subtle ways of achieving protection for domestic firms confronted with rising domestic costs (and thereby loss in competitive international advantage). As we have already argued, nontariff barriers are inappropriate mechanisms for domestic control of waste residuals resulting from consumption. Trade in intermediate products such as petroleum which yields residuals in the production process also should not be subject to tariff or nontariff barriers but be taxed or subject to standards only when used. However, if nontariff barriers are instituted by certain countries, then an attempt should be made to convince them to institute the least restrictive import barriers on commodities that these countries have a comparative disadvantage in producing. Also, if possible, fixed time limits on tariff or nontariff barriers should be encouraged.

Even though traditional tariff or nontariff barriers are not utilized by countries to mitigate the impact of domestic environmental controls, other more subtle forms of barriers to trade will undoubtedly arise. An example is the recent law in the Federal Republic of Germany (West Germany) restricting the lead content of gasoline to 0.15 grams per liter.[19] Ostensibly, the law was passed to reduce lead emissions from automobiles in West Germany although it has the simultaneous impact of restricting sales of other countries' automobiles in West Germany, which is clearly a nontariff trade barrier. West German vehicles can be easily adjusted to low lead gasolines, but several major Italian and French automobile makers' high compression engines cannot be so easily adjusted. Is this a nontariff barrier? We do not know, but the example indicates the potential complexity of deciding

[19] See Claire Sterling, "Depolluting Autos is Complex Issue," *Washington Post,* November 9, 1971, p. A18.

which environmental controls are barriers and which are not. We would recommend that the General Agreement on Tariffs and Trade (GATT) or a GATT-type of organization be used to analyze and arbitrate such barriers so that if possible, environmental control does not become the instrument of selective nontariff barriers.

Environmental Controls and the Developing Countries

Perhaps one of the most discouraging aspects of international environmental agreements is the feeling that such agreements between developed countries will have a negative economic impact on developing countries. There are several dimensions to the presumed negative economic impact. The first deals with the implicit assumption by developing countries that governmental expenditure of all types is relatively fixed in the developed countries and that environmental control costs in these countries will come, at least partially, at the expense of aid funds for developing countries. Thus, environmental control is viewed as a potential substitute for a use of expenditure normally earmarked for foreign aid by developed countries. Whether budgets are relatively fixed and the developed countries will actually view domestic environmental control as a higher-priority use of funds than foreign aid cannot be foreseen. However, a few very crude indicators can potentially be developed for the United States. A rough estimate of investment and other costs for a "substantial" reduction in environmental pollution in the United States is $95 billion for the next six years, or about $16 billion per year.[20]

This amount, if viewed as a percentage of the expected increase in gross national product (GNP) for the United States during the next six years, is substantial — about 35 percent.[21] Also, if one presumes that the entire environmental pollution program is going to be financed via subsidies by the United States government, then a $16 billion annual increase constitutes a sizeable expansion of about 8 percent in federal expenditure. Such a budgetary increase may very well induce some net reductions in foreign aid, but it is more likely to reduce or eliminate any net increases. What is overlooked is that it is doubtful that a substantial proportion of the total costs for environmental pollution reductions will be borne by the United States government. If the "polluter must pay" principle is adopted extensively, then direct and indirect subsidization for pollution control can be expected to be substantially less than 50 percent of total pollu-

---

[20] Estimate is taken from Allen V. Kneese, "The Economics of Environmental Pollution in the United States," in Kneese, Rolfe, and Harned, chapter 1.
[21] Ibid.

tion costs, or roughly $7 to $8 billion per year.[22] However, this amounts to only about a 3 to 4 percent increase in governmental expenditures per year which is unlikely to have a very pronounced negative impact on the level of foreign aid funds. As regards foreign aid, at least for the United States, the impact on foreign aid funds to developing countries will likely be smaller if an extensive set of emission standards and/or effluent charges system is adopted rather than a substantial subsidization system.

A second dimension of the potential negative economic impact of environmental control programs of developed economies on developing economies is due to the implied change in terms of trade between these two blocs of countries. If the developed economies adopt simultaneously a domestic charges or standards system for waste emissions control, this implies that some increase will occur in their export prices and some decrease in the profitability of investment relative to the developing economies. The normally expected impact would be a deterioration of the balance of payments in both current and capital accounts for the developed economies and improvement for the developing economies. Higher export prices would be expected to reduce exports, and lower profit rates would divert international capital flows toward more profitable ventures in developing countries. Alternatively, extensive governmental financing of subsidies programs in developed economies is likely to have the opposite effect unless subsidies are tied explicitly to waste emissions damages, according to the arguments we presented in section II. In the subsidies case profit rates will not decrease but will more than likely increase. On balance, subsidies related to reductions in effluent discharges will have an impact on export prices similar to but probably smaller than that of effluent charges but a different impact on international capital flows. Certainly, from the viewpoint of developing countries, emission standards or effluent charges adopted by the developed economies would appear to offer the fewest disadvantages in terms of both aid funds and trade repercussions. However, as will be discussed in section III, when export earnings adjustments and international income repercussions are considered, this tentative conclusion may or may not be correct.

Risking gross and potentially error-prone simplification, let us assume for the moment that there are three types of countries: developed, developing, and a third category containing countries which

---

[22] This calculation is made by presuming the United States government subsidies 50 percent of the change in costs for treatment of municipal sewage and 100 percent of the costs associated with separation of storm and sanitary sewers. All other industrial, municipal, and vehicular waste emissions control costs are presumed to be paid for by the emitter or some other nongovernmental entity.

are assumed not to participate substantially in international pollution agreements or to undertake very extensive domestic environmental control programs but which export commodities which are close substitutes for the developed economies' exports. Also, we assume that international competition for markets exists: between developed countries; to a lesser degree between developed and industrialized developing countries; and between developing countries. Competition for international markets between developing and developed or developing and industrialized developing is presumed to be relatively small. Thus, it is envisioned that there is a substantial degree of horizontal competition but not vertical competition between countries when vertical classification is specified by degree of development, i.e., level of income or income per capita. In this synthetic trading world it is assumed that export price elasticities of demand (a measure of the percentage change in exports demanded given a one percent change in the ratio of import prices) for particular countries increase (in absolute value) as degree of development increases.[23]

Finally, to complete this system of assumptions it will be taken as given that only the developed countries, and in certain instances the industrialized developing countries, impose substantial domestic pollution control programs which raise domestic and trading prices.

The first case to be considered is that in which all developed countries simultaneously institute waste emission control programs of varying degrees utilizing emission standards or charges. Clearly, all will undergo some reduction in exports since these countries' export prices will increase relative to their semi-competitors, the industrialized developing countries. Since export elasticities of demand are assumed to be elastic for the developed countries, export earnings will decrease for them. Likewise, for the developing countries with presumed inelastic demands for exports and declining relative prices, exports will increase but export earnings will also decrease. Alternatively, for the industrialized developing economies, rising prices of their competitors, the developed countries, may or may not lead to changes in export prices. However, it could be expected that these countries would have increased export earnings since export prices may be relatively stable but demand for their exports would increase.

The negative impact on export earnings of both developed and developing countries might be reduced or ameliorated if the industrialized developing countries were to adopt the strategem of standards and/or charges but implement them more slowly than did the developed countries. In the extreme case in which both developed and indus-

[23] For some evidence on this assertion see H. S. Houthakker and Stephen P. Magee, "Income and Price Elasticities in World Trade," *Review of Economics and Statistics*, May 1969 (Vol. 51, No. 2), pp. 111-125.

trialized developing countries simultaneously adopted relatively similar levels of nonsubsidized environmental controls, export earnings of all countries might fall.[24] However, such a decrease in export earnings in isolation tells us little about the impact on domestic incomes or the balance of payments of each group of countries. It only indicates that the amount of foreign exchange exchanged is reduced.

In the next section balance-of-payments and income impacts of domestic environmental controls are analyzed. However, before proceeding to impacts we should mention a third dimension of the special problems encountered by developing countries. This dimension arises with regard to threats of retaliation by developed countries to induce either industrialized developing or developing countries to impose more rigid environmental controls than they otherwise would consider. Retaliatory action such as trade barriers, which markedly influence international prices and thereby comparative advantage, should be discouraged for the many reasons outlined above. Only in cases of transnational pollution of a significant degree might there be some justification for potential threats of retaliation.[25]

III. NATURE AND MAGNITUDE OF MACROECONOMIC IMPACTS: BALANCE OF PAYMENTS AND NATIONAL INCOME

Introduction

In section II the long-term ramification for comparative advantage and competitive trading position of countries resulting from domestic environmental control programs were discussed. In this section we turn to a shorter time horizon and concentrate on the immediate or short-term effect of domestic environmental controls on two important indicators of social welfare for individual countries, national income or product and the balance of payments. Empirical estimates of the impact of environmental control programs on these two indicators are presented in this section. We omit explicit consideration of retaliatory actions by countries and concentrate explicitly on changes in national income and the balance of payments of selected countries resulting from the unilateral *and* multilateral imposition of environmental controls. Only those environmental controls such as standards and effluent charges which may have a substantial impact on domestic and export prices are considered in terms of empirically estimating impacts.

---

[24] That is, provided our assumptions on demand elasticities of the different blocs are valid.

[25] On this point see the discussion by Baumol.

An upward shift in domestic and export prices caused by one country unilaterally adopting environmental controls will induce adjustments in the balance of payments and national income emanating from at least two sources. First, substitution of relatively cheaper imports for domestic commodities will occur if: a) import and domestic-export commodities are substitutes; and b) if environmental controls on domestic firms result in higher domestic-export prices. Second, higher domestic and export prices through shifts in demand for imports and domestic commodities will influence the level of domestic production and thus domestic incomes. These initial shifts in domestic demand and income through multiplier-type repercussions will induce further adjustments in domestic income and imports.

The chain of economic events might be described as follows. A set of unilateral domestic environmental controls (related to effluent reductions) is imposed. This action increases export prices. The potential rise in export prices changes demands for exports, imports, and domestic products in domestic markets *simultaneously* via changes in the terms of trade. These changes in both foreign and domestic demand alter the equilibrium level of domestic expenditure and income. As both foreign and domestic incomes adjust to the changes in demand, if full employment is not achieved, multiplier-type repercussions will occur thus further altering the level of income and employment. A price-income adjustment system with foreign repercussions is thus hypothesized for measuring changes in the balance of payments and national income when there is less than full employment and in the short run no governmental actions are taken to remove the impact of unilateral domestic pollution controls on domestic or export prices.

The repercussions as structured are only intermediate in focus since the impact originates from an exogenous shift in export prices and concludes with the resulting adjustments in the balance of payments and national income. However, provided the government did not take remedial action on income, balance of payments, or the terms of trade via barriers to trade, a second adjustment would occur. The second adjustment would originate from the highly probable balance-of-payments disequilibrium caused by the initial shift in domestic and export prices. If the balance of payments was in deficit due to the price shift, normally we would expect a negative adjustment in the terms of trade so that balance-of-payments equilibrium (no deficit or surplus) would be achieved. The resulting movement in the terms of trade would not only influence the balance of payments in the direction of an equilibrium but also would induce further multiplier- and price-related adjustments to the level of domestic income via the mechanism described earlier. Our empirical results do not contain an estimate of this "second-round" effect which brings about balance-of-payments equilibrium. Thus, these estimates are of a short-run or impact nature and do not indicate the complete equilibrium movement of domestic income. What they do offer is an estimate of the degree of potential change in the balance of payments and national income that arises without considering the "feedback" of balance-of-payments disequilibrium on the terms of trade. Such a set of estimates, while not yielding reliable measures of national income or balance-of-payments adjustments, does indicate the potential direction of movement and the potential severity of environmental controls as a domestic policy problem. For example, if country y's estimated adjustment in national income is twice that of x's in percentage terms, then we can conclude that unilaterally imposed environmental controls will be a much more difficult policy question and require more extensive remedial actions on the part of policymakers in country y.

Assumptions and Basic Structure of the Empirical Model

In order to clarify the meaning and indicate the extreme qualifications of the empirical results given later in this section we present a very precise list of underlying assumptions used to develop the empirical model. Some, if not most, are fairly standard assumptions in the international trade literature for balance-of-payments adjustment models.[26] However, we present them hoping that the reader will become more fully aware of the basic structure and potential biases of the empirical model.

1) The trading world can be reasonably divided into six major trading blocs or countries: France, Japan, the United Kingdom, the United States, West Germany, and the rest of the world aggregated into one bloc.

2) It is assumed that a meaningful aggregation of different types of export, import, and domestic commodities is obtained by simply comparing the aggregate money value in real terms of all exports, all imports, or domestic consumption.

3) Adjustment of domestic and export commodity costs due to domestically imposed environmental controls is transmitted primarily through changes in prices and is not to any significant extent absorbed by losses in profits. If polluting firms tended to absorb these costs in profits and prices shifted very little, the impact on comparative advantage would be similar to the impact of subsidies discussed in earlier sections. However, an impact may result on international capital flows, and thus on the balance of payments, if domestic profit rates are substantially reduced.

---

[26] See, for example, Jaroslav Vanek, *International Trade: Theory and Economic Policy* (Homewood, Ill: Richard Irwin, 1962).

4) Exchange rates are pegged, and domestic monetary and fiscal policies are implicitly assumed to be operating to maintain constant interest rates and exchange-rate stability.

5) There is less than full employment in the domestic economy, and goods are assumed to be produced under conditions of constant marginal costs. These assumptions make the empirical model "demand-oriented" in that shifts in demand for domestic, export, and import commodities *completely* determine changes in the level of domestic output and income.

6) Domestic and export prices of the other countries and rest of the world bloc are constant in the unilateral case of imposing domestic environmental controls. In the case of multilateral adoption of environmental controls it is assumed that the net impact on any one country is the cumulative sum of the effects on that country of each other country imposing domestic environmental controls.

7) Estimated behavioral coefficients including marginal propensities to absorb domestic product, to export, to import, and to save and all import price elasticities and cross price elasticities of demand are constant or do not markedly change over the range of estimated domestic and export price changes.

8) The trading world is inherently stable in that the sum of the marginal propensities to absorb domestic product, import, and save equal one. If this were not the case, the empirical estimates of domestic income and balance-of-payments changes would not necessarily be toward a new equilibrium.

9) There are no compensating actions initiated by the countries selected or the rest of the world bloc when unilateral or multilateral environmental controls are instituted. Thus, such actions as tariffs or nontariff trade barriers which may be instituted unilaterally to protect domestic industries from foreign competition are not considered. Also, barriers placed on imported goods which have relatively high residuals generation in their use or final disposal are not taken into account. In consequence the estimates we derive later must be viewed as the probable *extreme* changes in income and balance of payments.

10) The base year selected for empirical estimation was 1968. Thus, all weights as regards export and import composition by commodity type, domestic and export price levels, and aggregate indices of the value of domestic consumption, production, exports, and imports relate to 1968. All estimates of coefficients were derived from annual data by country for the period 1952 through 1968. It appeared that 1968 was not a year of serious aggregate distortions in normal trade patterns.

11) All demand relationships for imports and domestically produced goods of all countries are assumed to be additively separable,

i.e., a shift in one variable affecting demand will not influence the magnitude of the effect of any other variable. (This is partially implied in assumption 7. It is restated here to emphasize the specific assumptions associated with demand.)

12) Demand for imports by country y from country x is assumed to be primarily determined by: the level of gross national income in country y; the terms of trade between country x and country y, i.e., domestic prices in y divided by export prices of x; and the terms of trade between country y and the rest of the world bloc defined as the import prices of y divided by y's export prices. All prices were expressed in index number form with quantity weights for 1968 by commodity type (the United Nations classification was utilized for identifying commodity types). Demand for domestic goods was presumed to be determined by gross national income and the terms of trade between the domestic economy and all other countries. A mathematical exposition of the demand relationships and other aspects of the impact model is presented in appendix 1.

Given this set of assumptions, an empirical model can be derived which will yield estimates of the change in the balance of payments and national income of the five countries and the rest of the world. Before proceeding to a discussion of the actual estimates we should make several statements with regard to the assumptions. First, if monetary and fiscal policies are operated so as to insure full employment and, perhaps, stable domestic interest rates, then the impact on real income from a shift in terms of trade due to environmental controls can be expected to be small, if not zero. Thus, the assumption that the government will take no unilateral countervailing actions (and proceed as just another producer and consumer in the economy) is perhaps the most restrictive one. However, unless the pattern of governmental actions is known in advance, no empirical estimation can be undertaken which accounts for this. And unless the government involved knows in advance the severity of the problem, it is doubtful if it can decide on the extent of countervailing action. Second, adding together into one dollar sum such diverse commodity types as agricultural products, electrical machinery, and petroleum does not allow one to discover which types of products will be affected most or least from changes in comparative international advantage. Also, such aggregations over commodity types for individual countries probably bias upward the estimated magnitude of change in balance of payments and national income but conceal partially the potential magnitude of change in the commodity composition of trade. This is due to the omission of considerations on adjustments within the country to changes in the terms of trade except at the aggregate demand level. Third, the division of the trading world into five major countries and the rest of the world introduced some inherent biases. For example, the European Economic Community (EEC) or European Free Trade Association (EFTA) trading blocs are not explicitly recognized. Also, preferential agreements or other forms of particular trading arrangement between these countries or blocs are not recognized by the division of trading blocs selected. In partial defense of the division it should be recognized that domestic environmental programs are likely to be decided on without substantial international negotiation. In light of this consideration and the fact that the countries selected represent a very large proportion of free-world exports the division appeared to be appropriate at least for an experimental model of the type described here.

Finally, it should be stressed again that given all of the qualifications set forth above, the resulting empirical estimates must be viewed as basically experimental at least at this stage of model development and testing.

Preliminary Estimates of Balance-of-Payments and National Income Impacts

In tables 1 and 2 the estimates of income and balance-of-payments changes in response to increased export prices are given. The percentage changes in export prices were calculated by taking estimated domestic increases in costs due to a substantial environmental control program by commodity type and weighting these cost changes by the dollar value of the commodity exported in 1968. Cost estimates and the weighting procedure are described in an earlier article.[27] These estimated export price changes are recorded in column 1 of tables 1 and 2 by country. It should be noted that we assumed all cost increases are completely reflected in export price changes. This is consistent with the assumption of the model that all commodities are produced under conditions of constant costs but requires severe qualification as was pointed out in section II.

Income and balance-of-payments adjustments were only calculated for the case in which the five countries unilaterally or, in selected combinations, multilaterally instituted "substantial" domestic environmental control programs while the "rest of the world" bloc as a whole had *no perceptible* change in export prices. Thus, the "rest of the world" sector taken as an aggregate was presumed not to participate significantly in domestic environmental programs which would raise export prices. This assumption may not be valid for certain relatively "developed" countries in Western Europe and elsewhere.

[27] See d'Arge, in Kneese, Rolfe, and Harned, appendix F.

However, given the degree of aggregation implied in using a "rest of the world" trading bloc, it appears reasonable to make this assumption.

A rather startling result emerged for estimated gross national income adjustments. For the United States, Japan, and France a unilateral export price increase resulted in a positive change in income for them as well as for the "rest of the world" bloc. Alternatively, export price increases (unilaterally adjusted) in West Germany and the United Kingdom resulted in a negative change in their domestic income. Also, if the United States, Japan, or France institutes unilateral environmental controls, the changes in income of all other countries as well as their own are positive. This occurs because of the multiplier nature, and the less than full employment assumption, of the model. An increase in export prices stimulates substitution to other countries' exports and away from the country with the price rise. But, expanded export sales and income of the other countries leads to *increased* exports sales by the price-raising country. This stimulation of export sales from increased incomes of other countries is greater than the reduction in income due to export price increases, resulting in a *net* positive change in domestic income. If full employment already exists, these results suggest that domestic and export prices will increase and thereby create domestic inflationary pressures. Note also that implicit in the model is the assumption that the balance of payments adjusts to a disequilibrium level which is consistent with the change in domestic income. The estimated negative change in balance of payments for all countries with unilateral export price changes (see table 2) indicates that the change in income is accompanied by and sustained by this deficit.

Given the assumptions underlying the model, we are able to calculate the cumulative effect on income of unilateral export price adjustments by all five countries. This process yields an estimate of the net change in income of each country if all five countries adopted price-changing environmental controls simultaneously. An estimate of this net change in income is recorded in row seven of table 1. Rows eight, nine, and ten contain the estimates of net change in income for multilateral adoption of environmental controls with Japan, France, and Japan plus France omitted from the multilateral decision, respectively. In the case of multilateral decisions involving all five of the countries or the subsets just specified, net income changes for all countries and the "rest of the world" were estimated to be positive. This result is surprising and should be taken at least initially as severely qualifying interpretations of the model's estimates. However, these very preliminary results raise some issues regarding the usually expected effect on incomes resulting from increasing export prices, or more importantly, from domestic changes in production costs. They certainly indicate that substantial research must be undertaken by any country before an adequate prediction can be made of changes in domestic income resulting from environmental controls.

In table 2 estimates of balance-of-payments adjustments are recorded for the five countries and the "rest of the world" bloc. In the unilateral case all countries had an estimated negative change in their balance of payments resulting from a positive change in export prices although the magnitude of change varied markedly between countries. With unilateral imposition of environmental controls by West Germany and the United Kingdom there were calculated balance-of-payments deficits for other countries as well. If West Germany unilaterally adopted domestic environmental controls which raised export prices, West Germany, Japan, and the "rest of the world" bloc would undergo a balance of payments deficit; if the United Kingdom unilaterally initiated such controls, the United Kingdom, West Germany, and the "rest of the world" bloc would probably undergo a balance of payments deficit. Only in the case of unilateral controls by the United States would the "rest of the world" bloc not be estimated to have a balance-of-payments deficit.

In the multilateral case in which all five countries adopt environmental controls simultaneously the *net* effect on the balance of payments is positive for the United States, the United Kingdom, and Japan while it is negative for France, West Germany, and the "rest of the world." For the various combinations of multilateral action the net effect can be either positive or negative depending on which countries are omitted except for Japan (with all positive changes) and the rest of the world (with all negative changes). It should be emphasized that there is a substantial variability in the estimated change in balance of payments among the countries with unilateral or multilateral shifts in export prices. However, for the multilateral case involving all countries none of the estimated negative changes in balance of payments exceeded one percent of 1968 exports.

Comparison with Other Estimates and Further Qualifications

In an earlier study one of the present authors reported estimates of income and balance-of-payments adjustments for the five countries.[28] The same export price change estimates were utilized in that study as are applied here. However, the previous model was much more aggregative in that it contained only one country and a "rest of the

---

[28] See d'Arge, in Kneese, Rolfe, and Harned, appendix F. Some of the results of the earlier aggregated model were also presented in: R. C. d'Arge, "Essay on Economic Growth and Environmental Quality," *Swedish Journal of Economics,* March 1971 (Vol. 73, No. 1), pp. 25-41.

TABLE 1. ESTIMATED CHANGE IN INCOME RESULTING FROM THE IMPOSITION OF ENVIRONMENTAL CONTROLS, FIVE COUNTRIES, 1968 (MILLIONS OF UNITED STATES DOLLARS)

Income Changes in Millions of Dollars and as Percentage of 1968 Gross National Income by Country

Export Price Percentage Increase by Country	United States Dollars (Millions)	United States Percentage	Japan Dollars (Millions)	Japan Percentage	West Germany Dollars (Millions)	West Germany Percentage	United Kingdom Dollars (Millions)	United Kingdom Percentage	France Dollars (Millions)	France Percentage	Rest of the World Dollars (Millions)	Rest of the World Percentage
(1) 3.6 percent by the United States	13,869	1.80	3,410	2.98	3,843	3.29	1,686	1.97	2,091	1.95	3,868	1.48
(2) 4.0 percent by Japan	1,606	0.21	1,594	1.39	394	0.34	225	0.26	235	0.22	411	0.16
(3) 4.0 percent by West Germany	−496	−0.06	−383	−0.33	−3,047	−2.61	−263	−0.31	−707	−0.66	−949	−0.36
(4) 4.0 percent by United Kingdom	−560	−0.07	−294	−0.26	−519	−0.45	−1,236	−1.45	−322	−0.30	−930	−0.36
(5) 3.7 percent by France	5,494	0.71	2,922	2.55	8,110	6.95	2,282	2.68	6,956	6.50	5,426	2.07
Sum of (1), (2), (3), (4), and (5)	19,914	2.58	7,249	6.33	8,782	7.52	2,695	3.15	8,254	6.77	7,826	2.99
Sum of (1), (3), (4), and (5)	18,307	2.37	5,655	4.94	8,387	7.19	2,470	2.89	8,019	7.49	7,415	3.55
Sum of (1), (2), (3), and (4)	14,420	1.87	4,320	3.77	671	0.57	412	0.48	1,298	1.21	2,400	0.92
Sum of (1), (4), and (5)	18,804	2.43	6,038	5.27	11,434	9.80	2,732	3.20	8,726	8.15	8,364	3.91

TABLE 2. ESTIMATED CHANGE IN BALANCE OF PAYMENTS RESULTING FROM THE IMPOSITION OF ENVIRONMENTAL CONTROLS, FIVE COUNTRIES, 1968 (MILLIONS OF UNITED STATES DOLLARS)

Balance-of-Payments Changes in Millions of Dollars and as Percentage of 1968 Exports by Country

Export Price Percentage Change by Countries	United States		Japan		West Germany		United Kingdom		France		Rest of the World	
	Dollars (Millions)	Percentage	Dollars (Millions)	Percentage	Dollars (Millions)	Percentage	Dollars (Millions)	Percentage	Dollars (Millions)	Percentage	Dollars (Millions)	Percentage
(1) 3.6 percent by the United States	—1,222	—2.66	454	3.13	292	0.94	152	0.76	233	1.37	91	0.13
(2) 4.0 percent by Japan	435	0.95	—274	—1.89	37	0.12	34	0.17	19	0.11	—251	—0.36
(3) 4.0 percent by West Germany	183	0.40	—35	—0.24	—970	—3.12	26	0.12	955	5.60	—157	—0.23
(4) 4.0 percent by the United Kingdom	63	0.12	160	1.08	—24	—0.08	—228	—1.12	162	0.96	—133	—0.19
(5) 3.7 percent by France	858	1.89	155	1.07	477	1.55	129	0.63	—1,393	—8.18	—225	—0.32
Sum of (1), (2), (3), (4), and (5)	317	0.69	459	3.16	—189	—0.61	112	0.55	—24	—0.14	—675	—0.97
Sum of (1), (3), (4), and (5)	—119	—0.26	734	5.06	—226	—0.73	78	0.38	—43	—0.25	—425	—0.61
Sum of (1), (2), (3), and (4)	—541	—1.18	304	2.09	—665	—2.15	—17	—0.08	1,369	8.03	—450	—0.64
Sum of (1), (4), and (5)	—301	—0.66	769	5.30	745	2.40	52	0.26	—997	5.85	—268	—0.38

world" bloc embodying all other countries. The estimates of income changes derived from the earlier model were larger in magnitude (except for the United States) and mostly negative in sign and with balance-of-payments changes positive. Disaggregation from a two- to a six-sector model had the impact of reducing the magnitude and changing the signs of the estimates. However, the sensitivity analyses reported on in the earlier study contained a range of estimates broad enough to include almost all of the estimates given in tables 1 and 2. Also, in the earlier study empirical estimates of elasticities and marginal propensities were collected from secondary sources which were not estimated using precisely identical data. In addition, estimates of elasticities and marginal propensities were not done simultaneously. Finally, and most importantly, the earlier study did not contain interdependencies between countries which have the impact of altering international shifts in demand. Thus, as was stipulated in the previous study, the earlier estimates could not be accepted without severe qualification.

In appendix 1 three tables list the set of estimated coefficients for each country including all marginal propensities to import, marginal propensities to absorb domestic product, price elasticities of demand for imports and exports, and cross price elasticities. Cross price elasticities reflect the impact of changing terms of trade between a country and the rest of the world on imports of that country from some other country or the impact on demand for domestically produced goods resulting from a change in the terms of trade with the "rest of the world." The estimates in some cases are not statistically significant from zero at reasonable test levels for econometric models. Thus, the empirical estimates in tables 1 and 2 are partially derived from a model which contains relationships not adequately observed in the historical past. In order to see how important such nonobserved but imputed relationships were the model was recalculated with all cross price elasticities constrained to zero. This resulted in very minor changes in magnitude of the estimated income and balance-of-payments adjustments and no significant changes in signs. Also, instead of constraining the model so that the sum of all marginal propensities associated with expenditure equaled one we used the original statistical estimates. This resulted in only minor changes in magnitude and sign. This would indicate, at least partially, that the estimates contained in tables 1 and 2 are not markedly affected by changes in magnitude of the estimates of coefficients (unlike the previous model). However, a relatively complete sensitivity analysis has not been worked out as yet for the model developed here.

The model described here probably yields a more accurate (though not necessarily highly accurate) portrayal of the unilateral and multilateral consequences of environmental control programs than the earlier model. The empirical estimates of coefficients are more compatible, the data analyzed is more homogeneous, and the structural characteristics of the model are much more realistic. More work needs to be completed before the empirical estimations and the model outlined here can be reasonably used as a basis of prediction and, most importantly, as a starting point for international assessment of the desirability of multilateral agreements on environmental control strategies. The model's results do indicate two relatively important conclusions: First, the impact of unilateral and multilateral environmental control programs is unlikely to be neutral in effect between countries, but it is crucially dependent on which countries decide to initiate environmental control programs; second, completely multilateral programs are likely to result in relatively small balance-of-payments problems between countries accepting them, at least in the short run.

IV. MITIGATING IMPACTS WITHOUT TRADE BARRIERS: IS IT A GOOD IDEA?

Introduction

We direct the present discussion primarily at the United States situation, but what is described could be utilized by other developed countries (or even developing countries) to mitigate partially the trade impact of environmental controls. Also, we focus on those situations in which the impact of a cost increase is initially on industry and secondarily on consumers. As we explained in section II, in the case of taxes levied on consumer goods (because of an external cost associated with their use or disposal), such as taxes on nonreturnable containers or automobiles, the situation is quite simple: These should be handled as excise taxes presently are. They should not be imposed on exported goods and should be imposed on imported goods when consumed domestically.

Emission controls or taxes imposed at the extraction or fabricating stage will, as we also discussed in section II, affect the basic price structure to one degree or another. Therefore, these cost increases cannot readily be excluded from the price of exported goods, nor should they be. There is no rationale for doing so since the external costs are associated with the production of the article rather than with its consumption.

As we have seen in the above analysis, if the major trading states moved multilaterally to impose controls on a somewhat similar scale, immediate or near-term effects on the balance of payments would be largely canceled. Aside from the adjustment costs which might be avoided by such action, there is good reason to favor more or less simultaneous action by the major industrial economies and to an extent by the industrialized developing economies since, in its absence, or even though all might favor vigorous action in their own countries, each may fear to act individually. But the United States, or any other country, can neither depend on this happening nor delay its own urgently needed programs in anticipation of it. Furthermore, some countries may well decide to provide subsidies to their industries to reduce the generation of residuals.[29]

The question that must be addressed is: "Should the United States move unilaterally to internalize the external cost of production?" We believe that this question must be answered affirmatively if we are to have a socially efficient economy. This general position should not be substantially affected by considerations of possible international trade effects. From the point of view of the domestic economy the case for making industry bear the external costs of production is compelling. At the level of national policy we can largely avoid the international question because, as our analysis above shows, the effects are likely to be minor (probably insignificant) relative to the many other influences which play on international trade.

This is not to say that impacts on particular industries, and especially on some specific plants, might not be substantial—indeed they probably will be. It is quite likely, for example, that some copper mines and pulp mills would close. But these are likely to be marginally profitable operations which are unable to meet the social costs of production even aside from international trade considerations. We favor a program of limited special adjustment assistance (adjustment to a situation in which external costs of production are internalized) not contingent on whether or not the problem for the firm results from its inability to meet either foreign or domestic competition.

Adjustment Assistance

While one can be confident that the adjustments resulting from a well-structured and administered program of internalizing external costs will improve the overall social efficiency of the domestic economy, there may be instances in which there is good reason to publicly assist

[29] Despite the present United States administration's position against such action (see *Environmental Quality: The Second Annual Report of the Council on Environmental Quality together with the President's Message to Congress* [Washington: Government Printing Office, August 1971]) it is already embodied in American policy to some extent through tax writeoff provisions. There seems to be a consensus developing among the major industrial powers (at least at the international conference level) that industry should in general bear the cost of residuals control.

the adjustment process. Basic to any such effort are, of course, policies which sustain a high level of employment generally in the economy. But even when this is the case, pockets of unemployment may persist because of geographical remoteness from employment opportunities or obsolete skills. This situation can be alleviated by policies which are directly targeted on the worker and by those which assist selected firms in adapting to the new situations. An appropriate way to pursue these ends would be through expanding and improving the program of adjustment assistance now available under the Trade Expansion Act. The act's adjustment provisions should be extended to cover all severe adjustment problems (in the sense that substantive long-term unemployment is likely to result) associated with environmental pollution control. A good summary statement concerning the present program is found in the recent report by the Commission on International Trade and Investment:

> Adjustment assistance . . . was introduced in the Trade Expansion Act of 1962 (TEA) to accomplish two specific goals: to alleviate injury stemming from increased competition from imports; and to facilitate the process of domestic adjustment by bringing about a more effective utilization of our manpower and capital. Workers were to be assisted in their transition to new jobs through allowances covering a limited period of retraining or relocation. Firms injured by import competition were to be aided in modernizing their plants and production methods and in switching lines of production through technical, financial, and tax assistance.
>
> Attainment of the first goal would ensure that particular groups in the economy do not suffer undue harm as a result of policies that increase the general well-being, and attainment of the second would improve the productivity of economic resources by enhancing their mobility and upgrading their quality.
>
> Unfortunately, these objectives have rarely been achieved by the current program of adjustment assistance because the program is too narrow, inadequate emphasis is placed on anticipating the need for adjustment, the criteria for eligibility have proved too restrictive, and time-consuming procedures have caused lengthy delays in delivery of benefits. There is little question that the extensive procedural and substantive detail enacted by Congress to limit the scope and prevent misapplication of the adjustment assistance program has unintentionally prevented its effective development.[30]

[30] *United States International Economic Policy in an Interdependent World; Report to the President, Submitted by the Commission on International Trade and Investment Policy* (Government Printing Office: Washington, July 1971).

Because the present transition to environmental controls will no doubt require some substantial adjustments with consequent possible pockets of unemployment we recommend that the Trade Expansion Act adjustment provisions (except escape clause relief) be expanded to apply to adjustment problems associated with environmental controls whether these are due to domestic or foreign competition. Furthermore, we suggest that these provisions be strengthened along the lines recently recommended by the Commission on International Trade and Investment Policy. Since the extension of these provisions is intended to apply to what we regard as essentially a transitional problem, it should be limited to a specified period—say, ten years. The commission's recommendations are aimed at making adjustment relief more prompt, effective, and equitable. We reproduce a brief summary of them in appendix 2.

There are other programs in existence which can be helpful to workers and firms during the transitional phases even though they are not specifically directed toward problems associated with environmental controls. The Department of Labor administers such programs under the Manpower Development Act. These are aimed at retaining and reemploying workers and are currently reaching about one million persons. In addition, the Economic Development Administration can provide loans, grants, and technical assistance to local governments and industries in economically depressed areas. Finally, the Small Business Administration (SBA) can make, participate in, or guarantee loans of up to $350,000 for the SBA share. These could be used by small businesses to modernize plants and otherwise control residuals. In view of the added adjustments which will have to be made in the economy during the transition period it would appear to be desirable to strengthen present retraining, reemployment, and small business assistance programs.

If possible, adjustment assistance and retraining programs should be geared to relocation in industries for which the United States (or for that matter any country) will have a long-run export advantage *when* residuals generation, assimilative capacity, and preferences for improved environmental quality are adequately taken into account. Such assistance would then tend to accentuate comparative advantage rather than retard it between countries, as might happen with continuously increasing subsidization for industrial pollution control regardless of the degree of competitiveness of the industry.

V. CONCLUSIONS AND SOME THOUGHTS ON THE "NEW PROTECTIONISM"

It is currently a matter of some debate whether the major trading states are poised on a course leading toward a new protectionist period.

During the past decade tariffs, and to some degree nontariff barriers, have exhibited a downward trend. Concurrently, however, specific trading blocs have developed such as the EEC and EFTA, which tend to expand trade within the bloc but diminish it with other countries. In recent years balance-of-payments deficits have induced some developed economies to adopt protectionist policies, at least for short-term intervals. Whether these and other signals indicate movement toward or away from a new degree of protectionism is a matter of discussion much beyond the scope of this article. What is pertinent is the possibility that domestic environmental protection will become the rationalization for greater protection. In sections II and III of this article we have attempted to demonstrate that such a rationalization cannot be substantiated on the basis of either long-term comparative advantage and efficiency or on likely short-term impacts on the balance of payments and domestic incomes of selected countries.

On efficiency premises there is little if any justification for tariffs or nontariff barriers applied to imports destined for consumption in the importing country. A much more efficient taxation device is through excise or other forms of taxes applied on the import *and* on domestically produced commodities of a similar waste-generating nature at the point of consumption or waste generation. If the waste residuals generated by the production of commodities create external costs and since these external costs are imposed on the producing country, they should be taxed or otherwise regulated by that country. In the spirit of no distortions in world trade, such as tariffs or other barriers, external costs should be fully reflected in export prices. We have argued that the decision by an individual country not to reflect such external costs in export prices is even more pervasive in distorting trade patterns than the imposition of tariffs.

From the standpoint of developing countries (largely the rest of the world sector in the model discussed in section III) the case for external costs being reflected in export prices for developed economies is particularly strong. Our calculations indicate that the terms-of-trade effect and the potential income and balance-of-payments adjustments are likely to be small in the short run with the added benefit of lessened pressures on channeling foreign aid to domestic environmental control in the developing economies. With reference to the United States experience in trade adjustment programs we have attempted to outline approaches to temper the impact, in the short run, of domestic environmental control programs with their costs reflected in export prices. A near-term loss may be encountered with such assistance programs. But this relatively small loss may be more than offset with long-run gains in comparative advantage adjusted for citizens' desires for environmental amenities.

We hope that international negotiation and the harmonizing of environmental control programs can proceed unhindered by unjustified unilateral decisions for protection of domestic industries which will result in inefficiencies in production that are international in scope.

APPENDIX 1: THE EMPIRICAL MODEL

In section III a verbal description of the empirical model used to calculate the shifts in domestic income and the balance of payments resulting from domestic and export price changes was given. Here, a highly simplified mathematical derivation of the model is developed along with three tables containing the marginal propensities and elasticities utilized in all calculations. The model involves two sets of equations in which all but price ratio variables are expressed in constant dollars, i.e., adjusted for secular drifts in prices. The first is for domestic demand for domestically produced commodities:

1) $M_{ii} = a_0 + a_1 (P_w/P_i) + a_2 Y_i$

where:

M_{ii} denotes gross domestic absorption of country i defined as consumption expenditure, investment, and government expenditure;

P_w/P_i denotes an index of import prices from the rest of the world divided by an index of export prices for country i;

Y_i represents gross national income in country i;

and a_0, a_1, a_2 are constants obtained by regression analysis utilizing data for each country for the period 1952-1968.[1] The second demand equation estimated was for imports of each country where the subscripts j and i denote imports of country i originating in country j:

2) $M_{ji} = b_0 + b_1 (P_j/P_i) + b_2 (P_w/P_i) + b_3 Y_i$

with:

M_{ji} representing imports of country i originating in country j;

P_j/P_i representing domestic or export price indices in country j divided by domestic or export price indices in country i;

P_w/P_i identical to the ratio defined for equation (1);

Y_i identical to the definition given for equation (1);

In addition to the demand equations specified a set of basic identities were postulated as follows:

---

[1] The estimated regression equations are not reproduced here, and the set of data utilized is not documented in detail. The authors will gladly make this information available upon request.

3) $Y_i - \sum_{j=1}^{6} M_{ii} = 0$ $\qquad\qquad$ $i = 1, \ldots, 6$

and

4) $\sum_{j=1}^{6} M_{ij} - \sum_{i=1}^{6} \dfrac{rP_j}{P_i} M_{ji} = B_i$ $\qquad$ $i = 1, \ldots, 6$

where:

$\quad$ B_i $\qquad$ denotes the current balance-of-payments deficit or surplus in real terms of country i;

$\quad$ r $\qquad$ denotes an exchange rate expressing the quantity of country j's currency it takes to purchase one unit of i's currency.

Substituting the demand relationships postulated in (1) and (2) into the set of equations (3) and (4) and differentiating the resulting system of equations with respect to P_i, we obtain a linear system. Before describing the result it should be noted that in a trading world by definition $\sum_{i=1}^{6} B_i = 0$. That is, the balance-of-payments deficit for all countries taken together must be zero. Thus, one of the equations causes the system of equations to be linearly dependent and therefore must be omitted in order to obtain an independent set of relationships. In the computational system the equation specifying B_i where i denotes the "rest of the world" was arbitrarily excluded. To illustrate the resulting system of equations we present it for five countries and the "rest of the world" where the only export price change is assumed to occur in the first country, i.e., $P_i = P_1$.

In matrix notation:

5) $$\begin{bmatrix} M & | & O \\ \text{---} & | & \text{---} \\ N & | & -1 \end{bmatrix} \cdot V = Z$$

where:

$\quad$ M $=$ a six by six matrix of one minus the marginal propensity to absorb domestic product for each country on the main diagonal and marginal propensities to import (with negative sign) country i's product by country j composing the remainder of the elements where i denotes row number and j column number, i.e., $j = 1, 2, \ldots 6$.

$\quad$ N $=$ a five by six matrix with each row containing the sum of marginal propensities to export of country i (row number) to all other countries composing the diagonal elements and marginal propensities to import (with positive sign) of country i's products by country j composing the off-diagonal elements of each row where i again denotes row number and j column number. Note: The row for the rest of the world is deleted.

O = a six by five matrix of zeroes.

-1 = a five by five diagonal matrix with all diagonal elements equal to minus one.

V = a column vector (of dimension 1×11) with dY_i/dP_1 for $i = 1, \ldots, 6$ as the first six elements and dB_i/dP_1 for $i = 1, \ldots, 5$ as the next five elements where the change in prices is for country 1. An analogous vector is obtained if the system is differentiated with respect to any other countries' price levels.

Z = a column vector (of dimension 1×11) which is different whenever the system is differentiated with respect to one of the five countries or bloc prices. We only discuss the vector when the first country's domestic and export prices are presumed to be exogenously changed. The first row of the vector contains the sum of all export elasticities of demand for country 1's products. The second through sixth rows contain the import elasticities of demand by country 1 for the other countries' products where row number indicates the export country; added to this is the weighted cross price elasticity between imports to country 1 and the terms of trade between the rest of the world and country 1. Row seven contains the weighted sum of all export, import, and cross price elasticities of demand for country 1's products. Rows eight through eleven contain the sum of import, export, and cross price elasticities of demand derived from the b_2 coefficient in equation (2) between country 1 and country i with the eighth row containing $i = 2$, ninth row $i = 3$, tenth row $i = 4$, and eleventh row $i = 5$. This sum was omitted for $i = 6$ since no balance-of-payments equation was included for the "rest of the world."

Taking the estimates of all marginal propensities and elasticities recorded in tables 1, 2, and 3 and inserting these into the M and N matrices and into the Z vector in the system specified by (5) yields a linear system of eleven equations and eleven endogenous variables. The empirical estimates of the magnitudes of the eleven endogenous variables including changes in income of the five countries and the rest of the world and changes in the balance of payments of the five countries, derived by solving this system for each country, are presented in tables 1 and 2 in section III of the text. It should be noted that the system of equations was recalculated for unilateral domestic and export price changes in each country and the rest of the world. Given the presumed linearity of the system, the total effect on incomes and balance of payments of all countries imposing environmental controls would equal, by definition, the sum of the effects from unilateral action by all countries.

TABLE 1. ESTIMATES OF THE MARGINAL PROPENSITIES TO ABSORB DOMESTIC PRODUCT AND TO IMPORT, SELECTED COUNTRIES, 1968

Exporting Country[a]	Importing Country					
	United States	Japan	West Germany	United Kingdom	France	Rest of World
United States	0.2200[b]	0.0283**	0.0193**	0.0276*	0.0192**	0.1250**
Japan	0.0101***[c]	0.1790	0.0032**	0.0026*	0.0016***	0.0732**
West Germany	0.0087**	0.0047**	0.2750	0.0214**	0.0430**	0.1445**
United Kingdom	0.0065**	0.0041**	0.0105**	0.3150	0.0087**	0.0598***
France	0.0016**	0.0014**	0.0347**	0.0173**	0.2070	0.0571
Rest of World	0.0353**	0.0846**	0.1511**	0.1887**	0.0800**	0.5400

[a] Each row contains one minus the marginal propensity to absorb domestic product (excluding saving) with i = j and marginal propensity to export from country i to country j (or import to j from i), with i ≠ j, where i indicates row and j column.

[b] Marginal propensities to absorb domestic product were calculated by subtracting the estimated marginal propensities to import and 0.05, to account for savings propensities, from one. Thus, for each country the marginal propensity to absorb is calculated as a residual. This procedure was necessary since the sum of the marginal propensities to import and consume domestic product derived from the regression estimates exceeded one, thereby implying instability in world trade.

[c] * indicates marginal propensity was statistically significant at the 10 percent level and ** significant at the 5 percent level using a two-tailed "t" test.

TABLE 2. IMPORT ELASTICITIES OF DEMAND[a]
SELECTED COUNTRIES, 1968

Exporting Country	Importing Country					
	United States	Japan	West Germany	United Kingdom	France[b]	Rest of World
United States	—	—2.18**	—1.17*	—0.70	—2.60	0.29
Japan	—1.12*c	—	—1.42	—1.98**	—1.30	0.77*
West Germany	—2.40**	—1.29**	—	—0.94**	—8.30	0.01
United Kingdom	—1.85*	—2.14*	—0.29	—	—6.80	—0.19
France	0.30	—0.68*	—0.59	—1.12**	—	2.03*
Rest of the World	—0.29	0.26	—0.18	0.21	—0.84	—

[a] Import elasticity of demand is a measure of the percentage change in imports resulting from a one percent change in the terms of trade between the importing country and the exporting country. The terms of trade are defined as a composite price index of the importing country's domestic prices divided by a price index of exports of the exporting country.

[b] The empirical estimates for France were derived using non-least-squares estimating techniques. In consequence these estimates are not strictly comparable to the others reported on in this table.

[c] * Statistically significant at the 20 percent level. ** Statistically significant at the 5 percent level.

TABLE 3. ESTIMATES OF CROSS PRICE ELASTICITIES[a] OF DEMAND
SELECTED COUNTRIES, 1968

Exporting Country	Importing Country				
	United States	Japan	West Germany	United Kingdom	France
United States	−0.099**	0.490	0.020	0.190	0.660
Japan	−0.124[b]	−0.053*	−0.090	−0.420	−4.740**
West Germany	−0.003	0.500	−0.189*	0.030	−1.080*
United Kingdom	−0.008***[c]	−0.110	−0.220	−0.054*	−1.450*
France	−1.040**	0.140	0.390	0.210	−0.036

[a] Cross price elasticity of demand measures the percentage change in imports or in domestic absorption resulting from a one percent change in the terms of trade between the "rest of the world" and the exporting country. The terms of trade were estimated by taking the ratio of an index of export prices of the "rest of the world" and dividing it by an index of export prices for the exporting country. Generally, if the "rest of the world" exports are substitutes for the exporting country's, the sign of the cross price elasticity should be negative.

[b] Most calculated cross price elasticities of demand were not statistically significant at the 5 percent or even the 20 percent level. In consequence the empirical model was also estimated constraining cross price elasticities to zero. The results were not markedly different from those reported on in section III, tables 1 and 2. Research is continuing in an attempt to obtain more precise cross elasticity estimates.

[c] Statistically significant at the 20 percent level. ** Statistically significant at the 5 percent level.

* Statistically significant at the 20 percent level. ** Statistically significant at the 5 percent level.

APPENDIX 2: BRIEF SUMMARY OF THE UNITED STATES ADJUSTMENT
ASSISTANCE PROGRAM AND RECOMMENDATIONS OF THE
COMMISSION ON INTERNATIONAL TRADE AND INVEST-
MENT POLICY

The Commission on International Trade and Investment Policy
identified two cases under which adjustment assistance can be obtained.
We quote from their summary document:

> First, a firm or a group of workers may apply to the Tariff
> Commission for certification of eligibility to apply for adjustment
> assistance. If the Tariff Commission finds that the injury require-
> ments of the law are met, it so reports to the President, who may
> then certify that the applicant is eligible to apply for relief.
>
> At that point, a firm seeking relief submits a proposal to the
> Secretary of Commerce, who certifies its eligibility to receive
> assistance upon determination that increased imports have caused
> or threaten to cause serious injury to the firm. Groups of workers
> apply for assistance to the Secretary of Labor, who must satisfy
> himself that increased imports have caused or threaten to cause
> serious injury to the firm. Groups of workers apply for assistance
> to the Secretary of Labor, who must satisfy himself that increased
> imports have caused or threaten to cause unemployment or under-
> employment of a significant number of workers in an afflicted firm
> or in one of its subdivisions. Individual workers must apply
> separately for benefits, and if they meet the strict criteria of the
> Act, they will be certified as eligible to receive those benefits.
>
> Second, a trade association, firm, labor union, or other repre-
> sentative of an industry may apply for "tariff adjustment"
> (escape-clause relief). If the Tariff Commission finds that the
> industry represented by the applicant meets the injury test of
> the law, the President may raise or impose import restrictions
> through the escape clause; may initiate adjustment assistance
> procedures as an alternative; or he may do both.[1]

The Commission on International Trade recommended that time
delays in handling applications be reduced by eliminating Tariff Commission investigation and findings except for escape clause action.
The commission thought it best to allow the executive branch to make
decisions about whether firms or workers have met the injury criteria.
We strongly concur since reducing delays under this assistance program would undoubtedly reduce pressures for trade barriers. For
improved assistance to workers the Commission on International Trade
recommends: a) making adequate amounts of assistance available as
quickly as possible after eligibility has been established; b) providing

---

[1] *United States International Economic Policy in an Interdependent World.*

greater incentives, including wider benefits, to accept training or relocation assistance; c) making allowances available for the full period of retraining, in addition to retroactive allowances paid during a period of unemployment while awaiting retraining; d) giving qualified workers the opportunity to pursue technical, professional, or academic as well as vocational training; e) relaxing the requirement concerning previous work and earnings, thereby enabling recent entrants into the labor force to qualify for the program; f) providing family health benefits for workers in the adjustment assistance program; and g) providing subsidies to allow older workers, who are not yet eligible for full social security benefits, to enter the social security program without reduction of benefits.

Adjustment assistance to firms can be provided under the Trade Expansion Act for "modernizing" existing plants and "developing new lines of more competitive products." The Commission on International Trade recommends that: a) operating responsibility be centralized to expedite the delivery of benefits; b) more attractive terms of financial assistance and tax benefits be provided; c) interim financing be made available between approval and delivery of assistance; d) adjustment assistance to firms be normally available only to small businesses; and e) United States antitrust legislation be altered to permit mergers of firms encountering difficulty because of competition of imports. We concur with these recommendations except for restricting adjustment assistance to small businesses in the case of loss in comparative advantage due to emission standards and/or taxes since these controls are likely to affect the competitive position of domestic industries characterized by high degrees of concentration and size as much or more than small businesses.

PART V

CONCLUSIONS

INTERNATIONAL INSTITUTIONS AND THE ENVIRONMENTAL CRISIS: A LOOK AHEAD

David A. Kay and Eugene B. Skolnikoff

DAVID A. KAY is associate professor of political science, University of Wisconsin, Madison, and visiting research scholar, Carnegie Endowment for International Peace, New York. EUGENE B. SKOLNIKOFF is professor of political science, Massachusetts Institute of Technology, Cambridge, Mass.

In the industrialized northern hemisphere we are assaulted daily with evidence of the deteriorating quality of the human environment: Rivers are closed to fishing because of dangerous levels of contamination; the safety of important foods is challenged; the foul air that major urban areas have been forced to endure is now spreading like an inkblot into surrounding areas. Lack of early concern about the implications for the environment of the widespread application of modern technology has allowed the problem to grow rapidly into a critical domestic and international issue.

Certainly one indication of the growing international public and political attention being devoted to the environmental issue was the 1968 decision of the United Nations General Assembly to convene a conference on the environment.[1] The speed with which the organization moved to convene this conference was markedly greater than that shown for earlier UN conferences on trade and development or the peaceful uses of outer space.

We do not propose to summarize here the points made by the contributors to this volume. Our effort, rather, will be to identify some of the implications for international politics and international organizations of the process described and analyzed in these articles.

I.

Central to understanding the drive behind the convening of the Stockholm conference as well as assessing the continuing effects of this new concern for environmental problems is the evidence that has

[1] General Assembly Resolution 2398 (XXIII), December 3, 1968.

developed on the imbalances and strains created in the global ecosystem
by the widespread application of powerful new technologies. These
imbalances and strains have created problems that are in many cases
global in nature and that will in all probability require solutions breach-
ing traditional political, sectoral, and disciplinary boundaries.

Many of these imbalances and strains have been identified. Examples are the 10 percent rise in atmospheric carbon dioxide over the
last century; the tremendous increase in the amount of waste products
which become pollutants, indicated by the fact that in 1968 solid wastes
in the United States amounted to 7 million automobiles, 10 million
tons of paper, 48 million cans, and 142 million tons of smoke and
noxious fumes; the estimated one billion pounds of DDT that have
entered the environment and the additional 100 million pounds that
are used each year in the face of growing evidence of the toxicity to
some forms of animal life of the concentration of such persistent pesticides in the food chain.[2] Although these and other indicators of
environmental imbalance have played an important role in pushing
environmental concerns to the forefront of major public policy questions, they have, perhaps more importantly, made us aware of how
little is known about the workings of the global ecosystem. While
written specifically about the state of scientific knowledge concerning
man's impact on climate, the judgment of the recently completed
Report of the Study of Man's Impact on Climate is apropos in describing the general state of knowledge concerning man's relation to
the ecosystem:

> During the past two decades there has been significant and
> encouraging progress by the scientific community in developing the
> theory, models and measurement techniques that will be necessary
> for determining man's impact on climate. We are, however, dis-
> turbed that there are major and serious gaps in our understanding
> of the complex systems that determine climate, and that data in
> many critical areas are incomplete, inconsistent, and even contra-
> dictory. . . . It is clear to us that without additional research and
> monitoring programs the scientific community will not be able to
> provide the firm answers which society may need if large-scale,
> and possibly irreversible, inadvertent modification of the climate
> is to be avoided.[3]

[2] See *Man's Impact on the Global Environment: Assessment and Recommenda-
tions for Action* (Report of the Study of Critical Environmental Problems)
(Cambridge, Mass: M.I.T. Press, 1970); *Environmental Quality: The Second
Annual Report of the Council on Environmental Quality, together with the
Message of the President to the Congress* (Washington: Government Printing
Office, August 1971); and *Problems of the Human Environment: Report of the
Secretary-General* (UN Documented E/4667).

[3] *Inadvertent Climate Modification* (Report of the Study of Man's Impact on
Climate) (Cambridge, Mass: M.I.T. Press, 1971).

One of the clear messages that has emerged from the process leading to the Stockholm conference is that, lacking clear knowledge of our ecological system, we constantly hazard man's future in a game whose rules we do not yet fully understand. Yet the same lack of knowledge makes it difficult to design specific policies and measures. This situation has certain important implications for the activities of international organizations. As many of the contributors to this volume have noted, there is a desperate need, on a continuing basis, for information, research, and analysis about the environment. The objectives of this research and analysis function should be: 1) to provide continuous, up-to-date information on what is happening in the global ecosystem; 2) to determine the likely effects of present trends and to establish tolerances; 3) to develop alternatives to, or modifications of, current practices when necessary; and 4) to establish hard data on the costs and benefits of alternative courses of action for political decision.[4]

In a fragmented manner many international organizations already have taken steps toward these objectives. It seems clear that as a result of the Stockholm process additional pressure will be exerted for the development within the United Nations of a recognized and impartial analytical capability for considering the environmental implications of ongoing and contemplated scientific and technological developments as well as for the development of the capability for making recommendations on the necessary public policies required by these developments. Both Richard Gardner and Brian Johnson in their articles have examined the various institutional shapes that this research and analysis function might assume as a result of the Stockholm conference. But what can be said about its implications for the United Nations system regardless of the exact institutional shape that it assumes?

Any movement toward increasing the responsibility of international machinery for collection, research, and analysis in the highly complex area of environmental affairs will increase substantially the requirements for the effective performance of that machinery. At present it cannot be assumed that the international secretariat of the United Nations system has either the quality or influence required for these new tasks although there are "islands" of technical quality and efficiency. Unless the quality of the personnel and the effectiveness of the institutions engaged in these new functions are clearly respected by governments, the scientific community, other international organizations, and the public, there is little hope that this research

[4] Eugene B. Skolnikoff, "The International Functional Implications of Future Technology," *Journal of International Affairs*, 1971 (Vol. 25, No. 2), p. 274.

and analysis function will be able to have a major impact on environmental developments. It is doubtful that such a level of quality can be developed without substantial institutional change, including a direct challenge to many of the hallowed canons of international secretariats, such as the concepts of career civil service and geographic representation. In very few areas of the United Nations system has effective performance been the standard against which bureaucratic form and organization have been tested. New patterns and altered forms of existing organizational patterns will surely be needed if international machinery of recognized quality and influence is to develop in this area.

Development of international machinery for research, analysis, and policy review of scientific and technological developments concerning the changing environment also is likely to have important implications for the relationship between the United Nations and member states. International organizations already perform a wide variety of regulatory functions, some are engaged in allocation of resources, a few even are engaged in the inspection and enforcement of agreed international rules. States have already delegated appreciable portions of their sovereignty to international bodies—more than most realize—(in addition to watching the erosion of their sovereignty in a multitude of other ways through the rapidly growing and largely unavoidable interdependence of national societies). The essentially boundless nature of the "environment" as an issue area is likely to further narrow the scope of unilateral, national decisionmaking and to increase the role and authority of international machinery.

"Environment" as an issue area has no simple bounds. To be concerned with assessing the impact of scientific and technological developments on the environment requires being concerned with the full array of issues affecting civilization, from disposal of waste to population growth, from the methods and amount of food production to the wise use of resources, from the transfer and control of technology to the calculation of the real costs of economic growth. This is thus not a concern with a new problem for societies but with the oldest and most central of all problems—the allocation of values within and between polities. Inevitably, as international institutions develop their concern and capacity for analyzing environmental impact issues, they will find themselves involved in many questions touching on major political, economic, and social problems.

In this connection it should be noted that the process leading up to the Stockholm conference was designed by the secretariat to go beyond the involvement of traditional diplomatic and government participants and to seek to draw into the preparatory process significant domestic and international interest groups.[5] This conscious effort to penetrate national societies was greatly abetted by the very nature of the issue. One can expect that the post-Stockholm concern of international institutions with environmental matters will involve them with closer and more sustained contact with nongovernmental elements of states than ever before. Such penetration of national societies can be a source of strength for international institutions as well as a source of tension with member governments.

International institutions have traditionally suffered, in their attempts to influence governments, from a lack of significant contact with domestic interest groups. In most cases, the International Labor Organization (ILO) and the European Economic Community (EEC) being the major exceptions, member governments have successfully maintained the claim that they should be the channel of contact between international organizations and their societies. If in the environmental area the responsible international organization is able to deal directly with iterest groups, such as the scientific community or environmentalists, the possibility of bringing added leverage on the policies of government could enhance the influence of that international organization.[6] On the other hand, direct contact between an international secretariat and potent domestic interest groups, which results in attempts to influence the policy of a state in critical areas, can also develop into a significant source of stress between member governments and the international secretariat.[7] On matters as complex as environmental issues, in which clearly conflicting values must be balanced, the national decisionmaker is likely to view as unwelcomed the efforts of an additional contender in the policy process. This is particularly likely in relatively closed polities, such as the communist states, and international secretariats may well find their efforts to develop links with environmentally significant domestic interest groups producing strong reactions from these governments. On the other hand, such development of interest-group politics on a cross-national basis could in time have profound effects on international affairs.

[5] See, for example, *Report of the Preparatory Committee for the United Nations Conference on the Human Environment* (UN Document A/CONF.48/PC.9); and *Statement by the Secretary-General of the UN Conference on the Human Environment* (UN Press Release HE/2, February 8, 1971).

[6] On this point see Maurice F. Strong, *Development, Environment and the New Global Imperatives: The Future of International Co-operation* (Plaunt Lectures delivered at Carlton University, Ottawa, Canada, 1971.) (Mimeographed.)

[7] For an example see Leon N. Lindberg, "Integration as a Source of Stress on the European Community System," *International Organization*, Spring 1966 (Vol. 20, No. 2), pp. 233-265.

II.

One of the most persistent problems surrounding efforts in the United Nations over the last four years to engage the organization's interest in environmental issues has been the reluctance of the developing countries. Joao Augusto de Araujo Castro, ambassador of Brazil to the United States, has expressed in this volume his strong fears that concern with the environment is being used in the United Nations to distract the organization's attention from major political issues that the United States and the Union of Soviet Socialist Republics now prefer to handle outside the United Nations and to limit the economic development of the developing countries and excuse the failure to provide them with adequate resources. Ambassador Castro also has forcefully argued here for separating consideration of the environmental problems of the developed and developing world.

The unenthusiastic attitude of the developing countries for greater United Nations involvement with environmental issues was recognized early in the planning for Stockholm. As Maurice Strong has written:

> Although environment has rapidly become a major preoccupation of both publics and governments in the industrialized countries, it is still endowed with no such magic in much of the developing world. Environment is still seen by many as a rich man's problem, a disease they would be prepared to risk if it is a necessary accompaniment to the economic growth which they want and urgently need. They are understandably concerned about how the preoccupation of the industrialized countries with environment will affect their priority task of meeting the basic and immediate needs of their peoples for food, shelter, jobs, education and health care. They have also been concerned that those whose industrial technology has produced the major part of today's pollution should assume the major cost of dealing with the environmental consequences. They want to be more sure before jumping enthusiastically on the environmental bandwagon just how it is likely to affect their own interests and their own priorities.[8]

We do not propose to assess the merits of the position of the developing countries—both Brian Johnson and James Lee have examined the development-environment nexus in their articles—but rather to point to a few of the implications of this view for international action on environmental concerns.

The developing states compose a clear majority of the membership of the United Nations. A position supported by a majority of these developing states will necessarily command attention. The coolness shown by the developing countries toward UN involvement with the environment illustrates the point. It is to be counted as a major success of the secretariat of the Stockholm conference that through diligent efforts involving near-continuous lobbying by Strong the developing countries were so thoroughly engaged in the pre-Stockholm process. The 1969-1970 fears of a developing country boycott of Stockholm have not occurred, at least until now, to a large extent because of this vigorous effort to take their concerns into account.

However, the constant effort of the secretariat to keep the developing countries engaged in the process came at a price. First, it did require an immense amount of the time of the secretariat—time that was not, as a result, available for concentration on technical issues or on the real issues confronting industrialized states. Particularly in the year before Stockholm private complaints have increased from the developed states that the conference secretariat has failed to adequately consult them as a result of its concentration on the developing world. Second, the secretariat has encouraged the developing states to believe that concern with development will not reduce the funds available for development but rather will increase them. This increase is to come in the form of a fund that will bear the cost of taking environmental considerations into account in development projects. This fund, if established, would be financed by voluntary contribution from the developed states.

The developing countries' fears that increased United Nations action in the environmental area will adversely affect their interests will continue to be a factor beyond Stockholm. Hopes that a large fund will be established to bear the incremental cost of taking environmental concerns into account in development planning may fail. They may initially fail because the prevailing attitude in the United States Congress toward foreign aid, in any form, is not likely to support a large United States contribution to such a fund. Over the long run such hopes may fail because at least some economic development projects may not be compatible with sound environmental principles, for example, the Aswan Dam.

The very nature of the United Nations political process will mean that the developing countries are able to ensure that their concerns are taken into account. Whatever continuing bodies are set up by Stockholm will emerge as subsidiary organs of the United Nations, a United Nations that not only places a premium on the concept of one state-one vote but one whose broad range of concerns facilitates inter-issue bargaining.[9] One can expect that the developing states will use their tactical advantage in the UN bargaining process to extract

---

[9] For a discussion of inter-issue bargaining in United Nations politics see David A. Kay, "The Impact of African States on the United Nations," *International Organization,* Winter 1969 (Vol. 23, No. 1), pp. 20-47.

the maximum advantage. If this does turn out to be the case and the procedures of the organization make possible the delay or manipulation of the international community's response to crucial issues of survival, a significant incentive will have been created for bypassing UN involvement with environment issues.

III.

We believe that the articles presented in this volume and the overwhelming weight of available scientific evidence are in agreement that the challenge of environmental management is of a long-term character. There are few final solutions to environmental problems, and the objective of international action must be to seek to establish processes and techniques for identifying environmental problems, developing solutions on a continuing basis, and providing a forum for the clash of differing priorities and values. However, the realization of the long-term nature of the challenge and of the substantial existing international action already underway should not minimize the importance of the policies and actions that must be taken now.

Increasingly, new technologies are global in nature, or the side effects of more intensive application of existing technology have international and global repercussions. In time, and not very far ahead, many functions—regulation, allocation, inspection, enforcement, adjudication, and operation—will have to be performed on a wide variety of subjects in an international arena. There is an early need for the establishment of international norms for effluents, for solid waste disposal, for tanker routing, for actions in the event of ship accidents, and for registration of the thousands of new chemical compounds introduced into the biosphere each year.[10] As Ralph d'Arge and Allen Kneese have shown in their article for this volume, the imposition of national environmental standards can have an important impact on international trade. Continued international trade in a free and orderly fashion soon will require agreement on environmental standards. In areas in which the effects of pollution are subtle and complex and control measures require unaccustomed domestic retraints the political problems will be serious. If limitations must be imposed on the total use made of specific technologies each year or on the spread and introduction of new technologies or if limitations are eventually required on the amount of forest or agricultural land that can be destroyed each year, then we will be seriously affecting areas never before subject to any form of international regulation (or in many countries even subject to national regulation). Limitations on research

---

[10] Skolnikoff, *Journal of International Affairs*, Vol. 25, No. 2, pp. 274-275.

and development itself may even become a serious political issue if a judgment can be made—as was asserted by some opponents of the supersonic transport—that the direction new technology may take would seriously exacerbate environmental problems.

The establishment of norms will require international decisions on the fair allocation of the burdens involved in obeying these norms. We live in a world of inequality, inequality of wealth, of technological processes, of resource distribution, of resource use, and of the impact of various forms of pollution. Who would bear the burden of a ban on certain forms of activity, such as the use of a pesticide: the producers of the pesticide in the form of lost sales or the consumers of the pesticide in the form of lost crops, disease, and higher price substitutes? The determination of the cost and impact of various environmental decisions and the fair allocation of this burden will require international action of a recognized fair and impartial character. Once norms are established and the burden of compliance allocated, monitoring and enforcement will be needed in many cases to ensure compliance and detect avoidance of critical norms.

Scant attention has been paid to the international conflict potential of environmental change. As awareness grows among the public and governments as to environmental alteration and the sources of such alteration, the possibility of conflict between states increases. Acid rain, polluted waters, a disappearance of fish from a traditional fishing area, tainted foodstuffs, and the inadvertent modification of weather are likely to become new sources of international tension in the future. Similarly, the growing conflict of interest between the developed and developing countries has the potential of exacerbating international tensions. International machinery will be urgently needed if these conflicts are not to lead to interstate violence.

While it would be encouraging to be able to conclude this look ahead with confidence that the international community is moving to establish the needed machinery to perform all those functions necessary if we are to manage effectively on a long-term basis the critical relations between man and his environment, such confidence does not appear warranted. The general performance of the United Nations system today, notwithstanding its effectiveness in some areas, leads to considerable skepticism that it provides an adequate base for expansion in responsibility without substantial modification. This is not just a question of the capabilities of international secretariats but more fundamentally a question of the willingness of governments to encourage the needed evolution and expansion of the functions and authority of the United Nations system in directions that constrain their own freedom of action. The experience on the road to Stockholm is not overly encouraging in this regard. At times governments seemed far more interested in debating, perhaps even at the final price of sabotaging the conference, the merits of the attendance of the Peoples' Republic of China (Communist China) or the German Democratic Republic (East Germany).

There is no easy alternative to seeking to use the United Nations system for dealing with global aspects of the environment. It may be necessary to build some new institutions outside the UN, especially in those subjects requiring high technical efficiency, with limited membership and patterns of control and influence quite different from that which prevails in most United Nations bodies. But the UN system offers the best, and only real, opportunity for providing an institutional base with widespread participation. This political goal is critical, not only because of the global nature of the environment but also because of its importance for any future growth of a democratic world order. Indeed, if the United Nations can demonstrate its ability to deal effectively with the range of environmental issues requiring international action, it could make an important contribution to revitalizing the entire United Nations system, particularly in the eyes of the major powers which have shown growing disenchantment with the organization in recent years.

Index

Brazil, 31, 310
    as source of manganese, 29
Brookings Institution, 41
Brown, Harrison, 23n
Brussels conference, 139
Brussels Convention for the Prevention of Pollution of the Sea by Oil, 90

Cambodia, 212
Canada, 31, 109, 198, 212, 213, 218, 222
    as source of minerals, 29
carbon dioxide, 212, 306
    concentration in atmosphere, 167
Caspian Sea, 117, 212
Castro, Jaoa Augusto de Araujo, 237
Center for Housing, Building and Planning, 78
Charter of the UN, 249
Chile, 198
China, 20
Choucri, Nazli, 9, 19n, 20n, 29n, 40n, 41n
chromium, 29, 42
Clawson, Marion, 255n
climatic changes, 166
Cloud, Preston E., Jr., 24n, 28n
cobalt, 28, 29
Codex, Alimentarius Commission, 89, 214
cold-war dynamics, 19
Colombia, 231
Commission for Social Development, 80
Commission of the European Community, 95
Commission on Human Rights, 79
Commission on International Trade and Investment Policy, 292
    report of, 291
Commission on the Status of Women, 80
Committee on Housing, Building and Planning, 194
Committee on Problems of the Environment, 149

Committee on Science and Technology in Developing Countries, 153
Committee on Space Research (COSPAR), 142, 146
Committee on the Challenges of Modern Society, 90, 95, 219, 232, 233
Committee on Water Research, 146
Communist China. See People's Republic of China
Conference on the Human Environment. See UN Conference on the Human Environment
Convention of the High Seas (1958), 85
Cooperative Study of the Kuroshio (CSK), 145
copper, 27, 29
correlates of growth, 33
cost-benefit calculus, 21
    criteria, 35
cost structure, externalities and, 269
Council of Europe, 90
Council on Environmental Quality, 214

Daddario, Emilio Q., 17n, 21n
d'Arge, R. C., 265n, 287n, 312
DDT, 49, 256, 259
    alternative policies for, 54
    in biosphere, 51
    time delay in, 65
Department of Economic and Social Affairs, 78
Department of Labor, 292
dependency indices, 42
developing countries, environmental controls, 275
    special concerns of, 258
Development Assistance Committee (DAC), 229
diamonds, industrial, 28
diseconomy, 267
Djakarta, 231
domestic external diseconomies, some observations on, 272

Rivlin, Alice M., 39n
Rolfe, Sidney E., 256n, 271n, 275n, 283n
Rosenthal, Albert J., 36n
Rousch, G. A., 30n
Rousseau, 242, 247
Royal Society, 139
Ruhr, 256
Russell, Clifford S., 255n

St. Lawrence River, 213
St. Lawrence Seaway, 225
San Francisco, 184
Santiago, 192, 231
Sauvy, Alfred, 18n
Scandinavia, 20, 211, 256
    metric coal equivalents of, 23
scarcity calculus, 35
Schultze, Charles L., 39n, 41n
Science and Technological Research Committee of the European Community, 103
Scientific Committee on Antarctic Research (SCAR), 143, 146, 155
Scientific Committee on Oceanic Research (SCOR), 143, 144, 146, 155
Scientific Committee on Problems of the Environment (SCOPE), 74, 150, 152, 158
    Commission on Environmental Monitoring, 151
Scientific Committee on Water Research, 146
Second UN Development Decade (DDII), 171
secretary-general of the United Nations, 202
Senior Advisors to ECE Governments on Environmental Problems, 200
Shelesnyak, M. C., 11n
Singapore, 212
Skolnikoff, Eugene, 202, 203n, 307n
Small Business Administration (SBA), 292
Socialist Federal Republic of Yugo-

slavia, 30
solid waste, flows, 49
    generation, delayed responses of, 59
    policies, alternatives of, 61
    pollution, 65
South-East Asian Regional Workshop, 189
Southern Hemisphere, 246
Soviet Union, 21, 30, 31, 32, 233. See also Union of Soviet Socialist Republics
    mineral resources of, 29
"spaceship earth," 86
Spain, 30
Special Committee for the International Biological Program (SCIBP), 147, 149, 155
Spinelli, Altiero, 96
standard of living, relationship to industrialization and energy consumption, 23
Stanovnik, Jr., 193
Sterling, Claire, 99n, 274n
Stockholm Conference on the Human Environment, 6, 233, 308. See also UN Conference on the Human Environment
Strong, Maurice F., 72, 75, 109, 151, 309n, 310
Study of Man's Impact on Climate, 74
sulfur dioxide, 210, 224
Surinam, 30
Sweden, 104, 109, 223
Swedish International Development Authority, 177
system dynamics, 39
systems-analysis, 49

tariff, 267
technological development, effects on population growth, 18
Thailand, 30, 31, 212, 227
Thirring, Hans, 25n
tin, 28, 29, 30

324   Index